Underwriting the Internet

How Technical Advances, Financial Engineering, and Entrepreneurial Genius Are Building the Information Highway

LESLIE S. HIRAOKA

M.E.Sharpe
Armonk, New York
London, England

Copyright © 2005 by M.E. Sharpe, Inc.

Library of Congress Cataloging-in-Publication Data

Hiraoka, Leslie S., 1941–
Underwriting the internet : how technical advances, financial engineering, and
entrepreneurial genius are building the information highway / by Leslie S. Hiraoka.
    p. cm.
Includes bibliographical references.
ISBN 0-7656-1517-7 (hardcover : alk. paper)—ISBN 0-7656-1518-5 (pbk. : alk. paper)
1. Internet. 2. Internet—Economic aspects. 3. Information superhighway. I. Title.

HM851.H57 2004
025.04—dc22
                                                            2004011432

Printed in the United States of America

The paper used in this publication meets the minimum requirements of
American National Standard for Information Sciences
Permanence of Paper for Printed Library Materials,
ANSI Z 39.48-1984.

∞

| MV (c) | 10 | 9 | 8 | 7 | 6 | 5 | 4 | 3 | 2 | 1 |
| MV (p) | 10 | 9 | 8 | 7 | 6 | 5 | 4 | 3 | 2 | 1 |

To the memory of
SHIGEO SHINGO
(1909–1990)
Pioneer of another industrial revolution

Contents

List of Tables and Figures

Tables

Figures

Preface

As the worldwide Internet transforms information dissemination and communications technology with considerable impact on society, there is little understanding of how its development occurred and why it spread so rapidly. Impetus for the Internet's growth derived from innovations in computer, software, and networking technology that yielded new user-friendly and marketable products and services. High-tech firms were begun by prescient entrepreneurs eager to commercialize these advances, and financing was supplied by angel investors, venture capitalists, and initial public offerings (IPOs). The arcane technology and specialized use of investment banks that underwrote the start-ups and brokerage houses that traded their securities were incomprehensible to most investors and policymakers, but as long as the stock market went up there were few complaints, especially since a New Economy had been born, fueled by strong productivity growth. A virtual cycle had apparently been created in which technical innovations were commercialized with bountiful financing from Wall Street that opened new markets, created opportunities for synergy through mergers and acquisitions, and produced enormous personal wealth for entrepreneurs who guided these fast-paced developments. The much-publicized fortunes made especially by Microsoft's founders and even employees in turn started the dot-com mania and IPO frenzy in which harebrained schemes were transformed into untold riches for a brief time. Corporate leaders in other industries jumped on the gravy train with their illicit initiatives. Efficiencies from the digital revolution could not possibly accommodate the collective greed, and the ensuing $7 trillion collapse destroyed not only the dot-coms and Enrons, but the retirement accounts of small investors as well.

The tragic consequences moved lawmakers to search for corporate governance reforms to restore investor confidence in capital markets. Such action is needed as the baby-boom generation approaches retirement at the end of the decade. Officials in Washington are also calling for cuts in Social Security and Medicare benefits to control mounting federal deficits and entitlement costs. With the nation's fiscal affairs in disarray, an aging population has been left to its own devices to fund its retirement. Many turned to the mutual fund industry, only to recoil as scandal engulfed it as well. With 401(k) pension plans also being mismanaged, what were savers and investors to do? Unable to rely on the government and these financial institutions, individuals will have to learn how to save and invest for their own future well-being.[1] Such a realization prompted the writing of this book, which encourages investors to consider high-tech issues as investment instruments because these are where opportunities exist for sustained growth and capital gains. Furthermore, much has been learned in the boom-and-bust cycle surrounding dot-com and telecommunications enterprises, and as early as 2003 survivors of the Wall Street crash had rallied.[2] Any excessive exuberance, meanwhile, was dampened in 2004 by a heated U.S. presidential campaign and mounting war casualties in Iraq. Abroad, continued strong growth in China, India, and emerging markets in Russia, Poland, and Hungary are presenting global opportunities for a new class of start-ups. Following established game plans, their entrepreneurs plan on commercializing the innovations resulting from the Internet Revolution. Most will end up as roadkill along the information superhighway but a few will grow to compete against Microsoft, Cisco, eBay, Amazon.com, and Yahoo! and in the process offer substantial financial rewards for their founders and investors.

There are of course considerable risks when buying shares in newly established firms, so such investments should be balanced in a portfolio composed of mainly investment-grade bonds and high-dividend-paying conservative stocks like utilities. Such a diversified portfolio has served my own retirement goals well. It also allowed me to capitalize on the irrational exuberance in equity markets following commercialization of the Internet and, just as important, weather the severe bust that occurred at the start of the millennium. For the sake of disclosure, Microsoft, Oracle, and Hewlett-Packard are the only stocks discussed in this book that are in and form a small part of my portfolio. It furthermore would have been better if the software companies were never added.

Before signing off, I would like to thank M.E. Sharpe for publishing this book and particularly its Executive Editor, Lynn Taylor, for recommending the manuscript to its Editorial Board. I alone am responsible for its contents, and consequently strongly advise readers that if you can't stand the stress of equity investing, keep your money in U.S. Treasury notes and bonds, government-insured savings accounts, and AAA-rated municipal bonds.[3] You will sleep better at night when stocks fall.

Underwriting the Internet

—— Chapter 1 ——

Boom, Bust, and Recovery

The Internet Age, like most industrial epochs, was belatedly discovered by the hoi polloi because it arose so suddenly in the mid-1990s and revolved around not only arcane technology but atypical, almost maniacal financing. By 1999 the Nasdaq stock market that underwrote much of the dot-com (as in Amazon.com) phenomenon had surged to such frothy heights that an implosion was all but inevitable, even though media hypesters were cheering on a New Economy emerging from strong productivity gains that they predicted would keep the United States on an accelerating growth path. The vast wealth, created and lost in the blink of an eye, seared the ecstatic rise and agonizing collapse into the annals of business history and kept the Information Revolution, even with its momentary burnout, at the top of government and industry agendas into the new millennium. Already the instantaneous, low-cost communication network connects innumerable offices and homes, crossing oceans and national borders to encircle the globe. As a result, the loss of trillions of dollars in the stock market plunge is having only a transitory effect, with bankrupt e-commerce firms being replaced by a new generation of high-tech start-ups intent on succeeding in a more subdued environment.

The outlines of this resurgence are visible as software companies like Microsoft, Oracle, and SAP AG, the large German business-applications software company, continue their intense rivalry for network dominance. They are being joined by IBM, with its successful forays into software and services distributed over the World Wide Web. Cable operators are simultaneously increasing the carrying capacity of their online networks to allow faster electronic business transactions, transmission of information files, and multimedia interaction in real time. Networking moreover is still in its infancy, with innovators continuing to plan and implement new breakthroughs for the growing global system. Why did these activities continue to advance in the midst of a financial debacle? In retrospect, the Internet by the late 1990s had become such an accepted medium in communication, financial, and entertainment markets that the crash on Wall Street slowed but could not derail its forward momentum. Once clicked on, the World Wide Web permanently altered everyday life. Its use moreover was the latest manifestation of the Information Revolution in computing, software development, and networking, most of which were enabled by America's heralded technology that was used to vanquish fascism in World War II. Later technological breakthroughs also helped overcome a fierce industrial challenge from Japan and win a more menacing Cold War with the USSR.

The Internet's gestation period coincided with the Pax Americana following World War II and ensured that the government's meddling in the private sector would be minimized because of the absence of a pressing national security concern like global conflict. Hence the various stages of the Information Revolution, as listed on Table 1.1, could proceed and accelerate under free market conditions. Consumer demand, for example, ensured the rapid adoption of the personal computer, and with these ubiquitous terminals, users accessed cyberspace even as the U.S. Department of Defense was relinquishing control of its highly classified Arpanet communications network that began its evolution into the Internet. Entrepreneurs initiated projects to make use of the novel information superhighway spanning continents and oceans and developed the software and hardware that would connect the government-released Arpanet to private and foreign networks. Once the United States placed its wide area network in the public domain, other nations quickly connected their systems in order to keep abreast of the technology and to meet their own business and societal needs. The deregulation movement of the late 1990s also prompted a brisk innovation that burst forth in the free-for-all Internet milieu, with millions clicking on throughout the world to implement personal or business agendas or simply to "surf" the Net to see what the fuss was all about.

Various think tanks were similarly moved to monitor the Internet tidal wave, and the Paris-based Organization for Economic Cooperation and Development (OECD) reported on U.S. innovations in information technology (IT) and financial engineering even as the Nasdaq crash was causing the demise of innumerable dot-com start-ups.[1] The industry's vicissitudes were also mirrored in the cover stories of *Business Week* magazine, with "The Internet Age" appearing on newsstands on October 4, 1999, and "The New Economy" issued on January 31, 2000, both of which focused on productivity gains from the IT Revolution that would

Table 1.1

Stages in the Information Revolution

Era	Period	Characteristics	Principal Firms
Main-frame	1964–1981	Vertically integrated systems centered on large mainframe computers	IBM
PC	1981–1994	Distributed processing with personal computers widely available	IBM, Microsoft, Intel, Compaq, Dell
Dot-com	1995–2000	IPO and venture capital financing of dot-com start-ups forms stock market bubble and ends in its crash	Netscape, Amazon.com, Yahoo!, eBay, Webvan, eToys, Excite@Home
Inter-net	1994–	Internet infrastructure developed in U.S. and extended worldwide; speeds communications and commercial transactions; increases productivity	AOL Time Warner, Cisco, Microsoft, Sun Microsystems, Oracle, SAP

Source: Kenji Hanawa, "'Information Technology Revolution' Leads the U.S. Economic Expansion," *Sanwa Economic Letter,* November 1999, exhibit 10. The *Letter* has ceased publication and was not copyrighted, and Japan's Sanwa Bank changed its name after merging with another bank.

dampen if not eliminate the boom-and-bust nature of the business cycle. After the stock markets crashed, the magazine attempted a reevaluation with a backpedaling issue on March 26, 2001, on how it was "Rethinking the Internet."

Erratic Central Bank

Even more stunned with the startling reversal was the Federal Reserve Board of the nation's central bank, which under its chairman, Alan Greenspan, had steadfastly attempted to curb the "irrational exuberance" of the securities markets by raising short-term interest rates no less than six times in the absence of inflationary pressures. Sagging under the Fed's heavy-handedness, stock prices topped out in March 2000 and then precipitously fell, forcing a shaken Greenspan to reverse course in 2001 by dropping interest rates by several percentage points in a futile effort to stem losses amounting to trillions of dollars. Wall Street analysts were quick to blame the Fed chairman for doing "too little, too late." One irate columnist compared Greenspan to the central planners of the Soviet Union for practicing the black art of price-fixing in the manipulation of interest rates in, of all places, Wall Street, the bastion of U.S. capitalism.[2] The "irrationally exuberant" remark was also a pompously obtuse expression characteristic of the central banker, which made him the target for all economic ills. Pundits quipped that a mutation of the mad cow pathogen wracking the English countryside had infected the Federal Reserve, giving it "mad Dow's disease" and a feverish desire to topple the Dow Jones industrial index.

The Fed's tight monetary policy, moreover, proved damaging when the sudden and prolonged slowdown caused the worst job loss—particularly affecting IT industries—in twenty years. Even as the economy revives, employers are reluctant to add to their payroll for fear that Greenspan will whiplash them again with another round of up-and-down interest rate moves. The Fed chief, after all, moved to end, in his words, "a once-in-a-generation frenzy of speculation,"[3] only to make a U-turn when the central bank began to worry about a deflationary spiral of falling prices that crimped corporate profits and business investments. While overly concentrating on excessive stock market prices, the Fed failed to adequately monitor bank-lending practices, particularly in their structuring of over-the-counter derivatives with corporate borrowers. Use of these contracts—also called swaps, options, and futures—quintupled in value to $29 trillion, a development applauded by Greenspan because they allowed business to hedge adverse price and interest rate fluctuations. There was unfortunately a darker side to this topsy-turvy growth even as the central bank chairman was successfully leaning on the Commodity Futures Trading Commission to refrain from regulating the secretive transactions.[4] Without the oversight, two of the nation's largest banks set up offshore entities that engaged in sham transactions with energy producers like the Enron Corporation to mislead investors and employees. This resulted in equity losses of $200 billion when the stock market crash eviscerated their stock holdings in the energy companies. The banks were forced to pay $300 million in fines and penalties in a settlement reached with the Securities and Exchange Commission and the Manhattan district attorney's office. Such deceptions were also involved in the bankruptcy of Enron, WorldCom, and Global Crossing, the transoceanic fiber-optic telecommunications carrier, wreaking havoc on the economy and on investor confidence and delaying economic recovery even after the Federal Reserve had shoved interest rates to near zero. As to why events had seemed to spin out of control, Greenspan, in testimony to the Senate Banking Committee, pointedly blamed corporate greed as well as fraudulent accounting practices:

> At root was the rapid enlargement of stock market capitalizations in the latter part of the 1990s that arguably engendered an outsized increase in opportunities for avarice. An infectious greed seemed to grip much of our business community. Manifestations of lax corporate governance, in my judgment, are largely a symptom of a failed CEO. . . . I was really deeply distressed to find that actions were being taken which very clearly indicated a lack of awareness of where the market value of accounting is.[5]

In his testimony, Greenspan failed to mention his trip to Dallas on November 13, 2001—weeks prior to the Enron bankruptcy—to receive the Enron Prize for Distinguished Public Service from Ken Lay, who was soon to become the epitome of corporate greed. It was probably because the chairman was too burdened with the Fed's lack of success in stimulating the economy. The Bush administration subsequently proposed massive tax cuts that are resulting in record budget deficits and the possibility of more inflation and yes, higher interest rates. With the Fed seemingly stuck on a merry-go-round, is it any wonder that business investment and hiring remained sluggish in 2003, despite an economic recovery?

Internet Advances Stall

The capital markets crash and economic downturn undermined but failed to stop the Internet Revolution, which had been underwritten by generous financing from Wall Street. While much of the funds were misspent in an orgy of corporate greed, approximately $14 trillion generated during the 1990s was used to develop the Internet's commercial infrastructure and launch start-up firms that processed myriad interactions on the World Wide Web. A major participant in this exuberant period was the Internet portal company Yahoo! that was founded in California's Silicon Valley in 1994. Its youthful founders witnessed its share price soar to $240 a share to give the small firm a market capitalization value of $150 billion and an immediate presence in technical and marketing circles. And even though its stock promptly slid down the other side of the price curve as depicted on Figure 1.1, the company had accumulated sufficient resources and brand recognition to remain a permanent fixture on the Internet firmament. Such spikes were duplicated throughout the high-tech sector, leading to massive layoffs and corporate bankruptcies. Business slowed so quickly that it prompted John Chambers of Cisco Systems, another high-flying company, to proclaim: "This may be the fastest any industry our size has ever decelerated," and he further characterized the adverse effects as being struck by a flood that comes every hundred years.[6] Cisco, however, also had sufficient reserves and managerial talent to survive the cataclysm.

While the two companies can be categorized as Internet firms, each was in a separate part of the burgeoning business, with Yahoo! deriving most of its revenues from banner advertising on its Web pages and Cisco manufacturing routers and switches—principal hardware items that form the backbone of the network—in addition to selling its proprietary operating system software that controlled its computers. In the ensuing downturn, Yahoo! earnings tumbled into the red as major advertisers scaled back on Internet ads, finding them not as effective as those broadcast on television. The company discovered that TV viewers were willing to tolerate commercials while watching favorite programs, but Internet users easily ignored the static ads while selectively absorbing the information that had brought them to the screen. Another negative repercussion for both firms was the demise of numerous start-up firms that had been major advertisers for Yahoo! and buyers of Cisco's products and services. In 2000, firm failures began with one to two per month, reaching 16 and 20 in June and July. By November and December, monthly failures reached a "flood" stage of 46 and 40, respectively, with the year's total coming to 210. The torrid pace continued into 2001.[7] By then, surviving firms were limping badly, and with equity prices plunging, there was no place to go for a quick capital infusion that could carry a cash-starved firm through what had become a very bleak period. The downward spiral fed on itself, with falling sales and earnings producing sell-offs in stock prices and finally layoffs and bankruptcies. The Wall Street plunge that began on March 20, 2000, reached bear-market depths one year later when Standard & Poor's five-hundred-stock index dropped by 22.7 percent. A drop of 20 percent defines a bear market, and the attribution has been given to nine periods since the massive crash of 1929. That debacle saw a much smaller stock market fall a numbing 86.2 percent, reaching bottom in 1932. It furthermore precipitated the Great Depression, thus spreading a long-lasting pain over ensuing decades. The severe times, moreover, were exacerbated by a phlegmatic

Figure 1.1   **Yahoo! Share Price**

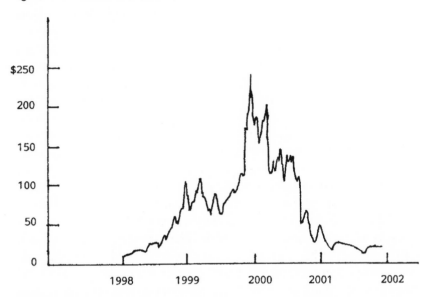

Source: "Going Down with the Dot-Coms," *New York Times*, March 11, 2001, section 3, p. 14.

Federal Reserve that adopted a tight monetary policy to purge equity markets of excessive speculation that had run rampant in the preceding Roaring Twenties. The central bank, at the time, did not know any better and consequently reverted to its traditionally conservative stance of administering bad medicine to a sick economy, unknowingly prolonging the Depression. In the current downturn the Fed has been impelled to move faster to combat recessionary forces, and it is pumping money into the economy to counteract the equity losses on Wall Street. Severe damage, however, has already been done, especially on the Nasdaq, where high-flying Internet issues like Cisco Systems and Yahoo! trade. That exchange fell a breathtaking 61.9 percent from March 2000 to March 2001, and wobbled near its lows for the following year and a half. Fortunately for American investors, other equity markets were not so wretchedly affected: The Dow Jones industrial average of big, blue-chip companies like IBM and GE fell only 13 percent in the same period. Nevertheless, the Internet bubble lured so many investors into high-tech stocks and out of more conservative issues that personal fortunes were severely impacted as investor favorites like Cisco and Oracle shares dropped by 75 percent, Intel by 60 percent, and Microsoft by 53 percent. Smaller firms were dumped by panicky individuals and mutual fund managers, with Yahoo! and JDS Uniphase, an optical networking newcomer, falling by 90 percent or more. In spite of the losses and ensuing layoffs, most of these enterprises remain viable businesses with sought-after products and frequently visited Web sites. They are hanging on in hopes of seeing better times, particularly as fiscal and monetary authorities move to stimulate economic activity with interest rate and income tax cuts. Others like Pets.com, eToys, Webvan, and Planet Rx (Internet seller of prescription drugs) were not so lucky. These e-commerce "shooting stars" burned through millions of dollars of venture capital and initial public offering (IPO) funds before crashing to earth without earning a dime for many of their investors. How could these supposedly knowledgeable individuals lose so much money that they had earned over many years of employment and even earmarked for retirement? "This is the central paradox of the dot-com phenomena: that a set of inspiring ideas about how to use new technologies and build new kinds of organization got transmogrified into a destructive orgy of speculation, greed and envy."[8]

In retrospect, the greed and hubris of entrepreneurs, venture capitalists, Wall Street stock analysts, and investment bankers should not overshadow the accomplishments of the Internet Age that saw the massive development of the new medium's infrastructure, allowing the Net to be clicked on by growing millions of people and businesses in every minute of a given day. Trillions of dollars of equity wealth have disappeared, but the American economy has suffered through only a mild recession of two consecutive quarters of negative growth. Interest rate and income tax cuts to counteract the downturn were enacted, and the United States is experiencing few macroeconomic destabilizing forces such as inflation that could stymie growth. The equity losses have compelled the government to regulate the various excesses that inflated and burst the Internet bubble, but its often clumsy ways of implementing change will probably have minimal impact on an industry that is changing so swiftly. Moreover, the securities business already has procedures for determining if investors have legitimate claims for recovering losses suffered at the hands of financial institutions. In actual practice, however, just resolution of these cases will be difficult because of the naive manner in which life savings were committed to highly risky investments, their victims suckered in by the overzealous way fragile dot-com issues were promoted. Class-action lawsuits are being filed at a rapid clip, but many of the start-ups whose shares were purchased at exorbitant prices are bankrupt and incapable of providing any type of settlement. While brokerage houses possess considerable financial reserves, they also have formidable legal departments to defend themselves against conflict of interest charges. Without deep pockets, the individual investor will probably not get much restitution. Such appears to be the case in Japan, which underwent a similar speculative collapse of its real estate and financial markets over a decade ago. Suffering through the 1990s in an economic malaise while the U.S. economy boomed, the Japanese were nevertheless inclined to muddle through the difficult times rather than slog through never-ending court cases or enact measures that might lead to additional instability. In the United States, policymakers should have been deliberating carefully now that they too were facing a lengthy slowdown induced mainly by a fuzzy-minded Federal Reserve Bank.

IT Revolution Bypasses Japan

Government mismanagement also lay behind most of Japan's headlong plunge from No. 1 to an also-ran position among industrial powers. High-level officials—like counterparts in the now-defunct Soviet Union—made the classical mistake of relying on existing institutions and outdated paradigms to handle their nations' crises that had been caused by major socioeconomic upheavals. Political party leaders and government bureaucrats who had risen to great heights by leading the way to superpower status—economically for Japan and militarily for the Soviet Union—were left floundering as the old remedies failed to work. Resources were squandered by the Soviet Union in a futile war in Afghanistan and in a vain attempt to outspend the United States in military weaponry. In Japan, make-work government programs failed to address major problems that dragged the economy down, such as bank loans that had become unproductive after the bursting of its speculative bubble. The United States in contrast eventually faced up to and extricated itself from the futile Vietnam War by ending the presidencies of both Lyndon Johnson and Richard Nixon, who were mainly responsible for building up and prolonging the conflict. In the savings and loan banking scandal of the late 1980s, federal officials removed inept bank managers who had made highly speculative investments and wrote off bank loans in timely fashion even if such action meant the liquidation of some powerful institutions. In Japan, unproductive loans were timidly addressed by banking authorities, resulting in a continued financial stalemate that stunted business development. This lethargic response can be traced to the incestuous relationship between government and business leaders that powered the country's ascendancy in the postwar period of the 1950s through the 1980s. As it atrophied, the aging coalition held on to power by choking off ideas required for the advancement of its information technology base. The lack of innovation resulted in a stillborn Internet Age for Japan even though the nation once led the world in semiconductors and consumer electronics. Its powerful government ministries, moreover, continued to operate in an archaic manner more attuned to the immediate postwar era when objectives included:

1. Rebuilding a war-ravaged nation with government sponsorship of select industries that were given access to investment capital and advanced foreign technology;
2. A cheap yen-to-dollar exchange rate that prompted massive export drives of inexpensive, high-quality goods to the United States;
3. Low-interest bank loans for favored businesses that financed the rebuilding paradigm;
4. Oversight by powerful government ministries—mainly the Ministry of International Trade & Industry (MITI) and the Ministry of Finance—which maintain control in important sectors like information technology and banking even though they are ill equipped to provide constructive guidance.

Flaccid Industrial Policy

For a poor, developing country like Japan in the postwar period, the advanced foreign technology and most of the blueprint for its industrial recovery were borrowed from the industrial workings of the United States, the superpower that had defeated it and its Axis partners. Unfortunately for the emerging Asian giant, the egalitarian underpinnings of the United States were not absorbed, leading to stalemate in the aftermath of the 1989 financial crash when the old leadership simply could not decide on a recovery policy. A constitution had been imposed by U.S. occupation forces, and during the ensuing Cold War it was used as a democratic façade, shielding the development of an industrial state with one-party rule. The status quo was so strictly adhered to, with prewar *zaibatsu* industrial groups reforming and leading the private sector under the aegis of the central ministries, that highly innovative firms like Sony and Honda broke from this hidebound mentality to seek their fortunes in the New World. The smug bureaucracy was unconcerned even though productivity advances wrought by the importation of foreign technology were slowing markedly, and the world stood at the beginning of the Information Revolution whose impetus would be led by small, eager start-up firms in the United States. Ragtag companies like Microsoft and America Online were nowhere to be found on the traditional Japanese landscape and, even worse, were not viewed as commercially significant. Rather, the industrial ministry (MITI) and the telephone monopoly (Nippon Telephone & Telegraph) busily cobbled together a grandiose but futile Fifth Generation supercomputer project that was expected to dethrone IBM as an industry leader. The goal was already dated because the personal computer was beginning its inexorable ascendancy, making moot any advances that may have been achieved with supercomputers.

Establishment Inertia

The misplaced emphasis on bigger, faster machines made by giant corporations was an easy mistake to make for an industrial state like Japan that once thrived on selecting and supporting major manufacturing companies that competed on global markets against America's IBM, GM, GE, and AT&T. The blueprint unfortunately neglected small, innovative firms that spearheaded the research and development of the Information Revolution. Such start-ups were not financed by large metropolitan commercial banks, and they had little recourse to stock market funds because nothing of the order of a Nasdaq or venture capital market existed. In this environment, a Silicon Valley of entrepreneurial, high-tech firms failed to materialize. The absence of reform and innovation in Japan's political and business hierarchy resulted from Washington's original ambition of turning its erstwhile enemy into an effective ally against world communism. Political stability and economic growth were encouraged, even to the extent that high-level elected officials like the prime minister came under the control of the Liberal Democratic Party (LDP) and its conservative business and agricultural factions. This situation fostered graft, nepotism, and political patronage, resulting in scandal as prime ministers rose and fell. This systemic decay had its origins in early postwar industrial gains for which the LDP and economic ministries claimed much of the credit, shunting aside business leaders who had negotiated with counterparts in the United States for the purchase and use of its vaunted technology. These individuals and firms also spearheaded Japan's international trade successes, resulting in the major rebuilding of its war-devastated economy. At this juncture, many of these pioneers turned their attention to global markets, especially in the West, moving cadres of Japan's elite managers abroad to implement business expansion plans. A "brain drain" subsequently developed that further nurtured decay in domestic institutions composed of lethargic career officials who were hardly qualified to lead the nation in the ensuing information maelstrom. In Washington as well, the government bureaucracy was devoid of much technical expertise, but American entrepreneurs never depended on it for inspiration or financing. Instead, the dispersed state of American authority, with its strong emphasis on the individual, yielded easily to the start-up of small high-tech and venture capital firms that had grandiose goals for changing the world. Their achievements would upend the industrial landscape.

In Japan, inertia ruled the day as the centralized power of its ministries spawned a rigid hierarchy in the electronics industry, with Nippon Telephone & Telegraph (NTT)—modeled after AT&T—at its pinnacle as a state-sanctioned monopoly. NTT surrounded itself with a few large supplier firms like Hitachi, Fujitsu, NEC, and Toshiba, and any company lying outside this inner circle of contacts and lucrative contracts had little chance of prospering. The few that did, like Sony, were too busy in other countries and rarely attempted to alter the ingrained business setup at home. The efforts at reform can be contrasted by the attempts of the United States and Japan to deregulate their telephone industries. In the former, AT&T was separated from its local operating units known as the Baby Bells, several of which have become major competitors of Ma Bell (AT&T). NTT was expected to undergo a similar dissolution but instead used its considerable power to thwart any dismemberment moves. The deregulation charade was heavily reinforced by an incestuous employment system that allowed high-level government officials to retire to paper-shuffling jobs at corporations regulated by their agencies. Within the private sector, executives at large firms would similarly move into sinecures at smaller affiliates. Together with a lifetime employment system at leading companies, the retirement shifts fostered an aging cohort of managers who held little interest in provoking change in industry deregulation or investing in new technologies that could upset their carefully laid plans.

U.S. Entrepreneurial Zeal

The result was the squandering of Japan's huge economic gains earned during the decades following World War II and few efforts were made at forming an entrepreneurial base, leaving it without innovators like Bill Gates, Michael Dell, Larry Ellison, and John Chambers, who were busily building high-tech empires in the United States and throughout the world. All would have been considered misfits in Japan since three of the four were college dropouts, and Chambers had a dubious employment record resulting from his dismissal at Wang Computers. Dell started his company while residing in a college dormitory and targeted no less than the IBM PC market by building a faster, cheaper computer with a thirty-day, money-back guarantee. In characteristic fashion, Dell used the Internet for direct sales of his PC after he realized that technically savvy Internet users formed a logical customer base for his computers. To implement the e-commerce channel, the young CEO initiated an intense www.dell.com campaign to integrate the Internet into all sales and information systems of the company as well as print the Dell Web address on all ads, business cards, and product packaging. The effort was supported by most employees because a corporate ethos had been created in which innovation and experimentation were accepted norms. According to Michael Dell, such action does not come naturally, even in the dynamic desktop computer business and consequently "To encourage people to innovate more, you have to make it safe for them to fail."[9] These attitudes characterized the Information Revolution in the United States and, as managers and policy planners in other advanced countries found, they are difficult to inculcate in most employees, who are naturally risk-averse and prefer to keep their positions secure.

An ingenious way of counteracting employee inertia has been the high-tech practice, used out of necessity by cash-strapped, dot-com startups, of awarding stock options to employees in lieu of monetary compensation. In this manner, employees became owners and participated in the equity bonanza when the firm went public and listed its shares on the Nasdaq. Total commitment was required by all members of a small enterprise and in many cases was obtained because, despite the high odds of a small, unknown company going public in the sale of its stock, such outcomes were increasing in the equity boom of the late 1990s, and cases of substantial wealth earned by even minor employees became routine. In larger companies like Dell Computer, shares in the firm were given to match employee contributions to their 401(k) retirement plans, again with the objective of blurring the lines between owners and workers. In Japan and other industrialized countries, stock distribution programs were rarely enacted, leaving employees and top managers often out of the money in any stock market boom. Intercorporate equity holdings and interlocking boards of directors were common, especially with major banks in Japan and Western Europe accruing considerable power because of their stock investments in other businesses. Corporate financial officers could be pressured into securing loans solely from the investing bank, which then charged high interest rates compared to funds obtained from other sources like the sale of securities. Equity financing consequently could not compete against the powerful commercial banks, and Nasdaq-type markets as well as venture capitalism never developed. In such a closed system, it was not surprising to see women and minorities kept out of managerial and supervisory positions and restrictions placed on imports and immigration. These placed a lid on innovation even after many countries began opening their borders to participate and share in the proceeds of the Information Revolution.

The United States has already "developed a rich set of institutions in both public and private sectors to support a very high level of technological innovations" that would make it "the most technologically dynamic economy" by far.[10] Innovative products and services, for example, can be readily launched by individual entrepreneurs and tested in consumer markets and quickly scaled up if the business proves viable. To support new competitors, antitrust action by the U.S. Justice Department has, over the years, helped shield young firms from being trampled by monopolistic power in the marketplace. These go back to the breakup of the Standard Oil Trust as well as the more recent deregulation of the national telephone monopoly under AT&T. Other cases undergirding the IT revolution include antitrust action against IBM and Microsoft, in which a slow-moving government has been provoked to marshal considerable resources in arguing the merits of increased and fair competition. Such operating conditions were even extended to foreign concerns, bringing innovative competitors like Sony and Honda to the United States as well as Chinese, Indian, and other motivated foreign students who came to study at U.S. schools, especially in California. Graduates and professors of Stanford University were instrumental in turning Silicon Valley near San Jose into a mecca for high-tech start-ups with available financing from individual "angel" investors and San Francisco venture capitalists who themselves achieved success with their own entrepreneurial initiatives and business plans. A virtual cycle thus developed in which foreign students enrolled in technical and business programs at West Coast colleges and readily found employment and entrepreneurial opportunities in surrounding high-tech areas. Products and services were earmarked for the dynamic electronics industry, with sales expanded to include foreign markets in Latin America, Europe, and Asia. This global trade reinforced ties to the Old World for immigrant managers in the form of customer links abroad as well as alliances with contract manufacturers and component suppliers, whose prices were much lower than what could be found in the United States. Software development jobs, as an example, were farmed out to low-cost centers in India and China. When successful entrepreneurs stepped down from running their own shops, many became investors and consultants to other start-ups, in the process contributing their considerable financial resources and technical and management expertise to the sustaining of this entrepreneurial cycle. Economic downturns also added to the competitive zeal by curbing marginal activity and spawning opportunities in more dynamic markets. Major retrenchment, for example, occurred in both semiconductors and computers, but failed to stem the giant strides in networking that followed slowdowns in the older industries. Traumatic financial setbacks also periodically visited Silicon Valley, and they include the October 1987 free fall of equity markets caused by the massive budget deficits of the Reagan administration, the 1994–95 Mexican peso crisis resulting in steep devaluation of the currency, and the Asian financial meltdown of 1997 that circumnavigated the world by causing the currency collapse of the Russian ruble and Brazilian real. In each case the Information Revolution has proceeded apace and will no doubt survive much of the devastation caused by the dot-com implosion that reached recession depths.

In the aftermath of the dot-com crash, capital spending fell sharply as business paused to evaluate Internet programs and initiatives in the more austere times. From 1999 through 2000, during the heyday of the dot-com mania, considerable investment funds were earmarked at even established firms for e-commerce start-ups by corporate executives who were responding to the intense media buzz and were fearful of being left behind. With little experience or expertise in cyberspace, these managers made major disbursements on software systems and server computer hardware that failed to favorably impact the bottom line. After the Nasdaq bubble burst, these inept officials together with their high-priced Web consultants were summarily dismissed from company headquarters. While subsequent write-offs have been huge, accompanied by a lengthening list of bankrupt dot-com companies, the bulk of corporate America continues to function normally, bolstered in large measure by consumer spending and home buying, accelerated by the Federal Reserve's interest rate cuts. Moreover, with the Internet industry still in its infancy and comprising only a small part of the economy, the American consumer continues to shop at traditional outlets and has not been unduly affected by the flameout of e-retailers. Other changes also occurred with the major Internet service provider, America Online, merging with a traditional media company, Time Warner, thus melding its e-business with more mainstream activities and diversifying its operating base.

Considerable carnage from the start-of-the-millennium implosions, however, occurred in two important sectors: Wall Street and telecommunications. In both, superstar stock analysts and investment bankers irresponsibly pedaled high-risk investments to a gullible public and were charged by regulators such as the U.S. Justice Department, the Securities and Exchange Commission, and the New York State attorney's office. Hypesters from major brokerage and banking houses inflated the dot-com bubble by issuing ecstatically optimistic recommendations that kept the initial public offering (IPO) market booming, in the process bringing in sizable amounts of fees and trading profits to their employers. Start-up firms with strong "buy" recommendations frequently had no earnings, and after an initial run-up in stock price, investors watched their gains disappear as newer issues grabbed the spotlight.

The staid telecommunications industry also partook of the Wall Street bonanza, with acquisitions, mergers, and the new Internet technology enabling newcomers like WorldCom and Global Crossing to challenge the venerable Ma Bell system. With billions of dollars raised from the sale of their securities, the made-over telecoms invested in ocean- and continent-spanning optical fiber networks, with tolls from the burgeoning Internet data traffic expected to pay for the huge outlays. With the dot-com meltdown, much of the costs were never recovered, leading to the bankruptcies of both Global Crossing and WorldCom and the drying up of capital funds. These events in turn resulted in mass layoffs of the technical geeks who were principal instigators of the Internet Revolution. Will their innovative ideas also be buried in the dour realities of the postcrash landscape?

Productivity Gains

The answer to the question is important because it will determine whether the incipient digital paradigm aborts or develops into a New Economy that accelerates the spread of knowledge and quickens the pace at which the new technology enhances the quality of people's lives. Up until very recently, much of the Internet Revolution was faddish, with greed whipping up an enormous amount of the now-collapsed froth. The popping of the bubble unfortunately meant that some worthy business plans were flushed with the detritus, but in a U.S. milieu characterized by considerable technical and financial acumen, new ideas will percolate from an increasingly diverse population base and from highly innovative institutions. Young entrepreneurs are already pushing plans at the frontiers of wireless services, online voice communication, and residential broadband access. In the telecom industry, increased activity and expenditures are being made as the network moves from voice to data traffic. In 1995, 95 percent of telephone traffic consisted of voice communication. That is expected to be supplanted by 95 percent of data transmissions in ten years. New entrants during this changeover are competing with the established Baby Bell firms for the lion's share of the new business. Innovation is also being galvanized by the faster obsolescence of equipment and software. Start-up vendors are offering improved products and services over the Internet to businesses which themselves must keep abreast of productivity gains made by competitors. The quickened pace of innovation results in faster growth for the U.S. economy, and this has been observed in the last decade by Oliner and Sichel.[11] The economists found that the IT Revolution not only contributed to growth but to greater labor productivity. Real nonfarm business output was estimated to have jumped from 2.75 percent to 4.82 percent between the periods 1991–95 and 1996–99. The rise was attributed to capital investment in hardware, software, and communications equipment—all fundamental sectors in information technology. Contributions from hardware to economic growth rose from 0.57 percent to 1.10 percent, from software, 0.25 percent to 0.63 percent, and from communications equipment, 0.07 percent

Table 1.2

Business Investment and Internet Usage

	1996	1998	2000
U.S. business investment ($ billions)	933.7	1,140.7	1,388.7
% spent on equipment and machinery	42.7	41.3	37.2
% spent on IT	31.6	33.5	39.9
Worldwide Internet users (millions)	38	142	257 (est.)

Sources: "Technology Investment Advances," *New York Times*, December 18, 2000, p. C4; "The Internet Is Revolutionizing Business," *Economic Policy Review*, Federal Reserve Bank of New York (October 2000): 86.

to 0.15 percent. These percentages reflect the greater acceptance and use of these three IT tools for streamlining operations. "In addition, the producers of computers (and embedded semiconductors) appear to have achieved huge efficiency gains in their operations." The growing IT use and computer production efficiencies are further estimated to "account for two-thirds of the acceleration in labor productivity from 1.53 percent to 2.57 percent in nonfarm business between the first and second half of the 1990s."[12]

Over a longer time horizon, beginning in the 1950s, when the first giant computer systems became available, processing and storage costs have fallen dramatically, resulting in more compact machines and inevitably their wider use in business and homes:

> Between 1950 and 1980, the cost per MIP (million instructions per second) fell 27–50 percent annually, spurring the use of computers as calculating devices. In a feedback loop, widespread adoption led to further price reductions as computer manufacturers rode up their learning curves. In the 1960s, computers became file-keeping devices used by businesses to sort, store, process and retrieve large volumes of data, thus saving on the labor involved in information-processing activities. The cost of storage fell at an annual rate of 25–30 percent from 1960 to 1985. . . .
>
> IT is likely to streamline corporate structures significantly by economizing on the number of workers employed in information and processing . . . eliminating the need for battalions of clerks, pools of secretaries, scores of purchasing and sales agents, and layers of supervisors and ad-

Figure 1.2 **Real U.S. Business Investment**

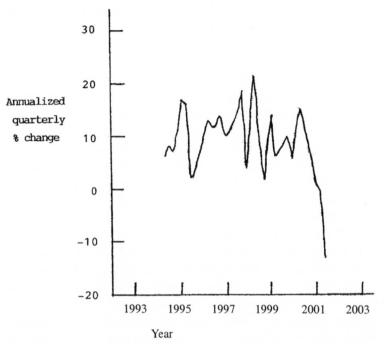

Source: Adapted from "Tougher Times Coming?" *Financial Times*, July 29, 2001, p. 1.

ministrators. Through IT, headquarters, design centers, plants, and purchasing and sales offices can be linked directly to one another. Over time, such major changes in business structure will inevitably raise labor productivity as it becomes possible to create more output with less labor.[13]

The expected rise in productivity materialized in the last half of the 1990s, accompanying a surge of investment in computers, other office equipment, software, communications gear and accessories, electronic components and services, semiconductors, industrial electronics, and photonics. Optimistic economists proclaimed the advent of the New Economy, but these pronouncements were dashed by the crashing stock market. Business spending coincided with these ups and downs, as shown in Table 1.2, and climbed strongly from 1996 to 2000 in overall terms and particularly in the percentage spent on IT categories. Figure 1.2 depicts the steep falloff in the annualized, quarterly percent change in real U.S. business investment resulting from the bursting of the Internet bubble and the telecom bankruptcies. The fall in demand produced by the Nasdaq collapse as well as rising interest rates left industry with considerable overcapacity in IT infrastructure that was built during the capital spending boom.

The resulting overhang has placed a damper on IT investments, but Internet usage continues forward. Close to 63 percent of American homes have access to the World Wide Web, and with its use in educational institutions and business becoming routine, the acceptance of the new medium will be reinforced by incoming students and employees as well as by technical advances that encourage its wider use. The interactive nature of the Internet moreover makes it a much more promising entertainment device than passive television viewing, with professional sports events showing a marked TV ratings decline that coincides with the popularity of interactive electronic games and chat rooms.[14] Social and economic development is similarly advanced by the Internet's use as an inexpensive information and communications network, especially as business globalizes and spurs international trade. In Brazil "the new Information Society Program aims to make technology services and job creation available to every citizen" via the Internet, while in Estonia, all schools are wired for network use.[15] The United Nations considers IT development in poorer countries so vital for their improvement that it is pledging resources, particularly in Africa to help combat the spread of AIDS and infectious disease that ravage the continent. Funding for these programs is also coming from private foundations whose largesse was swelled by the Internet boom on Wall Street. The dot-com crash may slow these efforts, but it could impel U.S. firms to seek markets abroad, where Internet use is accelerating, as opposed to domestic ones that are growing more slowly. On the other hand, as recovery continues, the larger, more lucrative U.S. market will again become center stage simply because opportunities abroad often prove elusive since so much infrastructural investment in e-commerce (already undertaken in the United States) needs to be made.

Internet Investment

In order to secure the expected productivity and profit gains, annual U.S. business spending as shown on Table 1.2 grew from 1996 to 2000 in overall terms and particularly in IT categories. The latter's increase was accentuated by the simultaneous decline of total equipment and machinery expenditures, leading to a greater relative increase for IT spending, which amounted to 39.9 percent compared to 37.2 percent for equipment and machinery. The greater percentage furthermore occurred for the first time in 2000, and its increase was abetted by substantial funding from booming equity markets as well as by the surging use of the Internet in the last three years, as indicated in Table 1.2. High-tech start-ups and established firms like Cisco and Amazon.com rushed to capitalize on the growing interest, with the firms being assisted by venture capitalists and investment bankers hoping to get some of the instant equity wealth being created. The vast majority of start-ups, including Amazon.com., had no earnings from operations, and despite this precarious financial position were taken public by reputable financial institutions. Endorsements from Wall Street's outspoken analysts resulted in record high share prices. The few firms with strong earnings, like Cisco Systems, had such a high valuation—$958.8 billion at its zenith on March 9, 2000—on its stock that for a short time it was the most capitalized issue on equity markets. Even with sustained growth, however, the lofty stock price could not be sustained because, as the dot-com mania imploded, many of Cisco's investors, employees, and customers disappeared or stayed on the sidelines. In the ensuing chaos, Cisco's excess production capacity and inventory stocks became albatrosses around its neck, with losses taken as these assets were written down in value and workers laid off. The bad times meant real trouble for related high-tech companies because Cisco was an integral buyer and supplier of sophisticated hardware for the Internet and had even developed an operating paradigm using the global Net as an instant communications link to its worldwide component manufacturers and customers. The company continuously matched supply with demand, and that theoretically allowed management to quickly respond to shifts in market conditions by increasing or decreasing operations. Overcapacity and excess inventory would supposedly never trouble the firm. Unfortunately, the paradigm had never been tested because the company had experienced only continued increases in revenues, earnings, and its stock price as IT investments and markets boomed. This fed the erroneous assumption that Cisco was immune to any slowdown, which Wall Street readily agreed with by sending its stock to record highs. Its premier position in the pantheon of Internet firms also added an aura that made the bust even more painful. The downfall began with an announcement in May 2001 of its first quarterly decline in revenues since the stock was listed on the Nasdaq in 1990, and an accompanying huge quarterly loss of $2.69 billion. The loss was attributed to a global slowdown, with orders in the main U.S. market falling by 20 percent in the first quarter of 2001. The turn of events constituted an abrupt shift from the torrid 32 percent increase in orders experienced in the second quarter of the preceding year. A steep fall in equipment prices also came with the sharp reversal, accounting for much of the red ink that resulted after a write-down of $2.2 billion because of excess inventory. The two main parts of Cisco's customer base were responsible for the dwindling business, with 40 percent less orders coming from mainly start-up firms that had hoped to use the Internet to parlay new telecommunications services. These were the high-tech weaklings with no earnings that succumbed quickly to the dot-com meltdown, with their ranks falling from 3,000 to 150. The more estab-lished telecom companies also reduced operations as the slowdown spread from Wall Street and Silicon Valley to Main Street. The doleful conditions forced Cisco to lay off eighty-five hundred employees from its workforce as its stock plummeted from $80 to $14 a share.[16]

New Doom and Gloom

Amazon.com, a high flier in e-commerce, suffered more than Cisco be-cause the large Internet retailer was never profitable and was kept finan-cially afloat by selling its securities on Wall Street. Its rallying cry was to use these funds to get big fast in order to overwhelm smaller competi-tors that Amazon knew would be entering its business. With $2.1 billion obtained from bond sales, the e-retailer of books, audio, and video ma-terial expanded online product offerings to include consumer electron-ics, lawn furniture, kitchen goods, and tools. Six warehouses were constructed in the United States to accommodate the increased inven-tory, and it began operations in three foreign countries. With the good times ending, Amazon reported a loss of $1.4 billion in fiscal 2000. The dot-com flameout moreover badly burned the investment community that, in turn, shut off financing for Amazon's deficit-ridden operations. Its future consequently looms ominously, because like the other dot-coms, Amazon's business plan of selling books and appliances over the Internet puts it at a disadvantage compared with retailers that have es-tablished stores as well as Web sites—Barnes & Noble to name one—to service their customers. Just as important, many of its competitors are operating in the black while Amazon is not. And Amazon's promises of future profits are falling on the deaf ears of individual and mutual fund investors who have already lost so much in the Seattle-based company's plunging shares.

The high costs of warehousing and home delivery of consumer goods afflicting retailers like Amazon led to the closing of the Webvan Group, an Internet grocer offering individualized shipment of online orders. Filing for bankruptcy in July 2001, Webvan never made any money on its flawed business plan of merchandising perishable goods and other groceries that had to be stored in warehouses costing $830 million to build. Orders would then be delivered by Webvan's own fleet of trucks and drivers. The expensive operations burned through $1.2 billion of investor funds that would never have been proffered had it not been for the exuberant dot-com times. The giddiness moreover surrounding this start-up was inflated by the celebrity status of its founder, Louis Borders, who had earlier established the bookstore chain bearing his name. He gambled on the mundane grocery business by dressing it up in high-tech fixtures complete with "intricate automated warehouses and computerized scheduling software" to guide his delivery trucks.[17] These steps would supposedly allow Webvan to compete against neighborhood supermarkets, where customers incurred their own selection and delivery costs by going to shop in person. The error in underestimating operational costs was further compounded by the assumed economies of scale derived from customer surveys indicating their willingness to use such a stay-at-home service. After Webvan began service, many initially used online shopping, but less than half placed a second order. Meals apparently could be better planned while shopping at the supermarket, where price and quality of foods could be easily compared. As these realities surfaced, Webvan undertook a $1.2 billion merger with a competitor and slashed expenses to conserve dwindling cash reserves. Borders, the company founder, also shored up his financial position by selling most of his Webvan stock for $2.7 million within weeks of the grocer's demise.

Media Hoopla Ends

Webvan's online business began in San Francisco, close to Silicon Valley, where so many Internet start-ups were headquartered that the city's downtown came to be known as Multimedia Gulch. The founders of these firms had usually attended universities in the Bay area, worked in nearby high-tech firms, sought financing from venture capitalists in the city, and were particularly attracted to San Francisco's bohemian style of living, which found its way into their corporate culture. For new entrepreneurs, the city was a logical launching pad because it was a media center with a plethora of publications heralding the Internet age. This gave the young firms and their novel products and services valuable exposure to a large, technically sophisticated audience. The magazine *Business 2.0*, for example, catered to an international as well as a U.S. clientele, with seven foreign offices listed on its editorial page—four in Europe and one each in South Africa, South Korea, and Israel. During the Internet boom the magazine's girth swelled with eye-catching, glossy advertising, paid for by Amazon and Cisco emulators attempting to stake their claims in the goldfields of e-commerce. The May 2000 issue was particularly hefty, containing no less than 472 pages. The May 15 issue of the following year, however, had an emaciated look with only 100 pages, with the soon-to-be-replaced editor lamenting the downsizing by commenting on how inevitable it was that the "hundreds of well-funded bad ideas inflating the great Internet stock bubble would eventually and spectacularly explode."[18] A 60 percent falloff in ad pages resulted in the absorption of his publication into the AOL Time Warner media empire based in New York. Other San Francisco periodicals were similarly affected, with *Red Herring* (mainly for venture capitalists) having 49 percent less advertising and ending publication in 2003, *Smart Business* smaller by 48 percent, and the unconventional *Wired* magazine thinner by 39 percent.[19] One of *Wired*'s more outlandish covers (December 1998) featured the blue-shaded face of Microsoft founder Bill Gates together with eighty-three reasons why the mogul's reign was over. The article proceeded to cite the firm's "funky karma" as the chief reason for predicting the demise of Microsoft's leader, even as the funky magazine's own well-being was being severely tested in the less euphoric times. In this, the business press was getting its own comeuppance for floating extravagant claims of little substance in order to increase advertising revenue and subscription fees from an audience not catered to by more mainstream publications. In the race to the bottom line, however, such magazines crossed into ethically dubious territory when they ignored the financial losses of dot-com firms and substituted other quantitative measures like rising revenues or number of Web site visits to justify outrageous stock valuations. In doing so, the media writers were mimicking their cruder counterparts on Wall Street who had concocted the new metrics to assure clients that the Internet bubble would continue to exponentially expand.

Cruder Counterparts

Stock analysts like Henry Blodget of Merrill Lynch made their reputations by boldly recommending unprofitable start-ups like Amazon.com based on the attention the bookseller was getting for its Internet moves and from optimistic pronouncements of future growth made by its colorful founder, Jeff Bezos (Bezos also made the cover of *Wired* in a story recommending that other entrepreneurs follow his lead). Blodget was one of the first forecasters to practice the black art of ignoring so fundamental a measurement as business earnings and luckily did so at the beginning of the bubble, when almost all issues began surging in price. In November 1998 he predicted that Amazon's stock, already expensive at $240 a share, would climb to $400 a share in twelve months. The hyperactive stock, moving wildly in the dot-com mania, reached Blodget's $400 lucky call in four weeks and proceeded upward to an astounding $600 a share. Outrageous predictions subsequently became the norm on Wall Street, especially from those analysts who worked for large brokerage firms that had merged or developed investment banking departments. Strong "buy" recommendations were given that generated trading fees for the broker, and the recommended company would return the favor by naming the affiliated investment bank as lead underwriter in the sale of its securities. Lacking meaningful earnings, dot-com start-ups like Amazon were always in need of cash infusions from the sale of its securities, and because the attendant underwriting fees were substantial, Wall Street analysts continued the courtship of these firms with wildly optimistic assessments. The reckoning for such action arrived when the Nasdaq tumbled, in the process shredding all of the Blodget-type pronouncements. Customers, who lost considerable amounts based on these recommendations, are filing complaints and seeking arbitration rulings at the New York Stock Exchange. One such dispute naming Merrill Lynch and involving Blodget has already been settled, with the investor awarded $400,000. The amount appears small compared to the analyst's $5 million in compensation from the brokerage firm, but the case is being followed by large numbers of similar complaints by disgruntled investors who suffered traumatic losses while institutions kept the Internet bubble growing with hot-air musings from their in-house analysts. It wasn't always this way. Responsible forecasters in the past usually put caveats on their stock picks, knowing that these decisions were based on a considerable amount of intuition and guesswork. A certain degree of professional trust was thus established between these firms and their customers that was torn asunder by the trillion-dollar stock market boom that lured masses of first-time, inexperienced investors. After the bust, regulatory bodies probed the conflicting claims to determine and enact reforms needed to eliminate the egregious practices.[20]

For their part, investors need to practice due diligence when venturing into an arena fraught with risk like a booming information technology stock market. Regulators, in addition, should be quicker in condemning obvious hucksters who peddle get-rich-quick schemes on Wall Street. Such action was needed, for example, in the numerous instances when analysts were recommending shares to their customers even as they or their firms were selling their holdings in the same security.

These misleading if not criminal practices as well as the leaden approach of federal regulators has slowed advances made in IT, as the doom and gloom of rising bankruptcies and lost investments bias the current business climate against spending on IT's infrastructure. Orders for IT equipment, which had been increasing at a torrid rate of 32 percent in the second quarter of 2000, fell resoundingly to a negative 20 percent by the first quarter of 2001. This accompanied a steep fall in equipment prices as well as in funding for start-up firms. Venture capital investments, for example, dropped from $103 billion in 2000 to approximately $40 billion the following year.

Much of the pessimism is misplaced, according to Andrew Grove, the sixty-four-year-old chairman of Intel, the world's largest microchip maker, who has stood at the helm of his company during the ups and downs of the IT Revolution. In the 1980s, Grove orchestrated Intel's strategic switch from memory to microprocessor semiconductors, in the process becoming an overpowering force behind the move to personal computers. This occurred mainly in reaction to the Japanese invasion of the U.S. memory chip market that was resulting in lower profits and market share for firms like Intel. Under Grove's leadership the company proceeded to concentrate on the more profitable microprocessor product area, which led to the Intel 8088 chip being selected for the new IBM PC. Grove sees similar opportunities in the aftermath of the crash, even though his company was forced to lay off five thousand employees and saw its stock value drop by a harrowing $300 billion. Despite the bust, Grove feels that much of the dot-com funding underwrote development of the Internet as a commercially viable meganetwork. Faster and easily accessible communication channels like e-mail translate into greater interaction among businesses—especially on a global scale—leading to greater productivity. He affirms: "And productivity is the key to everything—greater productivity increases economic growth. [Moreover] . . . a globalization of culture, of business, of communications achieves a level of pervasiveness that in itself will change the world significantly."[21]

—— Chapter 2 ——

Arpanet and PC Prelude

The Internet is not any one system or device but is rather a "network of networks." It uses software, communication protocols and routing and switching devices to link together a number of different terminal devices (PCs, phones, TVs) to a variety of communication channels including broadcasting, various cable systems, telephone networks, value-added networks and local or wide area networks.[1]

Its origins can be traced to 1969 when its predecessor, the Arpanet, was established by the U.S. Department of Defense (DOD). In the then–Cold War environment pitting the United States against the Soviet Union, the Pentagon built Arpanet as a "survivable communications network" that could withstand a nuclear attack by the communist superpower and assist in the launching of massive retaliatory strikes. More mundane uses included its role as a secure and efficient communication system that linked DOD-funded research centers on a day-to-day basis and facilitated the networking of expensive computer resources for use at different sites. Messages were transmitted digitally, in contrast to the old analog Bell telephone system, with lengthy messages broken down into packets by host computers at the point of origin. Interface message processors (mainly minicomputers) sent the packets between "nodes," and because the packets were individually addressed, they could be transmitted over different routes and reassembled at their destination. This allowed greater system flexibility, so that in the event a nuclear attack severed a route, surviving ones could be used. Alternate paths could also be used to bypass heavy traffic and delays. To determine if a given transmission had been successfully sent, the system's computers were programmed to check if it was received, and if not, a request to retransmit would be sent to the originator's host computer.[2]

The East-West Cold War furthermore assured that there would be adequate funding for the development of this vital network. The specter of a debilitating nuclear attack freezing vital communications stampeded both Congress and the White House—political institutions lacking technical expertise—into providing munificent sums for Arpanet, allowing its developers to incorporate new capabilities resulting from the digital revolution. These advances were.at the cutting edge of technology, and the liberal funding from Washington prompted research universities and think tanks like the Rand Corporation to embrace the initiative by proposing projects that had extensive computer networking and considerable software and interlinking requirements. Never one to question any buildup of Godzilla-like proportions, the high command at the Pentagon readily endorsed the initiative, in the process becoming dependent on the research community for Arpanet's development, which the brass could barely comprehend. In the early 1970s, moreover, Washington's military establishment—including its commander in chief—was being pummeled by losses in the Vietnam War, which ended in 1975 with the forced evacuation of the American embassy in Saigon. Before the fall, President Richard Nixon was impeached, and after the fall an interim president Gerald Ford would be defeated in his 1976 election bid for the White House. Both leaders, in addition to the catastrophic events in Vietnam, were facing calamitous problems at home wrought by the 1973 Arab oil embargo, which precipitated fuel shortages, economic recession, and hyperinflation. In the chaos, political and military chiefs had little time to oversee the Arpanet buildup except to rubber-stamp the effort and throw money at it. This enabled the network's development to systematically proceed, with leading researchers experimenting and making technical decisions that were untainted by political meddling. Its military classification also kept the public and press at bay.

Behind locked doors, progress on the national digital network spurted ahead, and although it was a government-sponsored, nonprofit project, its apparent usefulness gave several researchers a glimpse of the system's commercial possibilities. E-mail was one such "killer application" that began as a communication link between defense labs, and its use rose to tidal wave proportions on the Internet. Before the tsunami could develop, however, a number of computer and networking breakthroughs had to occur. One took place in 1975 when the first commercial personal computer made an unheralded inaugural in the United States, and the rapid spread of the desktop machines placed the computer's enormous power, which had been locked in corporate and government dust-free rooms, into the hands of the people. Heretofore the IBM mainframe—served by somber white-coated, high-tech priests feeding it key-punched card decks—had lorded over the Information Age, but its reign was coming to an abrupt end as use of the PC widened. Arpanet would even come under attack from adolescent hackers using their own PCs to crash their way into the military's secret communications system. The national network became more vulnerable in 1978 when it adopted transmission control and internetworking software protocols that allowed regional and local networks (which it had less control over) to gain access to the system. The smaller computers also advanced the linking of mainframe, mini, and desktop machines into networks in order to share data files and processing power. Large corporate and government agencies then took the logical step of connecting equipment at different sites to form enterprise networks, in effect mimicking what the military had done with Arpanet. As local networks hooked up, a broader and more diverse population of users came online, which raised anxiety levels about the system's security at the Pentagon.

Beginning of the Internet

Hackers and related problems prompted the Department of Defense, in 1983, to develop a highly secure as well as technically advanced Milnet to replace Arpanet. Because it was strapped for cash in the lean years following the Vietnam War, the DOD ended funding for Arpanet by simply disbanding it in 1990. Powerful public, scientific, and business users, however, would not stand for the loss of what had come to be a critical medium of communication in their lives, and they pressured the government, in particular the National Science Foundation, to come up with a substitute system. Unfortunately, money for a network bereft of military applications and competing against the Bell telephone system was difficult to come by, especially since the White House was now occupied by Ronald Reagan, who had pledged to end government intrusions in the private sector. The new president's fiscal initiatives also exacerbated the funding problem because they centered on:

1. A large income tax cut based on deductions permitted for individual retirement accounts (IRAs) that dried up revenues for other programs and produced massive budget deficits.
2. Huge defense expenditures that further added to the red ink and included the untested Strategic Defense Initiative (or Star Wars) missile shield to guard the nation against nuclear attack.

In such a fiscal environment, there was little money left for the politically weak National Science Foundation or for the network that had as yet limited commercial possibilities. Moreover, the inflationary pressures built up during the 1970s because of the petroleum shortages and in the 1980s by Reagan's spiraling budget deficits moved the Federal Reserve to adopt a tight monetary policy, resulting in high short-term interest rates.

Adding to the unsettling picture developing in the domestic economy was an immense wave of imports originating from Japan and landing on U.S. shores. Beginning as cheap toys and apparel shipments, Japan's industrial and trade renaissance grew in distinct steps from textiles to an impressive export list of ships, steel, chemicals, heavy machinery, and consumer electronic items that, because of their low price and high quality, took huge chunks of the U.S. market and drove many of its manufacturers into bankruptcy. Despite these inroads, most corporate and political leaders in the United States remained sanguine because three main industries—automobiles, semiconductors, and computers—remained firmly in U.S. hands. And it probably would have stayed that way had not the Arab oil embargo opened a gaping hole in the American market for small vehicles from Japan to drive through and fundamentally alter the world's industrial landscape. So important was the automobile to the economy that Reagan was forced to abandon his laissez-faire ideology and impose a quota on Japanese car imports to keep them from wrecking the U.S. auto industry. America now glimpsed the specter of a new superpower whose trade initiatives were reverberating in Detroit and Silicon Valley, at the NSF and the Pentagon, and at IBM headquarters on the Eastern seaboard. Detroit was particularly affected because Toyota, Nissan (Datsun), and Honda followed their trade blitz by constructing huge carmaking plants on American soil in an effort to keep their markets in the United States and dampen organized labor's opposition by employing U.S. autoworkers.

Japanese Electronics Challenge

Quickly following these inroads in motor vehicles, Japanese electronics manufacturers targeted the high-tech fields of semiconductors and computers heretofore dominated by the Americans. U.S. corporate executives and military planners were now no longer certain about the country's prospects, especially since the media was beginning to barrage the airwaves about the unstoppable juggernaut from the Far East and the widening technological gap developing in favor of Japan. The Pentagon felt particularly vulnerable because it was charged with the task of developing Reagan's missile shield that in turn was dependent on state-of-the-art semiconductor and computer components. It was feared that such advanced components were being controlled solely by the Japanese with synergistic gains achieved by manufacturers like Hitachi, Fujitsu, and NEC, which not only produced the high-tech products but also conducted extensive research on improving their performance. Japan's Ministry of International Trade & Industry (MITI) also pressed the drive for high-tech dominance with substantial financial funding coming from the nation's success in consumer electronics and international trade. In contrast, U.S. budget and trade accounts were deficit-ridden, leading to a massive collapse of stock markets in October 1987.

The turmoil in American markets made it difficult for then-small semiconductor firms like Intel and Advanced Micro Devices to compete against giant rivals from Japan. These industrial conglomerates had diverse revenue streams derived from booming consumer electronics businesses as well as from highly developed markets abroad. Profits from more mundane products like toasters and TVs financed R&D in semiconductors and computers and further underwrote the investment costs of fabrication facilities. In 1982 the Japanese scale advantages became quite noticeable in the dynamic random access memory chip segment of the $13 billion global semiconductor market. Technical advances were ushering in a new generation of chips, increasing their storage capacity from 64,000 (64K) to 256,000 (256K) units of data and necessitating new chip designs and production plants. In the prior 16K-generation of the mid-1970s, the Japanese acquired 40 percent of the market when U.S. companies failed to add manufacturing capacity because of the economic doldrums caused by the Arab oil embargo. The Asians built on this success by proceeding to capture 70 to 80 percent of the 64K chip market. Their fight for market share drove prices to such unprofitable depths that many U.S. firms were forced to abandon the competition even as they were further discouraged by the additional developmental costs of the 256K memory chip.[3]

More discouraging news was heard by U.S. manufacturers in October 1981, when MITI announced a ten-year program to build an advanced fifth-generation computer "that will be able to converse with humans in natural languages and understand speech and pictures [as well as] learn, associate, make inferences [and], make decisions" using principles developed in the arcane field of artificial intelligence.[4]

If successful, it would lead to computers that think, thus making a quantum leap over fourth-generation machines that processed instructions only in a linear manner. The new thinking machine would be driven by highly parallel processors that raised the speed of existing supercomputers from 100 million to 10 billion arithmetic operations per second. To achieve this second objective, the Japanese government together with six large commercial vendors launched the Super Speed Computing Project, which was funded for eight years at the rate of $100 million to $200 million per year. These efforts formed the foundation for the fifth-generation machine, with the two programs constituting a direct challenge to U.S. leadership and its flagship computing company, IBM. Remembering Pearl Harbor—Japan's surprise attack that started World War II—the Pentagon threw its concerted support behind a research consortium of government, academic, and corporate labs that were designed to maintain the U.S. lead in advanced technological systems. The concern further grew when DOD realized that such advanced computers were integral parts of its weapons research, aircraft design, and missile guidance systems. Supercomputers were so vital in such R&D that the government had embargoed their export. They were also used in research undertaken at American universities, but because their costs ran from $5 million to $15 million apiece, the institutions cleverly used the Japanese challenge to pressure the federal government into purchasing and maintaining the computers for their own purposes.

In the private sector, IBM remained more concerned about the thirteen-year-old government antitrust lawsuit filed against the company for dominating the mainframe market. It too used the foreign threat by getting the laissez-faire and pro-military Reagan administration to swiftly settle the case. The White House additionally intervened by granting "temporary" relief from Japanese competition in memory chips. This occurred in 1986 when a U.S.-Japan accord was signed that placed a price floor under chips sold in the United States and instituted an import quota mainly against shipments from Japan. The call for an Arpanet-type network was also answered in 1984 when funds were awarded to the National Science Foundation for a national networked system of supercomputer centers located mainly at academic centers. With the military abandoning Arpanet, the NSF seized the funding for linking the new centers with its own network called NSFNet. And although this effort was overshadowed by the Star Wars missile defense shield and by MITI's Fifth Generation computer program—both of which yielded extremely limited results—NSFNet steadily evolved throughout the United States and world to become the Internet as we know it today. Much of this development was hidden from public and politicians' view because it was shrouded in technical jargon involving sophisticated aspects of computer and systems networking. By the 1990s, however, the spread of the PC was allowing outsiders to glimpse what was becoming the Internet, which, like the goddess Athena of Greek mythology, appeared to materialize in all its far-flung glory from the brain of an ethereal superbeing. Its sudden appearance, moreover, is attributed to the media's concentration on loud, expensive, and ill-conceived programs, especially those supported by the White House, like Star Wars. At the same time, Tokyo's supercomputing efforts were being waylaid by the smaller, user-friendly desktop and laptop computers storming their way onto commercial markets, upending IBM's big machines and MITI's untimely technical offensive in supercomputers.

The Internet Revolution

Coinciding with the dramatic move to the small computer was the emergence of the Nasdaq stock market for small and medium-size firms that could not meet capital requirements for listing on the bigger New York Stock Exchange. While institutional investors like mutual and pension funds traded on the NYSE, individuals originally supplied the bulk of activity on the Nasdaq, which became the financial incubator of numerous high-tech start-ups like Apple Computer. Investors embraced its initial stock offering in December 1980 to such an extent that within a month's time its market capitalization of $1.8 billion exceeded that of Chase Manhattan Bank or Ford Motor Company. Apple's successful coming-out listing initiated the PC era and, through the spread of the desktop computer, the Internet revolution as well.

Its modus operandi also became a blueprint for advancing the information technology age as practiced by young, scruffy-looking entrepreneurs like Steve Jobs and Steve Wozniak, with their beards and sandals, who cobbled the company together in a Silicon Valley garage. Apple's prototype PC, not surprisingly, was assembled from off-the-shelf electronics parts and was small enough to be easily moved and demonstrated at computer shows attended by other young technical aficionados called "geeks" and "nerds" who knew if a product was worth buying. No pompous professor was needed to ascertain the technical underpinnings of the prototype, and funds from tight-lipped, buttoned-down bankers were not needed. As it grew, however, Apple did tap the coffers of small, nearby venture capital firms that had opened shop in Silicon Valley to finance fledgling companies like Intel. An early, shrewd VC investment of $57,000 in Apple grew to $14 million when the company was listed on Nasdaq. Talk of such fabulous returns traveled at the speed of the electron in money circles, firmly establishing venture capitalism and the Nasdaq market as financial connections to brilliant but slightly weird founders in the valley that became ground zero for the IT, PC, and Internet revolutions. Mainstream media as well as corporate and government bigwigs rarely comprehended the possibilities dreamed up by these upstarts, and the Japanese economy, for one, is still suffering from the oversight.[5]

Ascendance of Software

The rise of Nasdaq and the personal computer created a bleak future for the Fifth Generation supercomputer program by drying up commercial uses and corporate and government funding for big machines. Tokyo also became annoyed at huge research outlays of $35 million that produced few definitive results in the program's first three years and characterized it as too risky for additional support. Private electronics companies were reluctant to finance the shortfall, seeing little in the way of profits even if the project achieved some technical success. Japan furthermore lacked a Nasdaq national market, resulting in limited financing opportunities for entrepreneurs who had established Apple-type ventures that could produce PCs linking the country with the Internet. Instead, there was the conventional "salary man" who remained until retirement at Japan's corporate and bureaucratic helm, blocking innovative systems' work and usage. In the United States, equally lackluster counterparts at such corporate giants like IBM stuck with the mainframe, preferring to turn the PC over to others, namely Intel and Microsoft. In the process, organization men of both East and West were doubly finessed by major shifts in the computer industry that included product downsizing and the ascendancy of software in systems control.

> Japanese computer specialists and managers are not, and never have been, comfortable with software—it's intangible to them and its production is notoriously difficult to manage. [And unfortunately] most of the breakthroughs the Fifth Generation project must achieve are basically

innovations in software concepts. The Japanese lack a large corps of trained computer specialists. Their university-level training in computer sciences is mediocre—the best is just adequate, and the rest is bad.[6]

This timely warning made by an American computer specialist was naturally ignored by risk-averse government planners in Japan, who proceeded to cut funding for the nebulous area of software R&D at a critical juncture in the Information Revolution. In contrast, the importance of such developmental work was already being recognized in the United States and, as the following excerpt shows, was particularly suited for small, high-tech firms sprouting in Silicon Valley:

> Software is an important factor in information technology, exceeding four times the cost of hardware in large systems. The relative decline in hardware costs is shifting the focus of R&D to software. The term software refers both to the instructions that direct the operation of computer systems, and the information content, or data, that computer systems manipulate. An adequate organizing formalism or calculus for software creation has not yet been discovered. Therefore, the development of large, complex software systems depends heavily on the insight and creativity of systems designers and programmers. The methods presently employed to develop and test software are ad hoc, without a strong scientific basis. Thus, software systems are expensive to build and maintain, and can be unreliable in operation.[7]

Such problems plagued even IBM as it concentrated on developing its mainframe business and generally gave ancillary software to users that leased its big machines. With costs mushrooming in the mid-1980s, software engineering became more systematic, to allow its breakdown into discrete steps such as program specification and prototype design. In these processes, greater flexibility was incorporated into programs, allowing them to be used on equipment made by different vendors. The segmentation of software development also permitted small groups or individuals to work on different parts of the job:

> The segmentation or modularization of the software design breaks the problem into manageable pieces to maximize the ease of programming and testing the segments, and to facilitate the interchange or replacement of the modules to simplify maintenance. Proper segmentation is of particular importance because it has been demonstrated that as the size of the programming project team grows, more and more time is spent

communicating among team members and coordinating communication among program segments and less in actually writing code.[8]

Modularization of software development together with the spread of personal computers further eased the coding process by allowing job segments to be farmed out to freelance programmers. The Internet eventually permitted the downloading of code for testing purposes and offered an alternative sales channel, whereby a purchaser paid using a credit card. The PC meanwhile gave rise to independent software vendors who now, working at home or in small groups, developed application programs that were packaged on floppy disks costing $5 to $30 to make and sold for hundreds of dollars. Individual and corporate buyers eagerly sought the packages for use in word processing, spreadsheet tabulation, and tax preparation, and the number of software publishers ballooned to six thousand in 1983, with sales reaching $1.8 billion.[9]

Lotus Development Corporation with its pioneering 1–2–3 applications program in graphics, database management, and financial planning capitalized on these trends in the young industry as it developed stand-alone programs that ran on any hardware platform. Lotus's founder, Mitchell Kapor, worked as a radio disc jockey before starting the firm. He demonstrated that his unconventional background was not a drawback by successfully raising $5 million in venture capital before taking Lotus public in October 1983. The backing mainly came from Silicon Valley's leading VC partnership, Kleiner Perkins Caulfield & Byers (KP), with its prominent lead investor, John Doerr, handling the Lotus negotiations. During this quieter time for start-ups, individuals like Kapor and Doerr commanded scant attention in American capital markets, with the *Wall Street Journal* burying the news of Lotus's initial public offering on a back page. Doerr and KP were not mentioned at all. Considerable attention, however, attended Lotus's public listing on the Nasdaq, with the stock offered at $18, opening its first trading day at $22, and closing at $24.75. Its successful debut set the stage for the heavily publicized coming out of Microsoft in 1986, when its price on the day of its initial stock offering increased from $21 to $28 a share. The two firms subsequently battled in the software market, with Lotus leading Microsoft from 1983 to 1988, giving credence to what came to be known as "first-mover's advantage." This perceived head start prompted fledgling firms to rush to market with untested, bug-infested programs—snidely referred to as "vaporware"—that did little of what was promised by the vendor and its sales force. The Lotus IPO also showed that small, technical firms, begun on the West Coast away from Wall Street and managed by people with unconventional backgrounds, could gain the financial backing and services from investment bankers accorded bigger, blue-chip corporations. Comanaging the Lotus issue was the Silicon Valley VC firm Robertson, Coleman & Stephens, which, like Kleiner Perkins, had been established to serve technical start-ups in the area. In addition, the burgeoning business brought in mainline Wall Street bankers like Morgan Stanley and Goldman Sachs, with each investment house comanaging either the Apple or Microsoft IPO. IBM, the quintessential hardware firm, would also be dragged into software when in 1995 it paid $3 billion to take over Lotus to buttress its flagging capabilities. Such acquisitions along with feverish VC and IPO activity formed the essence of the Internet mania that stampeded ahead until it nosedived off a cliff at the end of the century.

IBM's Ancien Régime

IBM failed to foresee how corrosive the new personal computer would be on its mainframe business because it never expected its explosive growth. Other reasons behind the company's shortsighted behavior included the meager profit margins in the competitive microcomputer market, which paled alongside earnings from bigger machines. The corporate giant had also been accused by the federal government of exerting monopolistic power in mainframes and was therefore cautious about entering other computer areas. Reluctantly, it would be pushed into developing its PC by the publicized success of a ragtag outfit named Apple and its mercurial founder, Steve Jobs. Big Blue—as IBM is called because of its logo's color—came out with a personal computer in 1981 after hastily assembling it from components made by other companies. For the operating system software, IBM approached the small Microsoft Corporation in Redmond, Washington, not knowing that the latter firm did not have a suitable operating system and that it would surreptitiously buy one from a nearby vender. Big Blue further failed to obtain exclusive rights to the DOS (disk operating system), prompting Microsoft to sell it to other desktop manufacturers. These more nimble enterprises like Compaq and Dell then seized the lion's share of the growing PC market, in the process pushing aside IBM and paving the way for Microsoft's meteoric rise. The latter increased its chances for getting a stranglehold on the OS market by offering its DOS at low cost to these other PC makers, who in turn built high-volume computer sales by offering their PCs at cut-rate prices.

Development of LANs

As computer processing power spread with the helter-skelter installation of desktop computers, the logical extension presented itself of connecting the myriad machines at a given work site into a local area network, or LAN. The network offered distinct advantages to an organization because it facilitated communications between employees and allowed data stored in one computer to be accessed by another. PCs could also be linked to mini and mainframe computers in order to tap their greater processing power and data storage systems. Pioneering research on LANs began before the advent of commercial PCs, in 1972, at Xerox's Palo Alto Research Center. It focused on connecting workstations that were powerful enough to do complex technical jobs such as computer aided design and coordination of manufacturing processes that were formerly done by the larger, more expensive minicomputers. The workstation was compact enough to be individually operated, and because its tasks frequently called for the use of data located elsewhere as well as for consultation among engineers working on the same project, networking of the workstations became a necessity. Using these guidelines, efforts at the Palo Alto center resulted in the development of the Ethernet, a LAN that linked workstations and prototype PCs that were only beginning to be used in experimental systems such as this one. It was subsequently commercialized by the principal researcher of Ethernet, who left the center to form 3Com Corporation. Its network, like the PC and workstation, met with immediate commercial success and spelled more trouble for IBM in another rapidly advancing part of the computer business in which it had little to offer. Customers were now demanding more powerful, less costly, compact machines that could interact with other computers even though they were not made or leased by IBM. In 1980 such equipment already included minicomputers from Digital Equipment Corporation (the leading mini maker), PCs from Apple, and workstations from Apollo, with Sun Microsystems soon to join the fray with computers that could be networked with machines from other vendors. The torrid pace of systems innovation inevitably led to the ending of Big Blue's dominance with its stand-alone computers and proprietary systems revolving solely around its own machines. The mini, moreover, and not the mainframe, was already the computer of choice for developing the Arpanet since it had sufficient processing power for switching message packets along regional networks. It was also a lot less expensive and easier to operate, and these attributes further propelled the mini's use on the evolving Internet.

Internet Protocols

For the fast-evolving LANs, the next step lay in their connection to wide area networks (WANs) like Arpanet, which required the development of software protocols that allowed host computers on the LANs to send and receive messages to each other using the WAN. A second protocol was needed to coordinate transmission of packets between host and switching computers of a given local network and then on to another switching computer of the receiving LAN. It was difficult to establish a standard set of protocols in light of the variety of local networks that were to be linked—many with their own software already in use. Even on a given LAN, there could be computers controlled by different proprietary software. Fortunately, Arpanet, the principal if not the only wide area network, was still in the hands of the military, which was using it for communications purposes. To streamline the connecting of the LANs to Arpanet as well as quell the squabbling over protocol selection, the Pentagon unilaterally established the benchmark programs by selecting two familiar protocols that it had helped develop. The pair included TCP/IP, which stood for Transmission Control Protocol/Internet Protocol, whose development and testing had been closely monitored as well as funded by the Defense Communications Agency of the DOD. Selection by the government, furthermore, ensured that no private company like IBM or AT&T would exert undue influence over the formative stages of what would eventually turn into the Internet. Nevertheless, powerful interests were scrutinizing the wide area network and succeeded in getting Congress to pass legislation in the late 1980s that allowed them to transact business on the World Wide Web. By then the national WAN had passed into the hands of the National Science Foundation, and without the strict oversight of the military, the eased regulatory environment resulted in an explosive growth of software, hardware, semiconductor, and networking firms intent on making their mark in cyberspace.

IBM Falters

IBM, however, did not unduly benefit from the growing spread of commercial networks, even though it was a leader in desktop office computers as well as mainframes. In midrange or minicomputer markets, Big Blue was losing customers to Digital Equipment, primarily because it was difficult to network its equipment. Price wars also plagued the low-end or microcomputer market, resulting in meager profit margins for the IBM PC. A smaller home computer known as Peanut or PC Jr. was effectively stillborn at its launching in 1984. In networking, advances were bypassing its system of dumb terminals waiting to share time on a single mainframe. Newer networks of workstations were using powerful microprocessor chips that allowed the computers to work independently and not have to depend on the processing power of a bigger machine. Network software also permitted these smart terminals to interact with each other when needed. Such industrial shifts seriously impacted Big Blue's bottom line, with falling profits first hitting it in 1985 and continuing into 1986. The firm's top executives remained publicly nonplussed about the results, reassuring shareholders that after fifty years of profitable growth, the two down years were aberrations, which were expected to be succeeded by an upward move. Its fifty good years had furthermore brought the corporation staggering amounts of financial and technical resources that had already been used to quickly make its PC an industry standard and best-selling desktop computer model after its introduction in 1981. IBM attempted to build on this success by introducing an upgraded PC, the AT, in 1983, but encountered a software glitch, whereby the OS/2 operating system that ran AT's powerful 32-bit microprocessor was not deployed until 1988. Compaq Computer, meanwhile, launched its own 32-bit machine and went on to become a leader in the PC field.

The stumbling blocks, along with the structural changes, culminated in a massive $2.4 billion charge against current earnings taken by IBM at the end of the 1980s. It forced the computer maker to eliminate ten thousand jobs and reduce unneeded plant capacity for product that remained unsold. Big Blue was not the only large computer maker adversely affected by the fast-paced evolution of powerful smaller machines. Digital Equipment Corporation (DEC), the front-runner in minicomputers, came under fire from networks of advanced workstations made by Compaq and Sun Microsystems. Cost comparisons illustrate why the new systems were preferred: Ten workstations linked together had the processing power of a mainframe computer but cost only $300,000 compared to the latter's $5 million. Moreover, employees could work with their own computers, which greatly enhanced productivity compared to the shared use among ten people of a single mainframe.[10] The minicomputer was also inflexible, like the mainframe, and having less power, its role in the computer hierarchy would be eroded even faster by technically advanced PCs than in the case of the mainframe, which still served the needs of large corporate systems. DEC's slide would be so inexorable that it would be taken over by Compaq, the maker of small computers.

Formative IPOs

The upheaval affecting IBM and DEC signaled the beginning of a race among start-up firms to replace the leaders, with Wall Street opening its purse strings to fund high-tech enterprises like Apple, Dell, and Lotus. In March 1986, three small firms—Microsoft, Oracle, and Sun—went public within two weeks of each other, and their appearances greatly impacted the PC and networking industries. Of the three, Microsoft was associated with the older computer regime led by IBM because its operating system software ran Big Blue's PC. It would, however, make a major move onto the Internet in the subsequent ten years, using its PC base to launch its Explorer browser software that connected people to the Web. Its early alignment with IBM made its initial public offering (IPO) for listing on the Nasdaq a highly anticipated event, with the issue underwritten by the notable investment banker Goldman Sachs along with Alex. Brown & Sons. Its stock was offered at $21 a share and finished its first trading day at $28, and even though it had pre-IPO funds from venture capitalists, Microsoft's strong financial position derived from the booming PC market obviated the need for sizable outside investments in the young firm. As a result, its founder, Bill Gates, kept the lion's share of the company's equity and, helped by the stock's rising value, quickly became a multibillionaire and the world's richest person.

The day before Microsoft's debut, another West Coast start-up (Oracle) went public with its young founder, Larry Ellison, a college dropout like Bill Gates. Ellison's major contributions centered on the management decision-making tool of relational database software, which analyzed large amounts of information collected by computers to enable managers to project market trends or pinpoint problems for preemptive action. The demand for such software was so strong that Oracle's stock, concentrated in the hands of its founder, brought enormous wealth to Ellison, making him for a time the second-richest man in the world behind Bill Gates. Oracle's IPO, like Microsoft's, had pedigreed co-managers, and they included Merrill Lynch Capital Markets of the big brokerage house and Alex. Brown & Sons which had a leading role in the Microsoft stock offering. The Nasdaq warmly greeted this new listing by bidding up Oracle's stock price from its opening of $15 to $20.75 at the close of the trading day. Its sale of 2.1 million shares brought Oracle $31.5 million, less than half of what Microsoft raised the following day with its IPO. In the subsequent frenzy that characterized the Internet stock bubble, both of these 1986 IPOs, in monetary terms, would pale in comparison to the action of Netscape's initial offering in August 1995. The small software firm raised over $100 million from the sale of its stock even though the company had no earnings from its month-old business, centered mainly on its Navigator browser program. Despite the shortcomings, investors bid the price of Netscape's stock to $58 a share from its opening of $28. Sparked by this spectacular debut, the mania in Internet IPOs began its wildfire run through the canyons of Wall Street, feeding on the ever-present greed for the hypnotic wealth it was creating. Netscape's hyperbolic ascent, however, was short-lived. Akin to the rise and fall of a modern-day Icarus, the firm suffered a severe meltdown as it entered a software domain that Microsoft was set on contesting. Its splashy IPO, indeed, convinced Bill Gates that there were possibilities in the browser market, and he galvanized the vast resources of his firm for a frontal attack on the intruder, whose weak business fundamentals were easily overwhelmed. Netscape would be taken over by AOL, and its rapid rise and fall would be insignificant compared to Microsoft's evolution as a software powerhouse that was now making the transition from PCs to the Internet.

Microsoft Everywhere

While much of the public's attention was riveted on Nasdaq's (and Netscape's) boom and bust, the more important ascent of Microsoft over IBM and software over big hardware established the main industry trends of the IT Revolution. In both its PC and Internet business, Microsoft acquired and developed new technologies to compete in the changing milieu. Its innovative and upgraded software systems and successful marketing frequently left partners like IBM and competitors like Lotus in its wake. Its accomplishments, moreover, were grounded in understanding the distinctive nature of software, whose ethereal power, packaged on diskettes, was incomprehensible to an industrial old guard bent on building bigger machines to get bigger profits. Such size-oriented thinking undermined IBM's approach to the PC movement and allowed Microsoft and Intel (maker of semiconductor chips) to mine the riches exposed by this tectonic shift. Both companies shrewdly understood the implications of the transition and were nimble enough to implement plans for capitalizing on the altered environment. Intel's 8088 microprocessing chip was a landmark product packed with powerful capabilities similar to Microsoft's disk operating system (MS-DOS), and the two components became "the brains" of the IBM PC. Moreover, each part was frequently upgraded to give greater computer performance with software, in particular enhanced to take advantage of advances in hardware and systems technology. This ensured product obsolescence, forcing users to purchase upgraded programs in order to be competitive. In many cases, other vendors introduced new products because barriers to entry were low, with start-up and overhead costs minimal in the industry. Programs, once written, were easily reproduced, packaged, and commercialized. The heightened competition energized the combative zeal of founders like Bill Gates into continuously improving existing software and developing new products to ensure that Microsoft was not upended by an upstart firm the way IBM had been.

Possessed of a hard-charging manner, Gates embodied the high-tech manager who was driven by results and an intense desire for staying on top. His success at doing so during turbulent times can be attributed to the intentional establishment of Microsoft as a software company that was geared to tap the increasing power of the PC. With nearly total control over the company because of his equity ownership and forceful personality, Gates used his power to unilaterally allocate vital resources into areas that he anticipated would generate revenue growth. No decision-making by consensus or committees slowed him, and this style of management separated the high-tech firms—evolving at Internet speed—from older, more established enterprises. Microsoft's financial record clearly shows its heady evolution, with its revenue steadily increasing from 1975, when it was $16,000, to 1995, when it reached nearly $6 billion. Operating profit, moreover, never fell below 30 percent of sales from 1987 to 1995 despite the fact that it was a billion-dollar company. Only a strong leader with a flawless game plan could effect such a corporate performance, with due credit given to the revolutionary times that enabled Gates to so religiously pursue his agenda. The exceptional times also meant that other driven executives could accomplish similar feats, and a casual glance at Silicon Valley's recent past finds comparable achievements by Larry Ellison at Oracle and John Chambers at Cisco. Microsoft's impact, however, was more overwhelming because of its dominance in key IT areas. The antitrust lawsuit brought by the U.S. Justice Department is another testament to the considerable market power exercised by the firm, which was found guilty of anticompetitive practices. The judicial decision painted a picture of two companies: A small software start-up that with a great deal of luck and strategic planning by its founder obtained a stranglehold on the operating system for PCs, and an arrogant giant that used its monopolistic power in one market to bludgeon its way onto the Internet.

With the recent high-tech meltdown as background, the earlier Microsoft story of a struggling, young enterprise contains important lessons on how it accomplished so much while many dot-com start-ups failed. Microsoft realized from the beginning how to generate revenues from software and adroitly entered many of the areas that held the most commercial opportunities. Its move to secure the operating system for the IBM PC and reduce existing efforts in programming languages like Basic illustrates how Gates and company changed direction at critical junctures. Its small staff at the time had little expertise in OS; hence, the firm simply bought a prototype program from a nearby Seattle company and offered it as DOS (version 1.0) to IBM. The IBM PC quickly became the desktop standard, forcing other manufacturers to license DOS from Microsoft in order to produce IBM-compatible machines that were demanded by most buyers. The mass market win in PC software gave Microsoft a running start as well as substantial licensing fees, which the company used to increase its workforce to over one thousand employees by 1985. Launched in that year, Windows 1.01 would be one result of the expanded cadre of programmers who were hired to upgrade and write code for new products. Highlighting a graphical user interface, Windows made the still intimidating PC a much more user-friendly machine, especially for first-time buyers. The new operating system piggybacked on MS-DOS in order to permit application programs written for the older OS to be used with the new Windows system. It also featured a point-and-click method for accessing programs that performed word processing or spreadsheet setups, with these applications represented by an icon or small logo-type picture. The icon became the distinguishing aspect of the graphical user interface, and its ease of use made Windows a significant improvement over the MS-DOS interfacing that required the keyboard typing-in of characters. The screen pointer, moreover, was controlled by a hand-directed device called a mouse, with the arrow on the screen maneuvered by moving the mouse in the same direction. Clicking on a desired icon could be inputted from either mouse or keyboard.

Despite these advances, Windows was not an immediate hit because of technical and legal problems related to the graphical system that Microsoft licensed from Apple. Nevertheless, the firm, using revenues from MS-DOS, doggedly pursued the enhancement of both operating systems, and these focused on better file and memory management and improved graphics capability. MS-DOS also could run networking operations by 1984, and this evolved into Windows NT software for Internet client-server (big computer) information systems. In 1986 to 1987, MS-DOS and Windows were upgraded again to work with keyboards based on foreign languages, advancing the company's emphasis on international sales, which from 1986 to 1995 never fell below 65 percent of total sales. These continuing efforts at adding features and bringing forth improved versions of its most important products kept Microsoft ahead of the pack of other ambitious software firms intent on invading its markets. Product testing and debugging were also built into company operations to catch or repair glitches before or after product was shipped. Such bugs were the bane of all software competitors since many of them lacked the resources to incorporate adequate quality controls in their product development. Programs laden with defects were subsequently released, resulting in ruined reputations for firms that often had no choice in the matter because revenues for keeping the start-up afloat were desperately needed. This was never the case with Microsoft, whose coffers were overflowing. Its earnings were plowed into more revenue-generating ventures such as application programs and networking software. Improvements to the Windows OS were undertaken, leading to the eventual independence of Windows 95 from DOS. The earlier-released Windows 3.1 version had e-mail capabilities and allowed file sharing over networks that were spreading quickly, especially in the United States.[11]

Applications Programming

Coinciding with efforts to enhance its systems software, Microsoft—a small concern in 1982 with sales of $33 million—was forced to move into application programming simply because that was where the money was. Such software could be sold for at least five times the price of systems programs, and as a result total sales in applications stood at $1.89 billion, considerably ahead of system sales of $279 million. In addition to Lotus, Micropro with Wordstar, Visicorp with Visicalc, and Ashton Tate with dBase II became market leaders in word processing, spreadsheet formulation, and database management, respectively. Lotus and Visicorp even led Microsoft in sales—a far cry from the situation in software today. To counter these initial movers the company developed and sold its first commercially successful application program, named Multiplan, for use in spreadsheet tabulations. The introduction ran into unexpected distribution problems since Microsoft now had to package and market the diskettes through a myriad number of retail outlets rather than simply ship product to a few equipment manufacturers like Compaq and IBM. The PC maker installed the MS-DOS and assumed most of the costs of selling the machine. In applications sales, Microsoft in contrast planned and incurred all promotional costs associated with the task of persuading independent retailers to stock its diskettes. This proved difficult because Multiplan trailed sales of Visicalc and the new, improved Lotus 1–2–3 which attractively bundled spreadsheet with two other popular programs.

Moreover, as was common with a new product issuance, software glitches infected the Multiplan program, and Microsoft, reputation on the line, was forced to spend $200,000 to eliminate the bugs. Even with this setback, the Multiplan program was successful, and it was followed by Microsoft Word, a very strong entry in the word processing field, which it came to dominate. Realizing that Word would be a winner, Microsoft planned an aggressive introduction by placing demonstration disks of the program in *PC World* magazine. The giveaway cost the company $3.5 million but gained it widespread publicity, which Microsoft hoped to tie to its new Windows operating system. The powerful Windows OS with such features as point-and-click graphical interfacing would furthermore assist sales of the firm's application packages because these would work best when used in tandem. Independent software vendors were also encouraged to write Windows-based application packages, and to promote the effort Microsoft shared technical information with firms to give them a running start. Windows moreover was offered to PC makers for minimal royalty payments in an effort to make it a standard like MS-DOS, which further prompted more software-producing houses to rally around the Windows banner.[12]

In addition to these strenuous efforts, Microsoft began feeling the intense strain of supplying DOS to IBM, a job it had suddenly received in 1981. The computer giant furthermore was criticizing product it was getting from Microsoft, insisting, with all the clout that IBM can bring on a tiny supplier, that the latter improve the quality control of DOS production or else suffer the consequences. To placate its principal customer, Microsoft dipped into its financial reserves to hire competent program and functional managers as well as separate software development from testing to highlight and attack the bug problem. Defects, however, continued to plague the firm as advances in systems software were layered on earlier versions to accommodate applications programs written for the older software. Fortunately for the company, its operating system became a standard for the personal computer, and this forced even IBM to grudgingly accept it. Innovations in hardware also resulted in interactive complications since new code was needed to operate with the more powerful microprocessing chips. Testing rose exponentially when new software that itself was often defect-ridden needed to be experimentally run with old and new versions of other parts of the system. Testing, moreover, was always considered of marginal use—and this feeling was prevalent in almost all forms of production—because its value in the final package was hidden. Managers were more interested in meeting launch deadlines and production goals since these targets clearly had a notable impact on performance appraisals. Consumers on the other hand who bought defective product were quick to air their complaints in the media and with colleagues and take their business elsewhere. In such a charged environment, quality control problems could be resolved only by the strict attention of top management, a fact Bill Gates somewhat belatedly realized in 1989 as the bug problem spread. He allocated resources for a rigorous testing program to supplant the perfunctory examination of products as they left the factory's doors. Gates moreover had the power and loud demeanor to make everyone aware of his new quality standards, which specifically made all programmers responsible for correcting the defects in their coding. Such a zero-defect program was borrowed from Japanese automakers, which had pioneered the concept in their campaign to gain market share in the United States. Gates's subsequent yelling, of course, did not remove all defects, but it did do enough to impact the bottom line. A corrected Multiplan, renamed Excel, became the best-selling program in spreadsheet and graphics depiction and together with the new Word package for word processing, made Microsoft the leader in application programming. Windows 3.0 and 3.1 were released to rave reviews, and the popular Office package was developed that bundled three main application programs: Word, Excel, and Powerpoint for making presentation slides.[13]

These achievements—goaded by the yelling-in-your-face actions of Bill Gates—made the new corporate giant even more hated in information technology than IBM had been. Captain Ahab wannabes from the highly egotistical IT business began muttering about beaching this Moby Dick (Microsoft), which had replaced the Soviet Union (IBM) as the evil empire. In the resulting confrontation, industry antagonists became intent on stopping the Microsoft juggernaut from dominating the Internet and killing their efforts, one by one, as it had done with Netscape. They rallied to the government's side, despite their laissez-faire beliefs, in its antitrust case against Microsoft and organized to have Netscape bought by AOL after it had lost the browser war to Microsoft. In financial circles, moreover, the cabal of Microsoft opponents—Oracle, Sun, and AOL—was supported by the powerful venture capital (VC) firm of Kleiner Perkins (KP), which was intent on preventing the formidable software company from stomping on the start-ups it was bringing to market. In such adversarial circumstances, the VC industry and its principal practitioner, KP, attempted to level the playing field and allow innovative firms to implement business plans that advanced e-commerce and the Internet Revolution.

Early Venture Capitalism

In more harmonious times, as in 1986 when Oracle and Microsoft had their IPOs, the role of venture capitalism was a muted affair because these start-up firms were operating profitably and saw no reason to surrender equity ownership to what they often perceived as "vulture capitalists." Sun Microsystems fell in league with this wary line of thought even though its IPO, which had preceded those of the others by one week, was not as well received. Sun's stock price would close lower on its first day of trading because its workstations faced stiff competition from the older and bigger Apollo Computer company. Sun, however, had more resourceful people than Apollo as well as strong ties to important institutions. One of its founders was Vinod Khosla, an immigrant engineer from India who initiated the commercial linking of Sun's workstations along the lines of the Ethernet LAN operating at nearby Xerox and Stanford University, where Khosla had gone to school. The university, an incubator of managerial and technical talent for Silicon Valley start-ups, not only educated Khosla, who assembled Sun's prototype computers, but supplied an MBA graduate, Scott McNealy, who would lead the fledgling firm. Khosla helped obtain start-up financing from Kleiner Perkins and would later become a KP partner after leaving Sun. Its IPO was co-managed by a prominent San Francisco–based investment banker, Robertson, Coleman & Stephens, and this as well as the KP contact introduced Sun to many of the high-tech firms that would use its products.

Despite its ties to the financial industry, Sun's dependence on it for funding never amounted to much, which followed from the immediate commercial success of its workstations that brought in operating income of $598,000 and $3.7 million in its first two years. Furthermore, "Despite its reputation for zaniness on other fronts, Sun has always been a tightly managed company that meets its financial obligations."[14] Sun, like Microsoft and Oracle, was consequently a quality start-up, with profitable lines and aggressive managers who initiated R&D programs that kept the company at the forefront of its field. Sun's resources and managerial strength furthermore kept the young, unknown firm from splintering, even when it dared undertake the removal of Khosla as its chief executive, replacing him with McNealy. The executive upheaval could have been devastating for the company, but it took up the challenge because: "As 1984 progressed, people within Sun were becoming painfully aware that the company was outgrowing Vinod Khosla's skills as a CEO. It came down to his inability to deal with the primary capital of any knowledge-based company: people. Khosla was a visionary who didn't understand the down-to-earth reality of trusting employees to do their jobs."[15]

Khosla was also a powerful entrepreneur in Silicon Valley who had successfully founded Daisy Systems before joining Sun. He would go on to become a general partner at Kleiner Perkins and was dubbed "The No. 1 VC on the planet" on the February 13, 2001, cover of *Red Herring*. Sun Microsystems nevertheless made the difficult decision to proceed without Khosla because it was not beholden to outside funding sources and, like Microsoft, had the wherewithal to resolve in-house problems, develop innovative products, and win new markets. This independence furthermore ensured that powerful Wall Street forces would shy away from these start-ups with their zany, egotistically obnoxious executives, who were never interested in selling ownership stakes in their tightly held companies.

For mind-boggling returns, the underwriters had to wait for the IPOs of Netscape and Amazon, whose debt-ridden operations made them desperate for outside funding. The scenario thus evolved of investing in bottom-of-the-barrel companies with foolhardy but flashy schemes centered on illusory products and services. Seed money was even offered to founders based solely on an idea, as in the doomed Webvan case. Why would "smart" money from seasoned capitalists be so freely invested? For one thing, only the VC principals and founders understood the lack of substance underlying many start-ups, and since the shares were privately held (not listed on public stock markets), there was no requirement from regulatory bodies for disclosing the sad state of affairs. More often than not, breathless, self-serving press releases were floated announcing a revolutionary breakthrough in Internet technology to generate interest in the firm, along with confirming evidence that an in-the-know venture capitalist had taken a major investment position in the young company. The founders would keep a low profile after the VC investment, take what cut they had negotiated, and exit the company. The VC firm in turn got a fabulous return on its investment when the firm's stock was offered to the public and driven up in price by the hype of its "revolutionary breakthrough." Prominent Wall Street investment banks and brokerage firms chimed in with enthusiastic endorsements and would be rewarded with preferential shares not given to the hoi polloi as well as lucrative underwriting fees and trading commissions. The high-flying numbers attained for one VC investment in eBay, the Internet auction house, illustrate the stakes involved: In 1997, a $6.7 million investment in the auctioneer was made, one year before eBay's IPO. EBay, unlike other riffraff dot-coms, was well managed with thriving lines of business, and because of these attributes its stock took off. On the first day of trading, the value of the VC investment leaped from $6.7 million to $400 million and within an additional three months had surged to $21 billion, an increase of "100,000 percent in less than two years' time, making it the Valley's best-performing venture ever."[16] EBay may have been atypical as a profitable online business, but its return to its small coterie of investors became characteristic of the mad-money race that had begun on the Nasdaq. The madness notwithstanding, the Internet era did elicit major breakthroughs in hardware, software, and establishment of the electronic transmission network. Successful e-commerce ventures were launched, and together these developments ingrained the medium in business and society just as the railroad, telephone, and automobile did in prior industrial ages.

—— Chapter 3 ——
The Information Superhighway

Even with the spread of personal computers and the transformation of Arpanet into the more commercially oriented Internet, traffic on the spreading network lagged because it was mainly available to scientists and engineers at various research centers and not to the public at large. Most of the users were, furthermore, civilian workers employed by the U.S. military who conducted research that the armed forces was intent on keeping secret for national security reasons. Moreover, the fall of the Berlin Wall in 1989, signaling the death knell of Soviet communism, did not alter the surreptitious nature of these Cold War research programs that yielded few if any useful results. Final reports at any rate were duly classified and remanded into oblivion. As if the heavy-handed oversight by the military was not enough, the public's use of the Internet was also constrained by its highly arcane nature as well as by IBM's virtual monopoly of the computer industry that rested on the leasing of its mainframes to large organizations. Its emphasis on big, stand-alone machines proved to have a dampening effect on the networking of smaller computers, obviously because it did not want to foster an alternative architecture that undermined its main source of income.

Despite these obstacles, interest increased as the Cold War receded and commercial transactions were allowed on the Internet, which came under civilian (National Science Foundation) control. Users began surfing the World Wide Web, which was created by Tim Berners-Lee, with their numbers mushrooming to 130 million people by 1998 as browsers and other software aids became available. E-commerce ballooned to $22 billion, with online stock trading becoming a lucrative business undertaken by investors who had heretofore never clicked on a PC or maneuvered its mouse. What triggered these momentous changes, and why were they mainly confined to the United States?

Protocols Are Established

The Internet juggernaut can be better understood by examining the system and its components as they evolved to interact in a user-friendly manner that made the network accessible to an information-hungry public. In earlier Arpanet days, hardware consisted of host computers and interface message processors (minicomputers) in which the host formatted a message into packets and addressed each one to a destination computer. The processors then transmitted the packets, often over different routes to circumvent transmission bottlenecks. The system, to put it mildly, was not an easy one to use, and the advent of local area networks further complicated the hardware and software requirements of addressing and sending messages for communication purposes or for accessing information on another network. Growing numbers of individual computers—some of them workstations—were forming LANs, and more and more LANs were going on the Arpanet, resulting in incompatible connections. To handle the problem, routing computers replaced the interface message processor and, using updated routing tables, these computers transmitted messages to gateway computers on other LAN networks. An incoming message would be received by the destination gateway computer that in turn would send it to the correct computer on the LAN. Addressing requirements consequently had to specify the network and the particular computer on the network, and this entailed the use of two protocol sets that standardized the sending of messages. The first (Transmission Control Protocol or TCP) coordinated messages sent between computers on a given network, and the second (Internet Protocol, IP) oversaw transmissions between networks. The onerous updating of address tables inevitably crumbled under the weight of the exponential growth of host computers linked to the Internet and a more scalable domain name system was adopted. Addresses were disaggregated by domain such as .com, .gov, .edu, and .org, and special server computers maintained address databases of all hosts in the domain. Updated address tables consequently were maintained by only a small number of domain computers rather than all the hosts of every LAN connected to the Internet.

The TCP/IP standards greatly facilitated communications over linked networks, and the resulting increase in LANs connecting and forming the global Internet presented tremendous opportunities for routing computers, or routers, that soon formed the backbone of the spreading Internet. Routers, using the new protocol standards, had a cross-platform compatibility that allowed various computers—mainframes, minis, workstations—even with different software operating systems, to send and receive messages from each other. A second attribute was the ability to send information through the existing telephone system that spanned the globe, thus melding the substantial long-lines reach of telecommunications networks with the Internet. "This combination of intelligence—the ability to look into the packets and determine what to do with each—and a gateway to the outside world [by being able to access telephone lines] made the router the crucial device for the growth of the Internet once the World Wide Web appeared in 1993."[1]

In the mid-1980s, however, Arpanet and its smaller cousins, the local area networks, operated behind closed doors under the constant guard of military or corporate officials. Even the connection to AT&T's lines was not considered an asset because the telephone network was built with a different architecture than the packet messaging system of Arpanet. The cost of sending messages over long distances using Bell phone lines was also prohibitive, leaving e-mail confined to the Arpanet connecting a small number of research sites or within a local area such as a manufacturing facility, office complex, or university campus. Gateway routers and their software were consequently preempted by local telephone systems that gave callers easy and quick access to almost anywhere outside the local area. Dialing even overseas phone numbers had become routine, while computer messaging, in contrast, was difficult, especially for first-time users. Without Internet service providers and browser software, accessing information and Web sites was equally user-unfriendly, and considerable advances in hypertext linking, for example, had to occur before PC mouse-clicking reached tidal wave proportions.

In September 1988, moreover, the information technology revolution was still going through a transition consisting of the dethroning of IBM and the growing use of desktop computers with the rise of PC vendors such as Compaq and Dell. Establishments also concentrated on linking the 19 million desktop computers that had sprouted like weeds in the ongoing PC boom. Only 10 percent of these machines were tied into data-sharing and productivity-enhancing LANs, and corporate information officers were intent on securing the necessary hardware and software, including ancillary storage systems, that would bring more order and control in their workplace. Unfortunately for this endeavor, the industry had already split into two camps, with the first based on operating systems compatible with Microsoft software loaded on IBM's PCs. An incompatible, opposing group was primarily led by Apple and its Macintosh operating system. While Microsoft was too busy supplying systems software to PC manufacturers to develop programs connecting desktop computers, two other software firms—3Com and Novell, another leading supplier of networking software—quickly entered the breach. The founding executive of 3Com developed its Ethernet-like software at the Xerox Palo Alto Research Center, and after taking leave of Xerox, offered the program commercially in 1981 to organizations intent on networking their machines. By 1987, 3 Com's software was installed in 42,000 networks linking IBM-compatible computers, while the Novell program connected another 30,400. Both trailed the number of Apple-linked networks of 130,000, with the high incidence of such networks indicative of the great demand that existed for them in the workplace. Sales of Novell's networking software jumped 88.7 percent in 1987 to $182.8 million, bypassing 3Com in revenues. At about the same time, the start-up Sun Microsystems was battling Apollo Computer for the market linking workstations, and despite competition from the latter, its sales soared past $1 billion.[2]

Cisco Systems and Its Router

While networking proceeded at the local level, Cisco Systems, an embryonic supplier of computers that powered the Internet, waited in the wings fervently hoping that the increased activity would improve the sales of its routers and controlling software. Its hopes would come to fruition only after the World Wide Web (WWW) was launched, which took some time because the landmark software—that turbocharged the public's use of the Internet—was only then being conceived at a high-energy Swiss physics laboratory called CERN. The time delay proved fatal for the husband and wife founding team of Cisco who, like so many other Silicon Valley entrepreneurs, had come out of Stanford University. As graduate students, Leonard Bosack and Sandy Lerner, together with an engineer at the medical school, built some of the first routing computers to connect various departments at the university. Commercial opportunities beyond Stanford were immediately contemplated, but unlike other start-ups like Sun, Oracle, and Microsoft, the young couple's router did not have an immediate market. Financing for their company, which they named Cisco, therefore had to go through the plodding process of selling their business plan to surrounding venture capitalists, a disagreeable task that the other profitable firms could and primarily did avoid. Eventually a deal was struck with the VC firm Sequoia Associates of Menlo Park, led by Don Valentine, which offered Cisco $2.5

million, provided it transferred a one-third stake to Sequoia with accompanying rights to choose the top executive of the start-up company.
Sequoia also received the option to buy the ownership interests of the
founders, and these Machiavellian terms—normal in such VC deals—
effectively transferred control of Cisco to Valentine and his VC firm. At
the time, the founders were forced to accept such onerous conditions
because Cisco's future was in serious doubt, and few could foresee how
quickly moving events in Internet technology would transform the router
company into a high-tech powerhouse. The first signs of Cisco's bright
future appeared in 1990, the year of its successful IPO, but it was too
late for Bosack and Lerner to reclaim control of the firm. An outsider
was named president of the company, without their approval, and the
husband and wife entrepreneurial team—with the board of directors and
Valentine aligned against them—angrily exited the firm that was already
becoming one of the greatest start-up ventures of all time. This was
evident in the munificent cash settlement of $170 million that Cisco
paid the departing founders. The staggering payoff caused massive shifts
in the underlying dynamics of Silicon Valley, with savage warfare breaking out among the principals for control of those "geese that lay golden
eggs." Financial returns made by venture capitalists and individual, or
angel, investors began to assume Mount Everest–like proportions, and
their huge cash reserves effectively made them arbiters of entrepreneurial success in the Information Revolution. Don Valentine of Sequoia
Associates, as an example, sat on sizable amounts realized from earlier
lucrative investments in the corporate start-up of National Semiconductor and Apple Computer. This allowed him to present exacting terms to
hungry, naive innovators (like at Cisco) on a take-it-or-leave-it basis
with built-in clauses guaranteeing that control and a major share of any
profits went to the venture capitalist. These pernicious conditions kept
earlier entrepreneurs like Larry Ellison of Oracle a safe distance from
venture capitalists, and he could proceed to build his empire and aggrandize a personal fortune unencumbered by any liens on his firm.
Oracle's IPO, moreover, was launched with little fanfare compared with
Cisco's much-publicized listing in 1990. The billions of dollars involved
in later high-tech start-ups would attract swarms of immigrant engineers as well as computer science and business majors to the new California gold rush of establishing a technical enterprise. The feverish action
was undertaken to claim the billions of dollars being coughed up by
U.S. and even foreign financial institutions that resulted in the floating

of many fraudulent schemes that had little chance of becoming viable businesses. The intent, of course, was simply to get funding from angel investors, venture capitalists, and ultimately a gullible public. It would be initiated with the presentation of some abstruse idea that gained attention because it involved an Internet breakthrough. The investment process would end with the usual poor suckers stuck with worthless stock in a bankrupt company. The game plan successfully worked for a time because of the intense greed generated and the highly technical nature of the businesses that were being created. Both paved the way for Wall Street hype artists to induce a technically illiterate public into investing in the next NEW, NEW thing and perhaps retire with untold riches. The scams would have dissipated had it not been for the substantive progress that was actually occurring in transforming the Internet into a global communications and information medium. The router, computer networking, the advent of Internet service providers, and software development—particularly the World Wide Web, browsers, and portal programs—synergistically interacted to allow a host of commercial uses that swelled interest in the Internet. The soaring attention made investors more vulnerable to stock market gurus and their entreaties of getting in fast, on the ground floor of the next Internet killer "app" (hyped term for application) that was destined to hit Wall Street as an IPO. Technical jargon and electronic buzzwords filled the air, and in truth the technology underlying many of the substantive developments was so involved and complex that even inventors, such as Bosack and Lerner of Cisco, did not foresee all the far-reaching consequences of their accomplishment. In another principal area, there were such distorted accounts of the World Wide Web that its principal architect decided to write and publish his own account, *Weaving the Web*, to set the record straight.

The World Wide Web

Tim Berners-Lee, a professional programmer at CERN, was far from the madding crowd of money-grubbing stock analysts when he confronted and overcame the main stumbling blocks inhibiting a curious public from using the Internet. In his autobiography, he notes the situation as it was before the development of his program that came to be known as the World Wide Web: "The Internet was up and running by the 1970s, but transferring information was too much of a hassle for a noncomputing expert. One would run one program to connect to another computer, and then in conversation (in a different language) with the other computer, run a different program to access the information."[3]

This was the situation on the Internet, even with the use of TCP/IP protocols that facilitated the sending of messages but did little to improve the accessing of information stored outside the user's computer. In addition, the incompatibility of computers and data formats, the absence of an information space where documents could be posted, lack of an addressing system for locating data files, and software protocols for accessing information all held back progress in the transferring of information. Acknowledging these stumbling blocks, Berners-Lee, in 1990, began working on the software that facilitated the request and transmission of information over the Internet. The Web, as his innovative project was shortened to from World Wide Web, possessed these essential attributes that, with other contributions from the industry, enabled fast and easy sending of data files over the Internet:

1. An addressing format that identifies the server computer where the desired information is stored. Particular addresses are known as universal resource locators (URLs) and they begin with "http://www" followed by the server's and file's name where the information is located.
2. The hypertext transfer protocol, http as in the above URL, which controls how the server computer responds and transfers its information to the client computer that requested it.
3. A hypertext markup language, html, for composing Web pages and hypertext linkages between Web pages, to enable a user to go from one site to another by clicking on a highlighted term that contained an embedded address of the information source.
4. A browser program, also written by Berners-Lee, to access files that were on the Internet but whose server computer did not follow the http protocol.

With these software tools, an information space was created and called the World Wide Web, where data could be posted on server computers, given an address, and readily obtained by an inquiring client computer with the aid of a browser. At the time of the Web's creation, the Internet had been operating for decades with sizable amounts of data stored in its connected computers, and this substantial body of information would now be easier to access. To ease the Web's use and acceptance, Berners-Lee released the WWW programs in 1991, first to a few colleagues at CERN, the particle physics lab in Switzerland where he was employed, and then to the outside Internet community. The programs were quickly downloaded by digital cognoscenti throughout the world and used to surf this "thing" known as cyberspace. Information sources ballooned as more and more files were gratuitously posted on WWW, with Web sites of current stock market prices, sports scores, retail merchandise, travel routes, weather conditions, and news events attaining immense popularity and constant use. Enormous possibilities presented themselves for using the global network, and even though he personally did not benefit from any business arrangement, Berners-Lee believed that: "It was inevitable and important that if the Web succeeded, there would be a variety of free and commercial software available" for Internet usage.[4] His use of a graphical user interface, moreover, transformed information accessing that had heretofore depended on text-only hyperlinks and cryptic commands: "Using the Internet became easy and intuitive almost overnight. The number of users and the number of Web servers exploded. The early growth spurt in the mid-1990s reached 600 percent a year. Today, there are millions of servers, tens of millions of users, and hundreds of millions of Web pages."[5]

Leading this explosive growth was a dazzling array of advances in networking software for Cisco routers, Sun servers, AOL Internet service providers, Yahoo portals, AltaVista search engines, and most notably the Netscape Navigator browser. It became locked in a commercial and legal brouhaha with Internet Explorer from the software giant Microsoft. The browser and other battles continue in the new millennium as old and new, big and small forces attempt to dominate entry points and establish competitive positions in cyberspace.

The Mosaic Browser

Netscape's browser program had its origins at the National Center for Supercomputing Applications (NCSA) at the University of Illinois, which was established by the National Science Foundation as a response to Japan's Fifth Generation project. The PC boom upended both U.S. and Japanese supercomputing efforts as the big machines were superseded by the spread of desktop models. The scientific staff at NCSA understandably began flailing around for a new mission that would enable it to keep its government funding, and the networking of computers became a viable option, especially since NSF, its sponsoring agency, had taken over the Internet. This work could furthermore build on the WWW already created by Berners-Lee, and Marc Andreeson of the Illinois lab was directed to develop a browser that superseded the one written by the CERN programmer. Following the release of WWW software by Berners-Lee, such Internet-oriented projects became common in computer science departments at various universities like Illinois, where Andreeson was a student as well as a staff member of NCSA. Other browsers had already been developed at Helsinki University (named Erwise), the University of California, Berkeley campus (Viola WWW), and the University of Kansas (Lynx). Most of these programs could be downloaded from the Internet without charge, but a considerable amount of time and technical effort had to be expended on integrating the browser into a network as well as with the Internet TCP/IP protocols and software components of server and client computers. Internet use thus remained frustrating before and after the Web's creation, and commercial vendors were kept waiting for the easy-to-use software that would catalyze e-commerce: "But as difficult as it is to imagine, as late as 1992, there was no commercial Internet, no World Wide Web. Little was known about the "new media" market. And few businesspeople—especially in investment houses—believed that consumer networking was anything more than a fad, much like CB radios."[6]

The fledgling Internet service provider America Online still had no plan for bringing order to this amorphous and uncertain situation, and it was furthermore being threatened by a buyout from Microsoft. Bill Gates, CEO of the software company, was then interested in purchasing AOL for use as a beachhead in the event that online services became lucrative: His workers were more nonchalant about cyberspace: "As far as the Internet was concerned, the company seemed to have its head in the sand. [In 1995] most Microsoft employees paid little attention to the Internet, and some had not even heard of Netscape, browsers, or the Web."[7]

In such a milieu, Internet gamesmanship remained in the hands of the technically elite, but for those in this select group who possessed some business aptitude, like Andreeson, commercial goals were coming into sharp focus. The market for a browser became apparent as increasing numbers of Web users turned cyberspace into a rapid-response communication channel for critiquing ongoing software developments like those at NCSA. The launching of the Mosaic browser thus was aided by the constant feedback it received as it was being created and tested by online users. Based on comments from these testers, programmers at the supercomputing center embedded Mosaic with graphical color images that, like highlighted text, acted as hypertext links for accessing written documents, charts, and data. Mosaic was also designed for use with popular operating systems such as Microsoft's Windows, the Apple Macintosh, and Unix, which ran the X Windows System. Mosaic was released without charge by NCSA in November 1993, and by the following spring, a million copies of the browser had been downloaded. The wide acceptance of Mosaic proved too tempting for Andreeson, who set out for Silicon Valley where he teamed with veteran entrepreneur Jim Clark to form the Mosaic Communications Corporation. Clark had built an enviable record in the high-tech valley by establishing Silicon Graphics, Inc., which was noted for the dinosaur animation done by the firm for the blockbuster film *Jurassic Park*. Intrigued by the new Web developments that were causing a furor in the area, Clark left Silicon Graphics and was convinced by Andreeson to invest part of his personal fortune and expertise as a start-up manager in the new browser firm. Andreeson supplied the code for Mosaic and recruited members of the NCSA development team to work on its commercial upgrading.

As salary costs ballooned, Clark sought venture capital funding from Kleiner Perkins, the leading San Francisco VC firm, which put $5 million into Mosaic. This was one of the first investments for KP in the expanding Internet field, which would eventually total $300 million, making it one of the main sources of equity financing for dot-com firms. Payoffs for Kleiner Perkins began as these start-ups went public in the sale of their newly minted stock, which Mosaic did on August 9, 1995. Prior to the IPO, however, the University of Illinois, which had retained commercial rights to the browser program, began to license it to other software companies and forced Andreeson to drop the term Mosaic from its browser package and corporate name. The new company was renamed Netscape Communications Corporation and the Netscape Navigator 1.0 browser was released in December 1994. With its user-friendly features and free downloading, Navigator seized 60 percent of the market even though other brands, derived from the licensing of Mosaic, were already available. The successful release of Navigator paved the way for a spectacular launching of the company's stock in August of the following year. Five million shares were offered at $28 each, with the price skyrocketing to $87 and then falling back to close the day at $58.28. The investment banker Morgan Stanley Dean Witter underwrote the issue, and the big bank's Internet analyst, Mary Meeker, issued her usual enthusiastic endorsement of Netscape even though it lacked an earnings record. Meeker would quickly become the "queen of the Net" for her hyperbolic recommendations that, because of Morgan Stanley's prestige, frequently caught investors' attention, who followed through by bidding for the stock. This helped the underwriting business of her employer as well as boosted trading fees for the brokerage part of the bank. Numerous start-ups would follow Netscape's footsteps and have their IPOs launched by prestigious Wall Street houses. These small, unknown firms had threadbare business plans and were of course in dire need of the backing proffered by Meeker and her fellow analysts.

Unfortunately for the soon-to-be immensely wealthy entrepreneurs of Netscape, the market reception given both its browser and the firm's stock had unsettling repercussions for the young company's future. Within months of the IPO, Bill Gates of Microsoft initiated a massive corporate effort to develop a competing program. It would furthermore distribute it free to users by bundling it with its new Windows 95 operating system for PCs. Microsoft by then had built a monopoly in PC operating systems and had plowed much of the resulting profits back into the company. The result was what could arguably be described as the most potent capability in software research and development ever assembled. This was accomplished under the tight control and direction of its energetic chief, Bill Gates, who possessed shrewd business and technical instincts and tempered these with the constant fear that his company was turning into an enervating, lumbering giant like IBM. By being exceptionally zealous, however, the software company stumbled into the regulatory gaze of the federal government, which in June 1990 began an investigation into possible collusive deals restraining trade that Microsoft and IBM together had entered. No charges resulted from this first encounter. It was followed by a much more concerted move by the Department of Justice in 1997, after Microsoft with its bundled Explorer browser program eviscerated the early lead held by Netscape and caused its virtual collapse. To continue operating, a badly beaten Netscape agreed to be taken over by America Online.

The Bubble Paradigm

Even more than its near demise at the hands of Microsoft, Netscape is remembered today for how its IPO became standard operating procedure for fueling the Internet mania that resulted in a horrific crash in 2000. The bones of Netscape may have been picked clean by vulture capitalists in its fall, but Wall Street knew that the feasting would continue because there were hundreds of start-ups to take its place. More IPOs centering on Internet browsers, servers, portals, search engines, and graphical user interfaces were lining up to be parlayed to an ignorant, investing public. The overwhelming financial risks of purchasing shares in an untested start-up had always been known by investors because booms and busts chasing the instant money of a "revolutionary" idea had so frequently visited capital markets like Wall Street in the past. Dire consequences during such times resulted even for seasoned investors who failed to uncover the dark side of any hot new issue like Netscape. In this case, the specter of Microsoft hovering over the young firm was visible from the beginning and, moreover, Netscape had no operating earnings with which to prepare any counterattack. Who then made the decision to launch the firm with such hoopla that it brought on the ugly confrontation with Microsoft? The answer is obviously the founders, venture capitalists, and investment bankers who controlled the firm and who had the most to gain. Among them, L. John Doerr, general partner of the VC firm Kleiner Perkins, stands out particularly since KP's $5 million investment gained him a seat on Netscape's board of directors. From this position, his influence grew when he recruited the chief executive and other top officers of the browser company. The financial gain from KP's investment, moreover, could be realized only after a successful IPO of Netscape's stock, when the holdings of the VC firm were sold for a lucrative amount. A general partner like Doerr would take an estimated 30 percent of the capital gains resulting from his firm's investment, and for Doerr personally, this translated to over $100 million a year following Netscape's and other major IPOs.[8] These munificent sums undoubtedly encouraged him to actively push for a premature IPO: "In the summer of 1995, when Netscape was a year and a half old, Doerr worked behind the scenes to convince the company's management that it was the right time to go public. Doerr thought Netscape should raise money while the market was hot on the Internet, and, more important, an IPO would give Netscape's browser business a huge boost."[9]

Not all high-tech firms were rushed to market to get a "first mover's advantage," only to lack the wherewithal for maintaining any lead. Houston-based Dell Computer Corporation, for example, entered a highly competitive PC market led not only by IBM, but a nearby Texas company called Compaq. Following a modest beginning when its founder, Michael Dell, sold PCs from his college dormitory room, the firm's top executives decided in 1987 to take the firm public and searched for a suitable underwriter of its IPO. Most of the investment banks interviewed for the assignment were excited about doing the deal because Dell's business was growing rapidly, and the company had even established a foreign subsidiary in the United Kingdom. The underwriter moreover earned 7 percent of the capital raised in the stock sale in the form of fees charged to Dell. In this euphoric time, however, a cautionary note was injected by the large investment banking house of Goldman Sachs when it suggested that the young company postpone the IPO in order to more fully build itself up, away from the incessant spotlight of a publicly listed enterprise. Sudden downturns in the stock price or quarterly earnings could blindside Dell, and its management would be forced to spend inordinate amounts of time giving explanations of the bad news to the media and its shareholders. Dell wisely accepted the suggestion to postpone and sailed safely through the wrenching stock market crash of October 1987 as a privately held company. When the market recovered the succeeding year, Dell initiated its successful IPO.[10]

It should also be noted that the economic environment surrounding the Dell and Netscape IPOs, respectively, were markedly different, with Michael Dell considering a stock sale while Wall Street was shaken by huge deficits in the U.S. federal budget and its international trade account. The budget deficit particularly affected securities markets because it increased inflationary pressures and prompted the Federal Reserve to increase short-term interest rates. The deficit also provoked the specter of a bankrupt Social Security system as the nation faced a significant increase in the number of retiring American workers. Lower birth rates in the previous twenty years also meant that fewer people were available to replace the contributions of retiring workers. These uncertainties led to the crash of October 1987, which sent the Dow Jones industrial average plummeting to a one-day record loss of 504 points. The economic turbulence eventually led to the 1992 election of President Bill Clinton, who succeeded in bringing down the government's deficit and in the process inflationary pressures and interest rates. As a result, during Clinton's two terms in office, American equity markets experienced their greatest period of advancement, and the bubble that characterized the Internet era began to inflate at an astounding rate. Netscape, in 1995, floated the first big IPO to start the giddiest part of the boom, which ended in the 2000 stock market debacle. The crash followed rapid-fire interest rate increases of the Federal Reserve central bank, designed to curb Wall Street's irrational exuberance, and both actions were sufficient to send the United States into a recession. The tottering economy also received an explosive body blow on September 11, 2001, when jetliners hijacked by Arab terrorists slammed into and demolished the twin towers of the World Trade Center in New York's financial district and crashed into the Pentagon.

Precursor to the Boom

The terrorist attacks provided an exclamatory ending to a financial boom that was unsurpassed in the history of capital markets. Few gurus, if any, saw it coming because it had an ambiguous beginning in the economic turmoil of the 1980s. Washington, led by newly elected president Ronald Reagan, was attempting to move the economy forward following the devastation caused by high oil prices and recession resulting from the Arab oil embargo and Iranian revolution. The conservative president knew that his reelection depended on jump-starting the moribund economy, and he assembled a highly stimulating fiscal package of massive tax cuts and heavy defense spending. These produced huge budget deficits that tarred his administration and altered how Americans planned for their retirement. The deficits were largely responsible for the stock market crash of 1987, and they grew out of the $2,000 tax deduction given to taxpayers who contributed to an individual retirement account, or IRA. Because the growing deficits also threatened to bankrupt the Social Security system that financed most retirements, Americans began looking to Wall Street to secure a future that did not rely entirely on the shaky government program. The attraction of financial markets had begun because, in order to claim an IRA deduction, the average taxpayer had to deposit the contribution with a fiduciary agent like a mutual fund or brokerage account. This insured that withdrawals were not made until the account holder reached retirement. The account could still be managed by its owner, who decided in what instruments (stocks, bonds, mutual funds, money market funds, certificates of deposit) his or her money was invested in. Returns on the investment were tax deferred until they were withdrawn, ostensibly then to be used to finance retirement plans. In the process, intricate investment and tax considerations were thrust upon the average wage earner, who was further compelled to act wisely by the expected insolvency of Social Security. The uncertainty impinging on retirement plans increased when Washington's elected and bureaucratic officials—under the leadership of Alan Greenspan—moved to curry favor with the electorate by indexing Social Security benefits to inflation.[11] Although this was planned prior to the presidency that chose Greenspan to head the Federal Reserve, Reagan exacerbated the situation with his large tax cuts for individuals and businesses. The loss of revenue was substantial and it burnished Washington's image of fiscal irresponsibility. This image was further reinforced when the government was forced to rescind the tax deduction for IRA contributions because of the mounting deficits.

A clear indication was thus given to an aging populace that Washington, which could not keep its own finances in order, was giving the responsibility of funding retirement to the individual. An immediate need thus ensued for higher rates of return in case government benefits were cut and the possibility was advanced by brokerage houses and mutual funds—amid a steady drumbeat of negative publicity regarding the shaky Social Security system—that financial salvation could be achieved in equity investments. Even a member of the Federal Reserve's board of governors acknowledged "that the [Social Security] system will not simply evaporate as of 2038. But it remains true that if we don't change either the payroll tax schedule or the benefit schedule, then the system will, under present forecast, run out of assets in 2038."[12] Such pronouncements resulted in a rush of billions, if not trillions, of retirement dollars into private portfolio investments that was not interrupted by the 1987 stock market crash. By the end of the year, stocks had rallied sufficiently to regain ground lost in the steep downturn, which was then being portrayed by the media as an excellent buying opportunity. Over time, investors became adherents of buying on the dips, which indeed worked as long as stocks rose. In the bull market of the 1990s, equity investing increased from 21 percent of households at the start of the decade to nearly 50 percent by 1999. Equity mutual funds also benefited handsomely, particularly during the dot-com mania. In a two-and-a-half-year period at the end of the 1990s, a half trillion dollars were placed in these funds, lifting their value to an eye-popping $5.2 trillion.[13] Furthermore, when crises developed in foreign markets like the big Tokyo stock exchange, their investors joined in the mad dash to Wall Street, placing their bets on high-tech issues through the fully functional Internet. The rationale for its existence was thus becoming clear with every up-tick of the Dow Jones industrial average. Investors throughout the world could now participate in the U.S. equity boom because the World Wide Web provided ready access to online trading and easy-to-obtain financial information with the use of commercial service providers, portals, and search engines.

America Online

As the pot of gold at the end of the Internet rainbow came into sight, America Online was one of the first companies to offer access to cyberspace, even though as late as May 1993, Steve Case, AOL's chief executive officer, still looked at his outfit as a floundering enterprise that might cease to exist. The Internet's anomalous situation contributed to Case's shaky outlook because the network's backbone, NSFNet, was still owned and subsidized by the U.S. government, which prohibited online commercial transactions. This, however, did not prevent AOL and other businesses from offering their services such as e-mail and online chat rooms on commercial networks that had sprung up in regional areas of the country. The smaller systems lacked the national and international reach of the Internet that NSFNet was becoming, but their growth gave considerable impetus to the linking of these regional systems to NSFNet. Congressionally enabling legislation was subsequently passed in 1991 that allowed the private sector to commercially use the government-owned network. By then it was clear that, like the nation's telecommunications system, the Internet would function better if it were managed by independent operators to accommodate both individuals and businesses. The transition from government to private control began by connecting the regional networks to the Internet using gateway computers. Regional networks continued to own and maintain their own lines, and firms like AOL could now provide access to the Internet for a fee, thus transforming themselves into Internet service providers. Those parts of the Internet still government-owned were privatized, making NSFNet a redundant system that was disbanded in 1995. Privatization of the Internet had of course been eagerly awaited by America Online, because now it could offer its services to everyone on the Internet, and not only to users of its regional network. These services began in October 1989, with e-mail and the chat rooms for which AOL would become known as well as the usual information fare revolving around news, weather, sports scores, and travel tips. It was a tough beginning for the young firm because few people were aware of what an Internet service provider did, and fewer still had heard of Quantum Computer Services, AOL's initial name: "Analysts and investors were still unsure whether there was indeed a market for online services. Much money had been invested and much lost in a wide range of attempts at interactive communications—from interactive television to video text. Few experts were predicting big things in 1989."[14]

Companies attempting to capture the fruits of interactive television included the giant media conglomerate Time Warner under its chief executive Gerald Levin. Tens of millions of dollars were spent on equipment and software to experiment with the concept of video on demand. Through its widespread cable network, Time Warner attempted to market its large library of Warner Bros. movies and television programs to subscribers who paid for the service of viewing video transmissions on their TV sets whenever they wanted to. Trial runs in Florida commercially failed, however, as did Time Warner's attempt to become an Internet service provider. These results on the digital frontier forced Time Warner into a historical merger with AOL, whose online services grew explosively, especially in the late 1990s.

Prior to the momentous merger, however, AOL and its equally youthful CEO, Steve Case, had to first analyze the Internet morass and then develop a game plan to enlarge its subscriber base. This would give the Virginia-based firm some financial firepower that might keep Microsoft's Bill Gates—who was sniffing for opportunities in the company's backyard—from overrunning its Internet business. Fortunately for America Online, its new corporate name, which replaced Quantum Computer Services in October 1991, had a most impressive ring to it, which helped the company gain recognition while still a fumbling enterprise. The company moreover trailed its competitors, Prodigy and Compuserve, and all three online services were being considered for acquisition by Microsoft. Gates's company, with its monopolistic profits from the MS-DOS operating system, was furthermore in a position to buy all three firms. As a powerhouse in software systems, however, Microsoft decided not to buy any of them and chose to develop Microsoft Network, MSN, as its own Internet service. This added to a lengthening list of must-do projects that the Redmond, Washington, firm was undertaking, and fortunately for AOL and its competitors at the time, MSN was accorded a lower priority than the soon-to-be-launched Windows 95 operating system and the Explorer browser program. This gave AOL time and breathing space to overtake its two rivals and become the undisputed leader in Internet services before Yahoo! and MSN could get their acts together. The Yahoo! directory service—which first appeared in 1994—was a collegiate romp initiated by Jerry Yang and David Filo as students at Stanford University. Its purpose was to keep track of Internet sites that were of particular interest to the pair, and they never anticipated that the company they were starting would grow to have net revenues of $1.1 billion in 2000. As their enterprise grew, Yang and Filo hoped to keep their Internet service available to all without charge. In this, they complemented the aspirations of Tim Berners-Lee, whose WWW was freely released to the public. Such action contrasted sharply with the intense commercial battles that AOL encountered as it struggled against competitors that wanted to snuff it out. It consequently had little choice but to adopt a gutter rat's survival mentality and place financial sustenance at the top of its agenda, which was headed by an all-important IPO in 1992. The public listing was followed on May 11, 1993, by Gates's "buy you or bury you" ultimatum to AOL's Steve Case even as Microsoft's CEO was giving the green light to develop MSN, its own online service. AOL reacted with the mass mailing of its disks to American households, giving away free hours of its service and waiving the first month subscriber's fee for new users. It was a fateful time for AOL as it made a do-or-die effort to sign up a million users—all paying monthly fees to the enterprising but anemic firm—in its concerted attempt to escape being steamrollered by Microsoft.

It also proved to be a fortuitous time to begin an ongoing battle with the software giant because events occurred that strongly boosted AOL's Internet business. In 1991 the NSF, which oversaw the Internet, allowed commercial use of the medium. This was followed in 1992 with the free release of the WWW's program by Berners-Lee and in 1993 by the release of Mosaic, the graphical Web browser that eased accessing and rapid "surfing" of the World Wide Web. Furthermore, Bill Clinton was elected U.S. president in 1992 on a platform of economic reform with an immediate objective of balancing the federal budget to bring interest rates down. He made great strides toward these goals by implementing tax increases—highly risky for any politician to do—which prompted the Federal Reserve to increase the money supply and trigger the greatest stock market boom ever witnessed in the United States. One initial beneficiary of these moves was the nondescript firm with the grandiose name, America Online, which successfully sold 2 million shares in its IPO of March 12, 1992.

Dodging Oblivion

By then, however, scrappy AOL had escaped more perils than the peripatetic Pauline and dodged financial bullets from entrepreneurial concerns that preferred to see it dead. Under its earlier Quantum Computer existence, for example, a major creditor, Commodore International, froze its bank account in order to collect on a $1.5 million loan. In 1991 the privately held Quantum was offered a buyout from rival Compuserve for $50 million, which failed to win board approval because the amount was too small to give Quantum's backers a satisfactory return on their investment. Meanwhile, Steve Case was making headway in attracting funds for the firm's online services with the Tribune Company, parent of the *Chicago Tribune* newspaper, investing $5 million. More important, the commercial Internet and WWW's information space were rapidly evolving in the process, attracting significant attention from Wall Street. The earlier Dell, Microsoft, Oracle, Sun, and Cisco IPOs had whetted the appetites of the moneyed crowd, which knew little about operating systems, workstations, and routers except that great returns were possible from investments in such esoteric enterprises. Internet services were also beginning to warm the hearts of capitalists who sensed that a high-tech boom approaching the magnitude of the PC revolution was about to hit the Nasdaq.

Despite the Wall Street buzz, AOL's board was fearful that its youthful CEO, Steve Case, lacked the personal appearance of financial stolidity demanded by capitalist barons who were being asked to support the company's first stock offering. To ease their concerns, Case was temporarily replaced with another chief executive of older mien. The ruse worked, and the IPO raised $21 million, with the greater part, $11 million, going to nervous investors who were cashing their stakes before the public realized how bleak circumstances were at the fledgling company. The Internet service provider was still too small and technically incomprehensible for most investors, and even the *Wall Street Journal* failed to cover its IPO although it did note that it was one of the most actively traded issues on the day it went public. There were more alert observers on the West Coast, however, and like Bill Gates, they were ready to act. One interested investor was Gates's former founding partner at Microsoft, Paul G. Allen, who was "especially intrigued with AOL's focus on community and chat, and was eager to help it port its proprietary online services to the wider world."[15] His substantial wealth accumulated from his days at Microsoft enabled Allen to grab nearly 24 percent of AOL's stock and, through a tender offer, plan a takeover of the firm. This was thwarted by the issuance of stockholder rights that would have greatly increased AOL's outstanding shares if Allen went ahead with the takeover, forcing him to spend considerably more of his personal fortune to gain control of the company. It would also necessitate a messy proxy fight that, in the end, the reclusive Allen chose to avoid.

No such inhibitions deflected the acquisitive intentions of Bill Gates, who could use his company's vast resources—rather than personal money—in any buyout. More urgent tasks, however, were being undertaken in Redmond, which in the early 1990s was mainly focused on upgrading its Windows operating system. The launch of Windows 95 with its enhanced features was being designed to give Microsoft a means to lock up the PC market, and the desired outcome placed it front and center on Gates's hyperactive agenda. In the ensuing Sturm und Drang, an overlooked AOL was left off Microsoft's acquisition list, and even the Internet itself faded temporarily into the background. The turmoil increased in June 1990 when the Federal Trade Commission began an investigation of possible collusion between Microsoft and IBM in PC markets. While the FTC probe lapsed in August 1993, a more powerful agency, the Justice Department, began an antitrust investigation of the Redmond giant, which became the largest software vendor when it surpassed Lotus in 1988. Two major outcomes of the second action included:

1. A consent decree in July 1994 in which Microsoft agreed not to use its monopoly position in PC operating systems to enter other business areas like Internet commerce.
2. A challenge by the Justice Department that forced Microsoft to abandon its merger with Intuit, a smaller software developer.

In agreeing, Microsoft assumed that the Internet presented few opportunities and that the situation did not justify antagonizing the attorney general's office. Interest in AOL also lapsed, with Gates coming to the conclusion that his company could easily form its own online service, MSN, that would best innocuous rivals like AOL, Prodigy, and Compuserve. Moreover, the in-house development would keep Justice at bay, whereas an acquisition might provoke the department's wrath.

For AOL, the government probes provided a timely smoke screen that permitted it to develop its business without harassment from the software giant and from its MSN offspring. MSN was additionally handicapped by the PC-centric bureaucracy that Microsoft had become, with Bill Gates fixated on upgrading Windows while avoiding any bludgeoning action from Justice. An unencumbered AOL could thus develop its Internet service enhanced by the proceeds of its successful IPO.

Marketing Disks and Sex Chats

Oversight by conservative corporate parents also bogged down AOL's two larger competitors. Compuserve, for example, followed closely in the footsteps of its owner H&R Block, the noted tax preparation service, and steered clear of glitzy mass marketing of computer disks and steamy, online chat rooms that became hallmarks of AOL's rapid rise. Another rival, Prodigy, answered to the decorum and business interests of Sears, the national retailer, and IBM, its co-owner. When Windows, for example, was becoming a dominant operating system for desktop computers, AOL quickly made its systems compatible with the OS even though it was smarting from the contemptuous manner in which it had been treated in encounters with Gates and company. Prodigy, in comparison, delayed moves to woo the millions of Windows users because of its co-ownership by an aggrieved IBM, which had suffered from Microsoft's dethroning of its mainframe computer. Gates further inflamed the situation when he excoriated his staff to not let Microsoft evolve into the slothful enterprise that IBM had become. The latter's corporate lethargy had allowed Microsoft to elbow Big Blue aside, and in a somewhat similar manner AOL was about to do the same with the slow-moving Compuserve and Prodigy. In July 1993, AOL pounced on their lack of marketing verve and "began what has become one of the riskiest and most innovative branding campaigns of the digital age—the carpet-bombing of America with free AOL disks. The marketing plan ultimately sent out more than 250 million disks bearing AOL software to the mass market and was the principal tool in making AOL one of the best known names in cyberspace."[16]

AOL's Dark Underside

The disk campaign garnered 1 million subscribers by August 1994, a number that grew to 6 million by May 1996. The astounding increase rode in on one of society's more debauched aspects—that of child pornography, which did not stop with the exchange of sexually explicit pictures in AOL's privately networked chat rooms but included the criminal luring of children into pornographic activity. The sex-chat rooms, moreover, were a cornerstone of AOL's revenue stream because, prior to its institution of a flat rate fee, the huge hourly charges by sex-addicted visitors translated into significant profits that kept the company afloat during its formative period.[17] The ribaldry naturally spread its name over the gossipy network, attracting a tidal wave of new subscribers intent on participating in Luciferian activities. These could furthermore be conducted anonymously, from the privacy of one's own bedroom, resulting in few recriminations for closeted perverts who desired to hide their Jekyll-to-Hyde transformation. Disgusting as the sex chat between consenting adults may have been to prudish observers in the public at large, free speech was protected by the U.S. Constitution, and just as telephone conversations of a sexually explicit nature could not be banned, AOL's chat rooms were not closed by the authorities. The sexual revolution moreover had filled the airwaves with libidinous language, making parents the sole plausible overseer of what their children saw or participated in on the home television set or computer. In more public places, like movie theaters, entertainment, especially of a violent or shocking nature, readily overwhelmed latent Victorian attitudes, and AOL's chat rooms continued their magnetic attraction, helping to bring in 13 million monthly subscribers by 1998. In the process the company became the undisputed leader of Internet services, not only surpassing a lackluster Compuserve but eventually acquiring the former front-runner in a stock swap with WorldCom.

In its climb to Olympian heights, AOL was aided by the Netscape-Microsoft browser war that struck the start-up with a thunderbolt from "Zeus Gates" himself. The lightning rod was Netscape's IPO, which challenged the operating systems hegemony of Microsoft at a time when the PC revolution was yielding to the Internet Revolution. Netscape's browser moreover was seen by Microsoft as becoming a potential gatekeeper to the Internet, thus obviating the need for a controlling OS program at the PC level or in Internet access devices. The battle consequently began for the hearts and minds of big corporate intranet customers like the oil giant Chevron, whose information technology department was about to choose one browser for each of its existing twenty-five thousand desktop computers. In October 1996, Chevron selected Netscape Navigator, but replaced it with Microsoft's Internet Explorer (IE) the following year. Its chief information officer concluded correctly that Microsoft had more staying power than Netscape, and from a technical standpoint there were few differences between the browsers.[18]

AOL performed a similar switch for its horde of subscribers, licensing Navigator on March 11, 1996, and selecting IE as its standard browser the following day. The brisk about-face hid much of the corporate machinations now consuming the huge (Microsoft), quickly developing (AOL), and small (Netscape) Internet rivals. As is usually the case, with the playing field tilted toward the big and strong, the upstart Netscape would pay mightily for its misstep in not locking up the AOL account. AOL moreover was eager to team with Netscape after Microsoft announced the formation of its competing MSN service. Bill Gates, however, had already placed prime importance on his IE browser initiative, and partnering with AOL took precedence over the success of the fledgling MSN: "To entice Steve Case, the CEO of AOL, to make Internet Explorer AOL's preferred browser, Gates offered to put an AOL icon on the Windows 95 desktop, perhaps the most expensive real estate in the world. In exchange for promoting Internet Explorer as its default browser, AOL would have almost equal prominence with MSN on future versions of Windows."[19] As the following numbers illustrate, the Internet battle began when Microsoft, with its 90 percent share of the OS market, offered premier space on its successfully launched Windows 95 upgrade in an attempt to get AOL's 6 million (and climbing) subscribers to use its IE browser. Microsoft forged the alliance to attack Netscape's 90 percent share of the browser market and succeeded in bringing the percentage down to a near 50–50 split with IE by June 1998. More significant would be Netscape's quarterly loss at the end of 1997 following two years of dazzling growth, leading to layoffs and eventually to its takeover by AOL.

Sudden growth also taxed AOL's operations, to such an extent that its system ignominiously crashed on August 7, 1997. Microsoft, in an effort to energize MSN, introduced a $19.95 flat monthly fee for unlimited usage and forced a cash-strained AOL to match the move. The flat fee immediately increased demand and overloaded AOL's servers as the company scrambled to upgrade its processing capability. The browser-Windows deal with Microsoft also kicked in to swell demand, resulting in prolonged busy signals for subscribers trying to get online. The crippled system led to blistering attacks from media pundits even as AOL's managers worked feverishly to accommodate the rising demand. Despite the crash, excitement ballooned at the Internet service provider because the intense criticism and lengthening subscription list clearly meant that AOL had become the industry's front-runner. Having swallowed Compuserve, it would proceed to take over a faltering Netscape in 1998 and merge with Time Warner in 2000.

Netscape as Roadkill

As a front-runner on the information superhighway—with its spectacular Wall Street launch—it was fateful that Netscape would be steamrollered by Microsoft and end up as the Internet's first major roadkill. Its run furthermore was so short-lived that the start-up missed the giddiest part of the dot-com stock market bubble that it was instrumental in inflating. Perhaps because of its oft-cited technological prowess, the software company lacked the humility and flexibility exemplified by another struggling upstart, AOL, which enabled the latter to escape being overrun by Microsoft. In fact, AOL—realizing that it needed alliances to carry out its business—made repeated overtures to Netscape: one even before Netscape's IPO, when it offered to make a $300 million investment in the browser firm. It was contemptuously dismissed by Netscape, which was madly preparing to launch the Mosaic software that would propel the company to its August 9, 1995, stock debut. Thus began "Mr. Toad's wild ride," which the start-up's CEO remarked would require "seat belts and neck braces" for the young programmers who were racing to develop the landmark program.[20] "Even more surprising, Netscape later rebuffed opportunities [because it was 'too busy building this great enterprise software'] to reengage AOL. As much as half of Microsoft's early market share gains in browsers came from its deal with AOL."[21] A high-flying Netscape would similarly rebuff Microsoft when, in September 1994, the software giant proposed a $1 million licensing deal for the Mosaic browser. Two months later, Jim Clark, Mosaic's co-founder, reconsidered the ill-advised action and called Microsoft about a deal that included an equity position and representation for it on Netscape's board of directors. By then Microsoft was well on its way to licensing Spyglass's browser code in preparation for the development of its own Internet Explorer program that would crush Netscape. After the 1997 quarterly loss, a chastened Clark began the search for a takeover company, which led him to the corporate fold of a much stronger America Online.

The $4.2 billion deal was heralded on the front page of the *New York Times*, telling of a brave, new

> networked world in which the Internet is a limitless marketplace of infor- mation, entertainment, products and services. But for America Online— and for the big Internet players against which it will compete—the real potential gold mine lies farther down the road, perhaps five years away when people will venture on line for information or shopping not only from personal computers but also from inexpensive Internet appliances costing $200 each, pagers, cell phones and television set-top boxes.[22]

For their antagonist, Microsoft, the new alliance was a secondary set- back even though it strengthened the merger partners in both the browser battle and ISP rivalry. A bigger challenge for Bill Gates would be the massive Justice Department lawsuit charging Microsoft with monopo- listic behavior in slam-dunking Netscape. The action preoccupied the software giant for the ensuing four years, reducing significantly its role in the dot-com phenomenon that produced such early movers and shak- ers as Schwab, eBay, Yahoo!, and Amazon.com. These start-ups would come to define e-commerce by surviving the dot-com train wreck that destroyed most of their compatriots. For its part, AOL would stun the world by merging with the media giant Time Warner in the biggest in- tercorporate alliance ever, which dwarfed the Netscape takeover and was expected to strengthen its ability to do battle with Microsoft.

—— Chapter 4 ——
Dot-com Front-runners

While Cisco, Sun, Oracle, Microsoft, and AOL were gingerly building and plying their wares on the evolving information superhighway, a gaggle of dot-com speedy front-runners led by Charles Schwab, Amazon.com, Yahoo! and eBay zoomed ahead to test the limits of the new medium. Of the various e-businesses, financial services dealing with fast-paced stock trading were preeminent candidates from the start to capitalize on the race online. After all, instant price information and lightning-fast executions were hallmarks of the Net, which leveled the trading field between Wall Street professionals and those who were going about their lives at home or work. The terrorist attacks of September 11, 2001, moreover, made congregating in lower Manhattan a frightening possibility, prompting financial institutions to relocate offices to other sites, with the Internet used to keep everyone in touch. In addition, Nasdaq electronic trading had surpassed activity on the floor of the New York Stock Exchange, making desktop computers necessary fixtures in all brokerage houses. Laptop computers, cell phones, and handheld personal digital devices also enabled investors to trade securities while on the move. However, despite the spread of these mobile communicators, most barnacle-encrusted Wall Street firms chose not to embrace the online trading paradigm as it would have preempted the bricks-and-mortar branch office network that formed the core of their full-service franchise. The one-to-one interaction between brokers and affluent clients was grounded in what was thought to be potent in-house research performed by the likes of Merrill Lynch for investors too busy, lazy, or inept to do their own asset selection. For the aging, moneyed crowd—attuned to a nonelectronic era—discount investing using an impersonal terminal was decidedly a turnoff and at any rate, the careful handholding by empathetic brokers yielded bountiful fees from enduring cradle-to-grave relationships.

Against such powerful firms, the fledgling discount broker, Charles Schwab, would probably have remained a niche player, feeding on minor accounts brushed off by the more established houses. Ironically, the "little guy," who could afford to pay only discounted commissions and became the core of Schwab's clientele, held ambitions of amassing sufficient capital to admit him to more exclusive trading circles. Schwab accepted this reality when it upgraded its bare-bones, one-size-fits-all service to gold and platinum service levels for investors with assets exceeding $500,000 and $1 million, respectively. When it first began operating, however, greater trading volume with low commission rates remained the sine qua non for the upstart broker, and ensuing financial and information revolutions would go a long way toward building up its business. Prior to that, the discounter met so much resistance from the investing community—basically, lack of trust in an unknown firm—that Schwab sold itself to the Bank of America, one of the world's largest commercial banks and a San Francisco neighbor. The new parent failed to give it the financial backing it desired because the large bank itself was suffering from the process of disintermediation that swept many of its most-valued corporate customers from its cavernous halls.

Company treasurers were becoming adept at raising funds through the sale of securities and realized considerable savings by avoiding high-interest loans negotiated with arrogant bankers. Schwab thus deemed it wise to leave BankAmerica and proceed on its own. By then, activity on the Nasdaq National Market of small, high-risk start-ups had accelerated, passing trading on the American Stock Exchange, with which Nasdaq would merge. Aging baby boomers were seriously thinking about retirement and becoming aware of insolvency problems in the U.S. Social Security trust fund. Restructured company and individual retirement accounts, moreover, made it imperative that the average employee learn the fundamentals of investing. Otherwise, there would be no golden years. Timidly dipping toes in financially roiled waters, these neophyte investors were usually snubbed by big-time brokers or repulsed by loud, pushy account executives. Often their small accounts were churned, resulting in diminished net worth due to the payment of commissions for securities that fell in value. Small investors subsequently sought refuge at discount operations like Schwab, where sales agents were not paid by commissions and consequently were not hell-bent on coercing their customers into making ill-advised trades. Accessing market information also turned into a user-friendly exercise with the introduction of Schwab's Telebroker system, whereby clients obtained stock quotes and even traded using a Touch-Tone telephone. Because the process was automated, it did not further burden harried employees who manned switchboards that were constantly lit up by callers seeking to open new accounts. The automated system moreover cost pennies to operate and, significantly, led to Schwab's early adoption of online trading. In contrast, securities trading using the Internet was anathema for mainline brokerage houses, where business was generated by steering all inquiries to sales personnel, who had become a formidable force in the business because of their ability to generate fees and commissions for the firm. Without automating their systems, however, the old-line firms could not go after the sizable volume of new investors flocking to Wall Street. Moreover, commissions on trades were deregulated on May 1, 1975, reducing revenues from institutional trades made by large pension and mutual finds. The Wall Street firms consequently turned to investment banking and the underwriting of initial public offerings, IPOs, to cash in on the dot-com boom.

Going Online

Seasoned by the success of its Telebroker trading system, Charles Schwab proceeded onto the information superhighway to expand its electronic business in order to keep up with the rising trading volume. Its average daily online trades in 1996 would swell to 16,000 compared with E*Trade's 7,000, its nearest and much younger competitor. Since opening in 1974, Schwab had built a sizable customer base as well as a nationwide branch office network to attract walk-in customers in affluent areas. These underwrote the investment costs of its highly scalable automated systems that helped keep operating costs in line. As the PC revolution spread, other brokers were forced to make huge outlays to go online in order to compete for the big trades of institutional investors like mutual and pension funds. It was not enough, however, to get the fund business, and the established firms proceeded to give favored clients advance peeks at research done by the likes of Mary Meeker of Morgan Stanley and Henry Blodget of Merrill Lynch. Research was also intentionally skewed to promote the start-ups in order to secure future underwriting business. The inaccurate reports were then distributed to the public and, relying on them, large numbers of individual traders bought stock at suicidal prices and fell off the cliff when the dot-com bubble burst. Investment banks also purchased large amounts of the most popular IPOs for their own accounts and escaped significant losses because shares were dumped, sometimes on the first day of trading. Underwriters consequently not only received huge fees for taking the start-ups public, but with their insider's information, they successfully traded the same issues for sizable gains. Institutional customers were also attracted by the Wall Street bankers when they were offered participation shares in hot IPO issues. The big funds bought at the opening price and benefited from the early price run-up and, in return, gave their trading business to the banker. Smaller investors were not given such insider treatment, and they had to wait until the issue was listed and trading at frequently elevated prices. Euphoric praise for most IPOs was, of course, disseminated by star stock analysts, who were given wide coverage by the media because of the supposedly reputable firms that employed them. Aspersions were usually not cast on their flimsy analyses, even by seasoned reporters who knew that biased research had always been a part of the Street. *Business Week*, for example, was forced to lament, after the scandals were exposed, that "it was never much of a secret that analysts who work at investment banks often work against investors" of small accounts by giving out "insincere" stock recommendations.[1]

Another type of trading abuse led to a $100 million settlement payment at the end of 2001 by the broker Credit Suisse First Boston for giving favored customers greater amounts of highly sought IPOs that its investment bank underwrote. In return, the firm received kickbacks in the form of large commissions that were charged to customers in unrelated stock trades. Apparently CSFB was not satisfied with the $717.5 million worth of underwriting fees it received for bringing the high-tech firms to market, and concocted the kickback scheme to add to its take. Comparatively more infamous were the accounting practices of Enron, Global Crossing, and WorldCom involving billion-dollar investments in derivatives, swaps, and virtual partnerships that camouflaged losses on the corporate parents' income statement. Shareholders, duped by apparent increases in revenues, earnings, and cash flow, bid stock prices to record highs only to see them plummet when the irregularities came to light. Many employees lost entire pension plans because all their savings had been placed solely in their company's stock. After the Enron debacle, moreover, Merrill Lynch (as well as some large commercial

banks like JP Morgan Chase) came under congressional scrutiny for
financing controversial partnerships that the broker helped establish in
exchange for underwriting business from the energy company.

Painful Crash

The inexorable climb of Schwab's discount business increased pressure
on the large broker particularly after July 1996, when the bull market in
dot-com start-ups began its torrid run. Young, urban professionals, mesmerized by the "easy money" being made by high school and college
dropouts, abandoned plodding office jobs to become exuberant day traders. Equipped with a desktop computer and armed with the latest reports
from glib analysts, the inexperienced but highly hopeful investing cadre
began chasing the hyped stock of the day. For the most part these securities were from companies that had little in the way of sales, earnings,
physical assets, or managers who could run the company. Nevertheless,
the nonexistent attributes were of little concern to the novices, whose
interactions with any stock were brief—preferably in terms of minutes—
during which it would be bought at close to its low of the day and sold as
the price rose. All outstanding purchases were cleared (sold) at the end
of the trading day even if losses materialized. This reduced the risk of an
overnight surprise announcement that could torpedo the issue's price.
Success for the scheme ultimately depended on the frenetic trading that
was carried out on the Internet from desktop or smaller computers, causing huge intraday price movements in dot-com issues. The large number of volatile stocks furthermore required constant monitoring during
trading hours, keeping investors glued to their monitors in order to score
big quickly with a small amount of capital. The odds, however, were
stacked against them.

Their technique, after all, was closely related to other Ponzi schemes
that adhered to the "greater fool" theory, in which stock with little value
was pawned off on a sucker. Unfortunately, the day trader often turned
out to be the last buyer in the chain, with no one to sell to. There were
scattered instances when Lady Luck smiled on the little guy, but these
were few and far between because the smart-money pros, consisting of
venture capitalists, investment bankers, brokers, and institutional funds,
had already milked all gains from securities that often had little underlying value to begin with. Day traders and those investors with small
accounts were frequently wiped out in the process, but as long as the

dot-com boom continued, they were quickly replaced by another set of speculators willing to take their chances on Wall Street. Many elected to trade through discount brokers, which were severely impacted when the stock market bubble finally exploded. Bogged down by low commission rates, Schwab's bottom line plunged into the red as trading activity fell by 41 percent from more euphoric levels. Its stock price also tanked, falling below $9 a share, with the dire events necessitating layoffs. In 2001 the full-time workforce was cut by 25 percent as the firm suffered losses of $13 million in the fourth quarter of the year.

Merrill Lynch & Company, Schwab's older and more globally connected competitor, also saw its financial fortunes wither. An after-tax charge of $1.7 billion was taken to cover large cuts in the payroll and the closing of offices. Layoffs totaled fifteen thousand in 2001 alone as the firm scuttled ventures abroad, where it had invested mightily in hopes of forming a global empire. Most of the expansion came crashing to the ground as recession hit such foreign locales as South Africa and Australia, where the investments had been made. In Japan, the broker's retreat included the massive shutdown of twenty branch offices and twelve hundred layoffs. Henry Blodget, Merrill's Internet whiz kid, was similarly upended by the financial whirlwind, and he severed his lucrative relationship with the firm in November 2001. By then Blodget's lengthy list of buy recommendations was producing savage account losses for followers who had lamentably purchased such issues as eToys and Pets.com, two of Blodget's more inaccurate calls. In the new somber period, Merrill Lynch could ill afford to retain these untalented stock pickers who had tarnished its reputation and, more important, eroded the client base. With his lucky guessing days over, Blodget exited Wall Street to pursue other interests. Merrill gave him a severance deal of about $2 million, mainly to insure that its former star analyst did not support bitter customers planning lawsuits to recoup losses from the firm. Congressional committees, New York State's attorney general, and the Securities and Exchange Commission are also investigating the fuzzy-headed buy recommendations that doomed Merrill's many account holders.

In contrast, Charles Schwab's future is unclouded by the overhanging suspicions faced by full-service firms, whose research and advice were largely discredited by the crash's scandals. The discount broker never hired stock forecasters, until recently, because the margin for error was unavoidably high and the costs of good research excessive. Stock recommendations were also out of place at a lean discount broker with a highly automated, impersonal trading system. Schwab's payroll in 2002, for example, totaled 22,400, less than half of Merrill's 57,000 employees, allowing it to better weather the downturn following the terrorist attack. And although Schwab's trading volume may not reach the record number of 346,900 transactions executed per day in the boom times of 1999, it still is expected to increase from the 140,000 level to which it fell after the crash. The federal tax act of 2001, furthermore, is expected to favorably impact volume because it increased individual contributions to IRA and Keogh retirement accounts. It also enacted an education IRA for parents wishing to save for a child's college expenses.

Amazon.com: Getting Big Fast

While Henry Blodget may have gained mightily from his timely recommendation of high-flying Amazon.com, the principal and still standing beneficiary of the e-retailer's rapid ascent remains its founder and youthful chief executive, Jeff Bezos. In the postcrash doldrums, it appeared that he, like Blodget, would sink into oblivion, but the terrorist attacks and subsequent popularity of electronic commerce ensured that Amazon's franchise will continue to ply the information superhighway. And despite its ignoble stock price that trades in the mid-twenties instead of the high-flying hundreds of dollars per share, Amazon continues as a dot-com success story as opposed to the fly-by-night startups that crashed soon after their debut. The viability thus gives some credence to its founder's operational mantra of getting big quickly in order to capitalize on its first-mover's advantage. The company's early dominance of e-retailing indeed relegated latecomers to minor league status as it expanded its franchise to include popular consumer sales items and soaked up cash through stock and bond offerings. These financed huge warehouse facilities to better serve its expanding clientele. Bezos, moreover, had the energy and foresight to control most of this hectic growth and get Wall Street to pay for the expansion even as Amazon's bottom line remained drenched in red ink. Its net loss for the year 2000, for example, reached $1.4 billion, which included a write-down for bad investments of $343 million and interest expense of $130 million.[2] When the company initiated sales of consumer electronic items and toys, more distribution centers were added and the debt load climbed to $2 billion. This produced a scathing report on June 22, 2000, by a Lehman Brothers analyst who flagged the company's "weak balance sheet, poor working-capital management, and massive negative operating cash flow—the financial characteristics that have driven innumerable retailers to disaster throughout history."[3] This exceptionally blunt language about a Wall Street darling could only be made because the stock market bubble in Internet issues had burst and investors were stampeding out of the dot-com securities. Austere times came to Amazon as its stock fell from $85 a share to less than $10 in a matter of months, with no operating earnings to cover the onerous interest expenses. In January 2001, Amazon was forced to dismiss thirteen hundred employees, or 15 percent of its staff, and close a two-year-old distribution center in Georgia and customer service offices in Seattle, where the company is headquartered.

In a tacit admission that he had heretofore not taken investor concerns about corporate losses seriously, a chastened Jeff Bezos acknowledged that the job cuts and business closings were a direct response to the $545 million loss in the prior quarter. Moreover, the chief executive felt pressured into promising profits by the end of 2001. Grimly watching the dour report, Henry Blodget, still with Merrill Lynch and attempting to salvage his career as an analyst, opined that the worst for Amazon was probably over and assigned a grade of "B" to the company's recent performance.[4] He would have more to worry about even after departing Merrill. In April 2002, Eliot L. Spitzer, the state attorney general for New York, released e-mails written by the analyst deriding, in private, the same dubious start-ups that he had been enthusiastically recommending. This schizophrenic behavior was furthermore a common practice at Merrill Lynch, which led to misleading information being fed to its own customers. Why such duplicity? Apparently greed for the IPO gold tipped the venerable brokerage house into sacrificing its individual investors for munificent fees from underwriting the myriad new Internet issues that cascaded on Wall Street. The new gold could be mined, however, only if the IPO was bought by the public, and this depended on enthusiastic backing by the research analysts. Favorable endorsements were obtained because the compensation of these researchers was linked to the extent of their cooperation in boosting the sale of nondescript issues to the investing public. The conflict of interest was detailed in internal memos that were publicly released by state and local investigators. "How helpful analysts were to the investment bankers was central to their compensation and to their job security. . . . Firms typically provided analysts with a memorandum at the end of the year, identifying which [underwriting] deals they had been helpful on and guidance on how they could do better in the future."[5]

Indicted by its own memos, Merrill Lynch could only offer the lame excuse that the publicly released e-mailings were being taken out of context. They had, however, opened the broker to serious civil charges as well as endless litigation from clients who were duped by the conflicted research that was deemed fraudulent by the SEC and other prosecutors. On April 28, 2003, ten Wall Street houses including Merrill agreed to provide their investors with objective independent research and physically separate their research and investment banking activities.

Amazon Recovers

Paradoxically, the dot-com stock that catapulted Blodget's reputation as a star analyst was itself climbing out from the depths of the crash even as investment banks and their research departments were being swept into the gutter. On May 9, 2002, the stock of Amazon.com, without fanfare, reached a fifty-two-week high of $18.23, a far cry from the $400 per share price made infamous by Blodget's guess. In spite of the earlier boom times and obfuscating predictions, most investors in the Seattle e-retailer were already demanding that top management control runaway costs that led to a $323 million quarterly loss at the end of 1999. This represented a 543 percent increase in losses compared with year-ago results, but despite the blowup, Amazon and its Wall Street cheerleaders were able to explain away the red ink as necessary to expand the fledgling business. After all, it was absolutely imperative to keep the Internet boom rolling, with investment bankers knowing full well that the gushing red ink necessitated the underwriting of more debt issues to keep the dot-com firms afloat. Moreover, the financing from both institutional and individual investors was still forthcoming as evidenced by Amazon's stock price, which closed up at a lofty $69.43 on the day the loss was announced. As was typical during the frothy period of the Internet bubble, investors ignored the bad news and concentrated instead on the optimistic statements that peppered Amazon's earnings report. They included:

1. A 167 percent increase in sales resulting from a strong Christmas selling season during which the retailer introduced new online offerings in toys and tools.
2. The primary book business had its first-ever quarterly profit.

3. Marketing costs to sign up 3.8 million customers were only $19 per new account, with active customers purchasing $116 worth of merchandise per year.
4. Book sales for the period were up 66 percent and music sales increased by 136 percent while video sales surged 500 percent.

Amazon maintained that these results were achieved by upgrading its infrastructure, which incurred $108 million for distribution and shipping costs and $221 million for inventory that now included consumer electronics and home improvement goods as well as toys.[6]

In 2000 the full fury of the Internet meltdown hit and sent Amazon's stock price into single digits. For the fourth quarter of the year, encompassing the Christmas selling season, a subdued Bezos reported a woeful loss of $545 million, compared with the prior year's $323 million. No excuses were proffered. Instead, the chief executive moved to stem the losses with a thirteen-hundred-worker layoff that would lead to profits at the end of 2001. All the superlatives about this "giant of the Web," with its Internet franchise "recognized the world over," went flying out the window as well as the fact that it was "the most visited e-commerce Web site in America." The grim times necessitated a return to conservative practices in which only companies that increased the bottom line at a 20 percent or better rate would be supported financially on Wall Street. Never mind that "Amazon has the best reputation in the business for fulfillment and delivery" and that "its patented 'one-click' technology makes shopping delightfully simple."[7] The crashing stock market simply buried the dot-com rhetoric that had been spouted by consultants and academic gurus in books published by the likes of the Harvard Business School Press. Faddish titles written to cash in on the boom and now relegated to the dustbin include:

- *Net Gain: Expanding Markets through Virtual Communities*, 1997.
- *Innovator's Dilemma: When New Technologies Cause Great Firms to Fail*, 1997.
- *Blown to Bits: How the New Economics of Information Transforms Strategy*, 1999.

From such treatises came fuzzy concepts such as the "fear factor" surrounding "the specter of 'being Amazoned,'" in which established companies were toppled by "new economy" players like Amazon.com.

Older executives were particularly susceptible of being deemed technical deadwood that could be blown away by forces swirling on the World Wide Web. By the turn of the century, limpid earnings and collapsing stock prices smothered such hyperbole and sent the gurus into full retreat. One of their titles, *Leading the Revolution,* published, as usual, by Harvard Business School Press, in 2000, had its legs cut off before reaching the bookstore because no less a corrupt entity than the Enron Corporation was being hailed by the author as an exemplary enterprise. Enron had earned the attribution because of its "fluid organizational boundaries that allow skills and resources to be creatively and endlessly recombined."[8] The fluidity notwithstanding, a battered Enron is currently unceremoniously recombining itself in bankruptcy proceedings. It is also being investigated for accounting fraud, with former executives seen as purveyors of corporate deceit in their attempt to "Amazon" Enron by moving it into a new era of energy deregulation. Conniving executives, fawned on by HBS Press and other pundits as leading innovators, surreptitiously formed a plethora of corporate entities—readily approved by jejune boards and independent accountants—that artificially boosted earnings to enhance the financial interests of top management. The effort to conceal its complicity in such dealings led to the criminal indictment and subsequent conviction of Enron's auditing firm, Arthur Andersen, for impeding the government's investigation into the collapse of the Houston-based energy trader. Following the verdict, the government will now concentrate on investigating Enron itself as well as those who were responsible for its debacle. As belatedly chronicled by the *Wall Street Journal:* "The twin implosions of Enron and Andersen now stand as watershed events in a historic plunge in faith in American markets and corporations. In their wake, prosecutors and regulators have opened dozens of investigations into conflicts-of-interest among Wall Street analysts and the accounting practices of several major corporations, and prominent CEOs have been charged with tax evasion and insider trading."[9]

Paradoxically, Jeff Bezos was never bamboozled into believing the debilitating conceit that had so readily mesmerized others, even though he was often viewed as the poster child of the Internet revolution. Not simply a pencil pusher, Amazon's CEO had a sound background in online technology and business networking that was built during the late 1980s, just as e-commerce was developing. His first position, for example, following graduation in computer science and electrical engineering, was at a start-up firm in New York that developed communication links between U.S. and foreign securities traders. New York was also a publishing and media mecca, where plans involving the Internet were being seriously considered. In his third job, at a start-up hedge fund, Bezos actually worked on a project that centered on the electronic retailing of books. He enthusiastically recommended that an investment be made in such an enterprise because of the accelerating growth of Internet usage. Also appealing was the fragmented nature of the publishing industry, whereby even large houses relied on independent retail channels to distribute their titles. Bezos uncovered the possible efficiencies of selling books over the Internet, with sales paid for with credit cards and books delivered using independent couriers or the U.S. postal system. Although his employer rejected the investment idea, Bezos became addicted to it and resigned his position at the hedge fund in order to pursue his entrepreneurial goal. Based on his academic training and work experience, Amazon.com's founder realized that the software controlling his online Web site was essential to the successful launching of the new venture. To find the experts who would write the necessary programs, Bezos headed for the West Coast, specifically Silicon Valley with its abundant technical talent, and Seattle, where Microsoft was forming a global software empire. From the Valley, he recruited his new head of research and development, principally a programmer who could "build very fast databases." Seattle, where Amazon was based, supplied another software engineer who designed the Web site for the start-up retailer. Bezos meanwhile learned the fundamentals of the book business by taking an introductory course offered by the American Booksellers Association.[10] The preparation was followed by the debut of the Internet book business on July 16, 1995.

In the following month, Netscape stock was sold publicly for the first time, and Amazon's cash problems were solved until the end of the decade, when the collapsing stock market closed the purse strings to all dot-com ventures. For Amazon, however, it was off to the races with a heavily subscribed IPO showering money and media attention on the e-retailer of books. Also in play was the psychological fear factor that seized highly paid money managers who did not want to be left out on booming returns from Internet issues, even though they knew little about the medium. Amazon's lack of profits, moreover, was not a concern for most investors and business reporters at, for example, the *Wall Street Journal,* who waxed hot about the retailer's Web site, which offered "services that a traditional store or catalog can't match. An Amazon customer can romp through a database of 1.1 million titles (five times the largest superstore's inventory) searching by subject or names."[11] Profits were expected within "a year or two," an event that never materialized until the end of 2001, when a fleeting one-cent-a-share of earnings was announced by a desperate Bezos. During the salad days following the IPO, its CEO exercised considerable restraint, never willy-nilly spending the start-up's money even as his counterparts were using their Wall Street largesse to buy corporate jets and expensive geegaws. Operating costs were kept to a minimum by having publishers perform the task of promoting their own titles. Venture capitalists were also kept at bay, with their equity ownership a mere 11 percent at the time of Amazon's IPO. In contrast, Bezos and family members retained a controlling 52 percent stake in the company. These holdings, moreover, were seldom diluted by the issuance of more equity because financing for the rapidly expanding business was derived mainly from the sale of debt securities. Mounting interest expenses, of course, became a major concern following the demise of the bull market, and the problem was compounded by the losses from slow sales in nonbook product areas like music and toys.

As an economic downturn and wrenching bear market sent Amazon's stock reeling, its chief executive could no longer sidestep the burgeoning losses and delivered the start-up's inaugural quarterly profit (as promised) of $5.1 million at the end of 2001. The slim net income was earned on sales of $262.4 million, but its release took Wall Street by surprise as promises from other Internet ventures had repeatedly gone unfulfilled in the past. Many of these dot-coms were now folding, with equity losses suffered by investors exceeding $3 trillion. Amazon in contrast limped through 2001 with its one-cent earnings per share and followed that with its typical quarterly loss of $23.2 million at the end of 2002. Fortunately, market sentiment had improved from the prior year as, here and there, financial reports covering once high-flying stocks like Cisco and Oracle were indicating that the trough of the recession had been reached. The U.S. economy confirmed this in the first quarter of 2001 with gross domestic product climbing by 5.6 percent. The positive signs sent Amazon's stock price, in early May, to a yearly high as investors began sifting through the rubble of the dot-com implosion for surviving issues with notable brand names and capable management that might lead the way to the next bull market. Another explanation as to why Amazon survived the blistering sell-off came from the U.S. Department of Commerce, in statistics showing that even in the recession year 2001, online sales grew by 19 percent, to $32 billion. E-commerce was thus entrenched in the American economy, and electronic retailers like Amazon have become templates used by U.S. and foreign marketers for building sales. Indeed, so pioneering are its software systems that well-known enterprises such as Borders, Circuit City, Target, and Toys "R" Us are licensing its technology to, in effect, operate joint online stores with Amazon. These ventures also allow it to collect fees from other companies that advertise on its heavily used Web site, and this new source of revenue added $225 million to its coffers in 2001. Such income furthermore is expected to increase as other retailers realize that it is in their interest to link with the successful e-retailer as opposed to constructing a marketing channel that may not garner the attention of online shoppers.[12] And with the addition of major brand names, Amazon.com becomes a more sought-after online retailer featuring one-click shopping that obviates the hassle of traipsing through crowded malls and waiting in endless checkout lines. Amazon simultaneously co-ops other merchandisers when it offers their goods on its Web site in the same manner used by Charles Schwab when it began selling mutual funds from other firms on schwab.com. In so doing, both front-runners enhance their systems and software services while at the same time attracting more electronic customers and revenue.

Yahoo! Free, But Profitable

To the Byzantine development of the Internet came the quixotic Yahoo! whose characterization as a directory, search engine, or portal, or two of the three, or all three, is still unsettled. And because it was an enigma, it was the perfect vehicle for attracting the serious attention of Silicon Valley's geeks as well as buttoned-down capitalists from Wall Street. Technophiles immediately saw benefits in its goal to index the Net's burgeoning information files, easily empathizing with the twenty-something-year-old founders who were then engineering students at Stanford using the university's computer network to freely offer their directory service, which attracted as many as two hundred thousand nonpaying users per day. For breathless bankers in Manhattan, Yahoo! loomed as another Netscape, where enormous capital gains were to be had before the bubble burst. When forced by Stanford to develop and use its own computer facilities in 1995, the new enterprise reported a loss of $606,000 even though it had instituted banner ads that brought in fees of $1.36 million. In the boom times, however, the red ink meant little to investors who were lining up to throw money at the irreverent start-up, which had already supplanted Netscape as the "toast of the Valley." Wall Street's cheering endorsement came on April 12, 1996, when the Yahoo! IPO, led by the preeminent investment banker Goldman Sachs & Company, was oversubscribed at the offering price of $13 a share. Demand for the stock was so strong that it opened at $24.50 and finished the trading day at $33, to give the start-up a market capitalization of $848 million. Its founders, Jerry Yang and David Filo, would each be worth $165 million. Copycat competitors immediately appeared after the big bang to overtake Yahoo! but generally failed in their attempts.

With its finances set, the fledgling business remained vulnerable on its technical flank because it licensed the software for doing its searches from a Canadian firm. Without the input, Yahoo! could not put together its online directory. By the end of the last century, moreover, the number of search engines had soared to three thousand, and the intense competition among them had erased the need for Yahoo! to depend on any one service. In effect, a search engine uses a scanning program called a "robot," "spider," "bot," or "crawler" to extract key words from Web pages it partially or completely reads. The key words are then indexed to form the directory that Yahoo! placed on the Internet to aid anyone seeking a particular information file. AltaVista, one of its competitors in 1999, had an index referring to 250 million Web pages, which, while seemingly comprehensive, would prove as difficult to use as finding the proverbial needle in the haystack of its vast underlying database. The Yahoo! directory was much smaller and more efficiently organized, making it understandable for even first-time users, and this accounts for its popularity. Yahoo! also added content and services like stock quotes and e-mail as independent information sources rushed to post their news, data, or helpful tips on its widely scanned pages. This increasing depth of offerings in turn transformed the directory into a "portal," or first Web site seen by individuals contemplating a search of the Net. As a portal, users tend to spend most of their time with Yahoo! and this allows the service to charge more for ads based on the huge traffic its Web site continually garners. The volume can be seen in the number of visitors—40.25 million—it received in August 1999. The figure is sandwiched between users of competing portals, with AOL in the lead with 53.43 million and Microsoft third at 35.02 million. Amazon.com had the highest number of visitors in online retailing, but the number lagged behind the three leaders at 12.54 million. AltaVista was lower with 10.22 million users.[13]

With such an online base, Yahoo! quarterly revenues and stock prices zoomed, with the former rising from around $10 million in the first quarter of 1997 to $200 million in the last quarter of 1999. The time interval represented the heyday of the dot-com boom with unknown start-ups rushing to advertise their services on Yahoo! Web sites. After all, the directory or portal or search engine with its catchy name was the epitome of online franchises, and its viewers represented a segmented market tailor-made for the wannabes that sought to emulate its success. From these neophytes, Yahoo! garnered $459.1 million in ad revenues in 2000, allowing the company to post profits and sport a record high stock price of $237.50 a share, up from the $33 close on its inaugural trading day. These newly minted dot-coms were paying for this publicity with the same IPO funds that had initiated the Yahoo! start-up, with the arrangement becoming its Achilles' heel. As the new millennium began, the Internet boom turned into a bust, with debt-ridden upstarts folding at a maddening rate. The lean years had arrived, and like the situation at Schwab and Amazon, would absolutely stun the heretofore-lionized Yahoo! management.[14]

Spiraling Downward

Even as the dot-coms imploded in 2000, the Yahoo! executive suite consisting of the two co-founders, Yang and Filo, along with CEO Tim Koogle and president Jeffrey Mallett, expected the good times to continue and did little to change their pioneering modus operandi. Revenues after all exceeded $1.1 billion in 2000, with the main source coming from traditional advertisers like the auto companies. Services for non-dot-com activities brought in another $105 million, and these two revenue sources were expected to cover any falloff from dot-com ads. Top management was so sure of its business plan that even after the big merger between AOL and Time Warner was trumpeted at the beginning of the year, Yahoo! did not feel it necessary to follow suit and seek a merger partner. AOL as an Internet player was perceived as technically unsophisticated and really not in the Yahoo! league, while Time Warner was a staid media giant with few growth prospects. Furthermore, the latter was now expected to be a drag on AOL's earnings and stock price.

Yahoo! moreover was particularly proud of being one of the few start-ups with a profitable bottom line that was earned by a technically adroit, unorthodox, fun-loving corporate culture as manifested in its exuberant name. And management was intent on pursuing these easygoing ways as long as 180 million users per month clicked on its Web sites, which in 2000 were filled with $459 million worth of dot-com ads. Negotiating a merger or acquisition with buttoned-down investment bankers that could threaten this unique, even euphoric, enterprise was anathema for the Yahoo! inner circle, and this stubborn mind-set led to a breakdown of talks to purchase the online auction house, eBay, despite the compatibil-ity of the two firms. The profitable eBay also offered Yahoo! a means of diversifying its revenues since most of the auctioneer's income came from charging listing fees to sellers using its service. Rather than co-opt eBay's proven approach, Yahoo! arrogantly initiated its own auction Web site, and in order to catch up it was forced to offer sales listings for free. Despite the come-on, the effort remained puny compared to the front-runner, with eBay retaining its huge customer base through superior execution. As a result, 70 percent of items offered for sale by eBay was sold compared to only 18 percent for Yahoo!, which kept eBay's earn-ings and stock prices at lofty levels even as those of Yahoo! tanked dur-ing the dot-com bust.

The implosion struck Yahoo! in the first quarter of 2001, with sales falling 21 percent and losses for the year reaching $92.8 million. Its stock price plummeted to $16 a share, which together with the red ink foreclosed merger or acquisition possibilities. The bad times arose out of the precipitate loss of dot-com ads as detailed on Table 4.1. A whop-ping $360 million of revenues evaporated overnight, with the realiza-tion that the shortfall would not be made up in the near future. Beleaguered Yahoo! management was forced to dismiss 12 percent of its workforce and scrambled to implement a new game plan to keep the company from going down the drain. Koogle was replaced as chief ex-ecutive officer by Terry S. Semel, a longtime Hollywood mogul who had once been a co-CEO of Warner Bros. film studios, now part of the AOL–Time Warner media group. The appointment was an admission by Yahoo! that it now would have to charge for information and services because they were too costly to be given away. This strategic shift was further evident in December when Yahoo! made an atypically hostile takeover of HotJobs.com, the leading online job listing service with 6.6 million users. HotJobs's revenues came from charging employers

Table 4.1

Yahoo! Revenue Falloff and U.S. Online Advertising

| | Yahoo! revenue sources (in $ millions) | | | |
	Total revenues	Traditional corporate ads	Dot-com ads	Other sources	U.S. ad spending (in $ billions)
2000	1,110.2	545.5	459.1	105.7	8.2
2001	717.4	455.9	97.4	146.7	7.3

Source: "Going Down with the Dot-Coms," *New York Times,* March 11, 2001, sec. 3, p. 14.

monthly listing fees as set forth in yearlong contracts, with the arrangement not only producing steady income but gross margins of close to 90 percent. So eager was Yahoo! to acquire HotJobs that it increased its bid to $436 million in cash and stock in order to overcome a competing offer from TMP Worldwide.[15]

In the midst of the dot-com flameout, it may have seemed strange that Yahoo! was going outside itself to stay alive. Why, for instance, was it acquiring an online employment agency when the wretched economy was forcing it to lay off its own employees? Moreover, HotJobs's revenues were predicated on companies engaged in recruiting, an activity that had all but disappeared. Did it have some indication that the business cycle was bottoming out? Indeed, as a portal, Yahoo! was in an ideal position to glimpse any hints of a turnaround, and these came in the 2001 Christmas selling season when its online sales rose by 86 percent over year-ago levels to reach $10.3 billion. In the aftermath of the September 11 terrorist attacks, shoppers were increasingly using the Internet to buy holiday gifts, with video games, digital cameras, and toys being big sellers among the 210 million Yahoo! users.[16] With the return of shoppers, online ad spending headed upward, and Yahoo! and other portals pursued advertising dollars by animating with sound and eye-catching movements the banner ads that had remained almost invisibly still in the past. Yahoo!, for example, induced Pizza Hut to advertise its product by having the pizza slices fly around its home page, encouraging hungry viewers to click on the slices to get quick delivery. The more effective ads together with the recovering economy were expected to boost ad spending by 11 percent in the United States to $8.1 billion in

2002 over the prior year's $7.3 billion.[17] Yahoo! anticipated grabbing a large share of the increase because of its front-running status as an Internet portal, search engine, and directory. The HotJobs acquisition was also expected to add $13–$15 million in listing fees to the struggling company's coffers.

As part of its makeover, early 2002 witnessed the resignation of Jeffrey Mallett, the thirty-seven-year-old president of Yahoo! and chief operating officer, and the event signaled the end of the no-charge policy that had been the bedrock of its service. The roller-coaster ride of Yahoo! had been too much for shareholders, who now ordered top executives to make the singular pursuit of earnings together with the reduction or elimination of money-losing activities top priorities. The emphasis on profits meant the end of its freewheeling culture in pursuit of online pizzazz and cool innovations. In the transformation, an urgent search for more sources of revenues was briskly undertaken by the new CEO, Terry Semel, even as the old executive crew was being ushered out the door. In addition to the CEO and COO, departures included the top development officer, the communications chief, and executives in charge of international, advertising, and marketing areas. Acquiescing to the removal of these executives who had tirelessly and sometimes brilliantly worked for Yahoo! were its somber and still youthful founders, Yang and Filo, who were now in no mood to be glib television "talking heads" explaining the bitter downsizing of their beloved poster-child enterprise.

Semel too had no time for the media as he searched for operations to prune. One of the first to go was the auction business in Europe, which was being trounced by eBay. In contrast, its longtime joint venture in Japan formed with that country's Softbank Corporation continued its exponential growth even as the American parent faltered. Japan, as discussed in chapter 2, never went through the dot-com craze that seized Wall Street and consequently did not experience the meltdown of trillions of dollars in equity value that plagued the United States. In addition, Yahoo! Japan never developed the type of dependence on dot-com ads that its Silicon Valley namesake did, getting only 25 percent of its revenues from such advertising compared with 47 percent for the parent. Its popular Web site furthermore gets "nearly as many hits as its nine biggest competitors put together," a lead abetted by its innovative sponsors Yahoo! and Softbank, a Japanese venture capitalist firm.[18] In contrast, one of its rivals is a portal operated by the NTT group, the bureaucratic telecommunications giant once owned and partially regulated by the government. The nimbler Yahoo! affiliate has been able to make inroads against such competition by signing up traditional advertisers like retailers, restaurants, and travel agents that would normally have gone to the NTT offshoot because of the longtime telephone connections that NTT had with these establishments. Yahoo! Japan's marketing punch, however, was too formidable, and the neighborhood stores that are a fixture of Japan's economy flocked to the high-spirited portal, providing a solid base for its revenues. This in turn led to its remarkable triumph in the online auction business when no less than eBay was forced to abandon Japanese operations in February 2002.

While results were proving successful in the Far East, the U.S. competition was heating up with the entry of Google, a search engine wunderkind that, like Yahoo!, had its origins at Stanford. There, two doctoral students developed software that not only read and recorded key words of Net documents, but ranked the significance of the information as well. This permitted more efficient searches because applicable references could now be reviewed without wasting time on irrelevant material. The technology pole-vaulted Google's service to over 1.5 billion searches per month—in 74 languages and 32 countries—compared with approximately 600 million for Yahoo! The lead convinced AOL to make Google its exclusive search engine, to be advertised to its 35 million subscribers for a percentage of the revenues that Google got from the arrangement. Its profitable beginning moreover enabled the new search engine to shore up its top management with the recruitment of Eric Schmidt, CEO of the software company Novell. The experienced executive was needed to coordinate the rapid growth and handle negotiations with AOL and even Yahoo! which licenses Google's software for $7 million a year. In addition, hardware was set up to include five data processing centers each, with ten thousand servers to do the online searches.[19]

An IPO for the privately held Google remains at the rear of Schmidt's agenda because of the subdued underwriting climate. The downtrodden Nasdaq National Market has in contrast presented the financially stronger Yahoo! with opportunities to acquire high-tech firms at rock-bottom prices. In December 2002 a $235 million cash acquisition was made for Inktomi, a competitor of Google's Web search technology, and the following year Overture Services, a provider of search ads, was taken over. Two and a half years ago Inktomi's stock reached an all-time high of $231 a share and, following the crash, could be purchased in the ensuing bear market for a mere $1.65 a share. This acquisition shored up the Yahoo! technical base and added a new revenue source because Inktomi charges businesses for listing Web sites in its search engine's index. Hefty fees are collected from large enterprises like Amazon.com, which has a multitude of pages describing its myriad product offerings. Fees arise whenever a user clicks on a listed Web site.

In the first quarter of 2003, the new revenue sources for Yahoo! expressed themselves in a 47 percent increase, to $282.9 million over quarterly revenue for the preceding year. Advertising revenue grew by 38 percent; fee-based services by 61 percent; job ads and fees for listings by 89 percent. These increases were mirrored in the bottom line, with net income returning to the positive territory of $46.7 million from a year earlier loss of $53.6 million.[20] The profitable numbers allowed Yahoo! to return to Wall Street and successfully float a $750 million bond issue, with proceeds earmarked for the enhancement of its search services. Rival Google, of course, still lacks entrée to capital markets and must rely on operating income to battle the bigger Yahoo!

EBay Über Alles

EBay's stock debuted in September 1998 in a much more receptive period for IPOs than even a year later when it could have easily been sucked under by the dot-com implosion. Investors, stunned by the meltdown, turned their backs on the next Big Thing that would revolutionize the world. In 1998, however, few had an inkling of the impending bust, and eBay easily raised $6.7 million from venture capitalists, hired a competent but nonflamboyant chief executive officer—Meg Whitman—and offered its stock to Wall Street to the same rousing acclaim that had greeted Yahoo! and Amazon. The media attention furthermore elevated the founders of the earlier start-ups to the status of rock stars, a path that Whitman and eBay's founder, Pierre Omidyar, wisely chose not to follow. Both leaders were more involved in diligently refining an effective business strategy that shored up the young auctioneer's financial base in the event of an economic downturn. A fee-based system charging sellers was developed even though most electronic retailers like Amazon were pursuing a get-big-fast strategy with giveaways and massive discounting. Amazon also incurred considerable debt in order to extend the range of its product offerings and build distribution centers that packaged and shipped the, at times, bulky merchandise. By the time of eBay's IPO, moreover, the bloom on the Internet rose was fading, with numerous start-ups exhausting their capital and going out of business. Whitman witnessed this up close when she was featured on the cover of the August 6, 2001, issue of *The Industry Standard.* Already anemic from the falloff in advertising, the business magazine that purportedly offered "intelligence for the information economy" was tottering badly and within weeks would cease publishing. With a dying gasp, it proposed to its readers that Whitman, one of the few dot-com executives who could show solid bottom-line results, now "wants to conquer the world."[21] Ruling the world, however, had become decidedly passé especially since Yahoo! and Amazon were moving to crush eBay by launching their own online auction sites. A clash of titans was about to start even though eBay sought to finesse the challenge from the two larger combatants whose own equity values were wilting under assaults from the stock market.

EBay's founder, Pierre Omidyar, had furthermore begun the business not to overwhelm any front-runners but "as a public service, offered free to whoever wished to use it" as an improvement upon existing "online classified for selling personal items."[22] He built the system using his own programming expertise and an ordinary Internet service account that connected his home computer to the Web. Omidyar moreover had already become a millionaire by founding eShop, which was then sold to Microsoft. He thus had few thoughts of personal aggrandizement but still possessed the experience for managing the growth of his auction site, especially when his Internet service fees jumped due to the increased usage. To cover the rising costs, sellers were charged a nominal fee based on a voluntary honor system and the revenue collection proved so successful that eBay, as the start-up was called, atypically began life as a profitable online endeavor. This shoestring approach became the foundation for the company's earnings, with minimal amounts spent for soliciting participants and nearly all inventory/distribution costs borne by the sellers. Satisfied customers repeatedly used the site and extolled its merits through e-mail, in the process raising the number of registered users from 5 million in 1999 to 45 million in 2002. The gross amount of merchandise sold rose accordingly, from $0.5 billion at the start of 1999 to over $3 billion four years later. And because each sale meant fees for the auction house, the greater business translated directly into operating income, allowing eBay to escape the Yahoo! trap of garnering enormous online traffic that paid no tolls for surfing its information sites and linkages. EBay's fees naturally elicited bitter complaints from users who had become accustomed to the Net's freebies, but as long as they pay up and continue to use the service, eBay will assess the tolls. After all, it has its own costs to cover and breadth of service to maintain, which it intends to expand by dealing in more auction items such as those related to sports, home and garden, travel, and entertainment events. The expansion furthermore will be overseen by two employees, and the small overhead arises because "EBay has no inventory. Nothing to ship. Nothing to warehouse. No carrying costs. No obsolescence. No pick and pack."[23] The company's first CEO, Meg Whitman, was so endeared by these virtual attributes that she quit her $600,000 per-year position in Massachusetts for the lower-paying post in the San Francisco Bay area after which eBay was named. In the recruitment of its CEO, the fledgling auction house wisely shunned the rocket scientists, glib entrepreneurs, and charismatic visionaries who were running amok in Silicon Valley and spouting off on the airwaves, and instead got an experienced executive who stuck to the game plan of selling collectibles over the Internet and made it work. The execution went particularly smoothly because the business offered large profit margins—predicated on the above low operating costs—and easy scalability, again because it had no need to build stores and warehouses. Still, sustained profitability was no simple task, as Yahoo! and Amazon discovered when they attempted to establish their own auction sites. Both were left in eBay's wake when Whitman began offering new, brand-name goods made by notable manufacturers like IBM and Sun Microsystems while retaining its large individual sellers' base for dolls, jewelry, and used cars. Whitman bridged the diverse groups by not playing favorites and "subjects a Fortune 500 corporation to the same rules as a high school kid in Des Moines selling a few baseball cards—no volume discounts, no preferred placement, no exclusive deals, no escape from sometimes merciless member feedback. In I.B.M.'s case, though, it didn't hurt that eBay agreed to buy $50 million worth of software at the same time."[24]

To further seal the IBM deal, Whitman personally met with the computer maker's chairman and president to convince them that the slowing economy and competing online business from Dell Computer should prompt Big Blue to list its PCs on eBay. The marketing advice from the genial CEO swayed IBM executives, and the electronic auction site is expected to sell a billion dollars worth of its desktop computers in 2002. This large volume exemplifies how significant

Table 4.2

Stock Prices After the Meltdown

Company	Close on July 1, 2002	Prior 52-week Stock Prices	
		Low	High
eBay	58.58	40.48	72.74
Charles Schwab	11.00	8.13	19.00
Amazon.com	13.55	5.51	20.40
Yahoo!	13.63	8.02	21.35
AOL Time Warner	13.51	12.75	53.30

Source: Wall Street Journal, July 2, 2002, section C, stock market tables.

big-selling items such as PCs, books, and cars have become for eBay as opposed to collectibles, with two-thirds of its sales coming from the conventional retail categories. It has thus corralled the main parts of the online auction market even as Yahoo! and Amazon floundered. Further moves include more items sold with a fixed price, in effect challenging Amazon's franchise. To keep AOL out of auctions, eBay promised to place $75 million worth of ads with the Internet service provider. In truth, AOL, like Yahoo! and Amazon, had fallen on hard times, as witnessed by their low stock price, and probably could not challenge the auction house even it wanted. In particular, the ISP remains bogged down by the lack of synergy that was supposed to accompany its merger with Time Warner.

Comparing their stock prices to eBay's (see Table 4.2) at this point is bound to be disheartening for Schwab, Yahoo! and Amazon, whose founders overzealously expanded in the dot-com euphoria. While paying for this overoptimism, these entrepreneurs nevertheless managed to build successful franchises on the new medium without resorting to the deceptive, even fraudulent, practices of the energy trader Enron, its auditing firm Arthur Andersen, and the Wall Street analysts who recommended stocks of failing companies. As a consequence, Amazon and a few others remain reputable leaders even in the bubble-busted environment of the early 2000s. Schwab, for example, is aggressively promoting its new stock evaluation system in which reviewed issues will be graded on an "A" to "F" basis, with as many A's awarded as F's. This counters the optimistically skewed recommendations given out by mainline brokers during the boom of the 1990s that were used to ingratiate themselves with investment banking clients. Schwab pointedly states that it has no investment banking business that might taint the grading process, and consultants who field queries from investors are not paid by commissions based on the trades they handle. Schwab thus minimizes the conflict of interest that caused a large part of the losses suffered by investors in the tech-wreck.

Amazon and Yahoo! stocks have also taken it on the chin, but they were never in cahoots with brokers or auditors to artificially boost their earnings. Amazon in particular was very up front about its costs and strategy for emphasizing growth at the expense of profits. The Internet was in its infancy, and Jeff Bezos, its founder, was fighting off challengers who were planning to nibble away at his enterprise. And who can blame him for such an attitude? Bezos began the e-retailer when Microsoft was sundering IBM's leadership in computers and then going on to violently squash a fledgling Netscape. Can anyone blame executives at Amazon.com and Yahoo! for having paranoid feelings in the face of these smashups on the information superhighway? They were often forced to navigate among the wreckage of start-ups that folded within months of their IPOs while steering clear of marauders like Microsoft, which could inadvertently or intentionally torpedo their prospects. In this Mad Hatter's race, Yahoo! and Amazon needed to achieve a viable presence on the World Wide Web as well as economies of scale if they were to escape being flushed away along with the dot-com losers. And despite the drawbacks associated with their plans, both remain dominant survivors of the boom and bust and as such can proceed to build their enterprises with hardware and software resources that can now be acquired at bargain-basement prices.

EBay has also shaken off copycat followers that never had much of a chance in the electronic marketplace except to peddle their stock to investors at outrageously hyped prices. QXL.com was such a money-losing auction site, which had aspired to match eBay's market capitalization of $25 billion. In this endeavor it had the enthusiastic backing of Thomas Bock, an Internet analyst from SG Cowen, a regional financial firm that had taken the British-based firm public. A classic pump-and-dump routine followed during which early investors like venture capitalists and the company's underwriter hyped the stock as the next eBay, hoping the attention would cause the stock price to spike upward, at which time the big investors cashed out. Bock initiated action with a prediction that QXL would hit $333 a share when the market was valuing the stock at $20. The egregious prediction sucked in the *Wall Street Journal,* whose coverage helped the stock climb briefly to $171 a share. Near this high point, exiting investors caused the price to snap, sending the auction service plummeting until it reached a new low in June 2002 of $1.00 a share.[25] Such price behavior characterizes almost all of the roadkill that was strewn along the information superhighway, and the best and the brightest of these colorful but lost causes are analyzed in the ensuing chapter.

—— Chapter 5 ——
Dot-com Roadkill

The roadrunners of the last chapter that became the giants of e-commerce now walk more demurely among us, earnestly rebuilding or, like eBay, methodically expanding their franchises within the new constraints. Shareholders, aghast at the extent of their losses, still have residual value in their investments and at the very least can tearfully pray for the return of the information, Internet, digital hoopla that might send their holdings heavenward. Others do not share such hopes. Their securities have gone up in smoke and all that remains are the bitter lessons these smash-ups offer to the next generation of players in capitalism's principal casino. The difference between the survivors and the slain centers on the lack of value in enterprises like Webvan, eToys, and Excite@Home, a result of the merger between the portal Excite with the Internet service @Home, which were imitators as opposed to revolutionary start-ups on the order of eBay, Yahoo!, and Amazon.com. The era's frenzy blurred the distinction but as the Internet's novelty wore off, the weaklings simply tumbled off the Net and folded. Without operating earnings, the late dot.coms attempted to survive on the sale of securities in the manner of Amazon.com but failed to build a viable business before the Federal Reserve and Wall Street shut off the money spigot. The end came so suddenly that employees and individual investors were financially savaged as stocks crashed, eviscerating savings and stock options awarded employees by the cash-poor companies. Even managers and founders were swept away and together rued the critical miscalculation they made in assuming that their sand castles would escape the sea's relentless pounding. One prominent flameout was eToys, which had a red-hot IPO in May 1999, only to declare bankruptcy in March 2001 after failing to earn a profit during its short existence.

In retrospect its IPO, like all start-ups that began life in the late 1990s, represented an artificial landmark that Toby Lenk, its founder, mistakenly presumed augured success in the new millennium. The optimism was easy to come by since none other than Goldman Sachs & Company underwrote the issue, and buy recommendations came from Henry Blodget clones. The stock roared from the starting gate at $20 a share to close at $76.56, giving the online retailer a market valuation of $10 billion and its founder a personal worth of $850 million. The security offering added $191 million to the dot-com's treasury even as its financial statements sported a net loss for the first nine months of 1999 of $141 million based on $128 million in sales. The loss was dismissed by euphoric venture capitalists like Idealab, which had also acted as an incubation for eToys and saw its ground-floor $200,000 investment in the start-up soar to $1.5 billion. Idealab shrewdly sold a portion of its eToys stock for $47 to $70 a share, for a profit of $193 million. The shares had cost the VC firm a half cent apiece. Sitting atop this windfall, Idealab blithely encouraged eToys to sink all of its capital into building the "biggest, the best and the most expensive toy site to cement its place in the emerging pantheon of Internet stores."[1] It could indeed offer expansive advice because the venture capital firm had sold only 3.8 million shares of its holdings and was expecting billion-dollar returns on the 14.5 million shares it retained. EToys executives readily concurred with the ebullient outlook and promptly began the construction of a 150,000-square-foot headquarters that was funded by a new round of securities sales. Thus was eToys "amazoned" into pursuing a massive buildup based on wildly optimistic sales and profit forecasts that never materialized.

Getting Amazoned

In addition to the boost given the young company by its surging stock price, eToys experienced exceptional sales growth from $30 million in 1998 to $150 million in 1999, which its founder attributed to innovative marketing software that segmented its product line by age and type of toy. Top management seized on the early success and predicted that sales would double in 2000 and double again in 2001, reaching profitable levels of $750 million to $900 million in that year. This was of course the same talk coming out of Amazon.com, with the principal distinction being that already in 1999 the giant Seattle retailer had over ten times the sales volume of eToys, based in Los Angeles. Amazon was also a moving target. In order to double its sales, it decided to sell other brand names over its Web site in time for the Christmas shopping season. Pokémon toys and thirty-five hundred different video games, including titles from Nintendo, were sold in direct competition with eToys. A joint venture was also formed between Amazon and Toys "R" Us after the store chain was rejected in an attempt to go online with eToys. Amazon's expansion furthermore forced eToys into making huge outlays for advertising and distribution facilities in order to retain its market share against the much bigger rival. In the prior 1998 Christmas season, both online marketers had been overwhelmed by strong sales, and Amazon decided to build new automated warehouses with each capable of shipping a million boxes a day. These would process orders not only for toys and books, but also building supplies, consumer electronics, and computer hardware and software, which made up its new product offerings. To gain the attention of holiday shoppers, Amazon tripled its promotional budget to $90 million, "more than doubled its staff, to 5,000, and quadrupled the computer power that runs its Web site."[2] It was moving swiftly to keep its lead not only against the myriad online newcomers like eToys, Barnesandnoble.com in books, and 800.com in electronics, but also against established chain and discount outlets like Circuit City and Wal-Mart which were opening storefronts in cyberspace. Amazon moreover had a $1.5 billion war chest to finance what its CEO proclaimed was the "fastest expansion of distribution capacity in peacetime history."[3] Thus was the challenge formatted by Amazon for the 1999 Christmas selling season, which smaller companies like eToys had to emulate or they would fall behind. The strong growth of e-commerce and ready funding on Wall Street also attracted a gaggle of toy retailers such as KBKids.com, Smarterkids.com, and Toysmart.com, which diluted everyone's market share, in the process making it impossible for eToys to attain its optimistic sales projection. Just to stay even, it increased its promotional outlays by 30 percent, leaving nothing for the bottom line.

Despite the intense competition, Toby Lenk, founder and CEO of eToys, expected to get enough of the huge $55 billion U.S. kids market to stay well ahead of the pack and appease creditors and investors. After all, there was that enormously successful IPO in May, and his game plan had been ratified by a board loaded with Harvard and Stanford MBA graduates. Lenk himself had earned a Harvard MBA, worked as a corporate planner at Disney, and was convinced that costs would eventually be controlled even as his marketing budget ballooned. The savings, so he thought, would come from outsourcing the distribution-and-handling function, but this resulted in highly publicized delivery glitches of Christmas gifts not reaching the intended recipients on time. As a consequence, eToys was forced to make a massive investment in a new distribution facility for the 2000 do-or-die Christmas season even as it failed to match the economies of scale that the bigger Amazon had achieved. For example, promotional costs for the latter was 11 percent of sales while for eToys it was 37 percent. Similar numbers also held for Web site costs as a percentage of sales.[4] The grim comparisons notwithstanding, eToys was cheered on by Wall Street even as Jeff Bezos of Amazon was adding to his merchandise categories. Its IPO underwriter, Goldman Sachs, elevated the eToys stock recommendation to an outright buy, sending its price up by 10.5 percent for the trading day. Such action convinced Lenk that better times were ahead, and he consequently failed to part with any of the 10.5 million shares that he had received as the start-up's founder and top executive. At its peak price of $86 his stake was worth $850 million, placing Lenk on *Fortune*'s list of the forty richest people under the age of forty. That was back in October 1999, when sales were building. The bubble then burst on Wall Street and sent the price of eToys from $85 a share to $7.56 by April 2000. Investment bankers were now in no mood to peddle the securities of the online toy seller, especially since it had no earnings to cover the huge expenditures for equipment and property incurred in its battle against Amazon. It thus teetered on the brink of bankruptcy, with its last chance to remain solvent resting on the 2000 Christmas holiday season in what had become a very crowded toy-selling field. All would-be Amazons furthermore were just as hard-pressed financially as eToys and promptly engaged in wicked rounds of price-cutting in order to survive. EToys had hoped to garner $220 million in sales, but because of the competition ended up with only $130 million. The revenue shortfall meant that the company would run out of cash in the first three months of 2001, and in view of this, laid off 70 percent of its workforce in January. It also turned one last time to Goldman Sachs for "new investors, a buyer or a viable restructuring plan" that would save the company and keep it operating despite its debt load of $274 million.[5] This recourse did not materialize. In short order remaining employees were dismissed, its Web site closed, and its stock, trading at nine cents a share, was delisted by the Nasdaq National Market. "When the company finally did expire, Lenk—the 'captain of the ship' as he liked to say—went down with it. At the end, he was still holding 10 million shares."[6]

Stillborn Start-ups

For Toby Lenk, the error was not in selling his stock—he is contemptuous of those who did—but in blaming others for the death of eToys, whose concept was dubious to begin with. Its short existence proved that it could not compete, and top management lacked the wherewithal to make a needed course correction. It was not atypical in this regard because the vast majority of its e-business siblings faced extinction after being hatched in the minds of Internet visionaries whose short-term preoccupation rested on attaining IPO liftoff. This was usually forced on the founders by pre-IPO investors like venture capitalists and underwriters, who were never interested in the drudgery of building an ongoing enterprise, but in recouping their investments. More tellingly, the pumping up of the stock prior to its IPO took away the time and energy of top management just when the fledgling concern was at a critical juncture in its development: "They call it a road show. Think of it as two straight weeks of whoring yourself to every single major institutional [mainly pension and mutual fund] investor you can, doing whatever you have to do to raise the money to go public. It we weren't going to go public, we'd run out of money. It would mean the instant death of the company."[7]

Institutional investors, in contrast to naive founders, also knew that there was a closing window of opportunity during which funds could be raised, since many had experienced such effervescence before in, for example, the PC revolution that made Microsoft a titan and turned computer-makers Osborne, Sperry Rand, and Amdahl into also-rans. Entrepreneurs on the other hand were easily convinced that they would be the next Bill Gates, especially after millions of investment dollars were raised by their jerry-built enterprises. For eToys the conceit was enhanced by its birth in a specialized venture capital group called an incubator, where Internet start-ups were mass-produced under one roof. Efficiencies and experiences were transferred down the line as companies in later stages of development became templates for younger ones that then steered clear of the perils that had trapped their predecessors. In addition to the guidance, the hatchlings were provided office space, financial, computing, and accounting services, and even the recruitment of top executives from successful start-ups begun at the same incubator. Funds were also raised from entrepreneurs who had earlier struck it rich establishing high-tech ventures and were now eager to award seed money for stakes in the Internet Revolution. These experienced investors were offered seats on the board, with some getting veto power over even top management, as was exercised in the early days of Cisco Systems.

Incubators were frequently led by a young, charismatic founder in the mode of a nonstop-talking Bill Gates, spewing ideas faster than he could think regarding the next great concept in e-business. Futuristic and revolutionary, these concepts were never battle tested but nevertheless readily accepted by greedy investors looking only for the next Big Bucks liftoff. EToys was such a start-up, and it originated in Idealab, an incubator founded by Bill Gross, who raised $1 billion during the dot-com mania in order to bring his ideas to rapid fruition and "turn the venture capital business on its head. Instead of raising money and waiting for ideas to walk in the door, he'd generate the ideas and then go raise the money from the VCs."[8] In 1999, two explosive, takeoffs that of eToys and GoTo.com, a search engine also nurtured by Idealab, gave credence to his thesis that a mere $200,000 could be used to transform an idea into an operating asset worth billions of dollars, at least as measured by a frothy stock market. Both launchings canonized Gross as a New Economy prophet, who like the legendary King Midas, could turn dross into gold. Blessed with such a touch, Gross delved into his billion-dollar war chest, which had been filled by the likes of Dell Computer, T. Rowe Price, BancBoston Capital, and others lining up at the start of the millenium for a chance to strike gold. Following his initial success, salivating investors began leaning on Gross to take Idealab itself public, so that they could then cash in their 13 percent stake in the incubator. Gross remained unperturbed by the fleet-footed plans of these would-be deserters and further prophesied that their withdrawals would not be missed. That was before he lost $800 million by promoting zany ideas that were to be his next eToys success story. From the incubator's fund, $110 million went to Eve, a seller of beauty products online, Scout Electromedia took $16 million, $60 million backed Homepage.com, Z.com entertainment received $10 million, and $220 million was invested in GoTo.com in anticipation that once the search engine reported profits, its stock price would zoom upward from its $80 a share purchase price. Armageddon unfortunately intervened in the spring of 2000, and the Nasdaq sent the stock down to $10 instead. Idealab's own IPO was shelved, and Gross was forced to throttle back the expansion plans that had led to plush offices not only in Silicon Valley, but in New York, Boston, and London as well. Financing for most of the branch offices was curtailed if not abandoned, and a bloated staff of idea generators was cut from 250 to 100. The company was rapidly morphing into another carcass on the on-ramp to the Information Highway.

Mounting Roadkill

Even as Idealab fell into its death throes, wild-eyed imitators were dash-
ing in to get in on the easy money, as did novice entrepreneurs seeking
funding for their hackneyed schemes. The media was wall-to-wall with
fresh young faces babbling about a new concoction that would turn not
only the founders into billionaires but members of the audience as well.
After the crash, these talking heads were never heard from again. But
corporate America never forgot about the staggering sums raised by
neophyte entrepreneurs like Bill Gross, even though they quickly dismissed him as foolhardy for burning through $800 million in the blink
of an eye. In the selective remembrance, the dark side of the Internet
force, characterized by unbounded avarice, grabbed the captains of the
staid telecommunications industry by the throat. Their mouths were agape
after witnessing the Amazons and Yahoo! skim a fortune from the use of
their telephone networks while they stood by, restrained by heavy-handed
regulators. Compatriots in the energy sector were similarly mesmerized
by the likes of Gates, Gross, and Jeff Bezos and pursued deregulation so
that their moribund industry could innovate, compete, and reap the rewards of true-blue capitalism. Thus on the revolutionary foundation built
by the Ciscos and Microsofts was dumped the ten-ton deadweight of
leaden industries in energy and telecommunications which, for the past
generations, had spawned little of consequence, but could now see the
way to a brand-new economy overflowing with riches from the same vein
that had sent the dot.coms heavenward. At the end of these hallucinatory
horizons lay not only the collapse of their companies but the very visible
stick of Big Government, which was grabbed from Washington's closet to
club the rampant fraud and duplicity wrought by the Enrons, Arthur
Andersens, WorldComs, and Global Crossings. How could the gold at the
end of the Internet highway revert so quickly to roadside trash?

   Invidious comparisons with the original innovators readily convinced
latecomers that they too possessed the stuff to wreak the same magic.
Many appeared to be leaders, and they used their limited attributes to
talk the glib talk about reinventing the digital world. Speeches were full
of visionary goals, but solid results never materialized. One such follower in the incubator venture capital business was Jake Winebaum who,
like Bill Gross, decided "to produce enduring companies in rapid-fire,
assembly-line fashion, like so many Ford sedans"[9] and formed
eCompanies to ride on Idealab's coattails. Because it was launched prior

to the dot-com flameout, eCompanies easily raised $160 million and within a year cobbled together a grab bag of thirty-three start-ups with names like eHobbies, Charge.com, and Business.com, an online directory similar to Yahoo! As the Nasdaq collapsed, projected revenues for Business.com fell from $10 million to $2 million and it began to list badly, managing, however, to remain above water. The same could not be said for ten other start-ups begun by eCompanies, including eHobbies and Charge.com. By October 2000, with wretched times upon him, Winebaum abandoned most of his "serial entrepreneuring" even as eToys closed and Idealab was losing $800 million. Although their endings were tragically similar, glaring differences existed in the output of the two incubators. Idealab brought forth eToys, which proceeded to aggrandize a stock market capitalization as high as $10 billion. ECompanies claimed no such success for the $160 million of other people's money spent on Winebaum's illusory visions.[10]

Venture capitalists too were brought down as IPOs failed, with general and limited partners blaming each other for not so inconsequential losses climbing into the billions of dollars. Litigation hit Idealabs as minority investors like the T. Rowe Price Science and Technology mutual fund charged Bill Gross with mismanagement in the loss of one-half of its $1 billion investment. Hoping to recover some funds, plaintiffs sought liquidation of the incubator. In such ways the plug was pulled on the VC industry as returns plummeted 32.4 percent for the year ending September 2001, and headed much lower. With the few good years now viewed as lucky strikes, limited partners like the state of Connecticut's pension program sought not only to curtail commitments of $475 million, but the return of a major portion of the $200 million investment made in the Forstmann Little VC firm. Elsewhere, limited partners simply cashed out, using huge discounted valuations to lure vulture capitalists into purchasing their stakes. General partners, who managed the funds, fought the sell-off because they would have to write down the value of their capital base. This deleteriously impacted their fees, which were a percentage of the firm's capital.[11] A smaller base also reduced the coverage of overhead costs that ballooned during the bull market as VCs spent lavishly on highly paid personnel and expensive furnishings and services. As the money evaporated, managing partners desperately hoped for a market turnaround that would save the firm from a humbling downsizing and closing of operations. After all, these individuals were supposed to have awesome forecasting powers, but in the end they failed to catch the fundamental shifts that bludgeoned the industry. They, like the start-ups, overestimated the boom's longevity and planned on hefty returns even as the quality of their security offerings was deteriorating. An awful reckoning has consequently set in to pay for these mistakes, which will probably reduce the ranks of VC partnerships by about 50 percent.

A Boutique Bites the Dust

Robertson Stephens, a heralded underwriter of Silicon Valley wunderkinds, ended its investment banking operations in July 2002 after no buyer was found for the high-tech boutique. A major dealmaker in the PC, Internet, and dot-com bull markets, Robertson was a charter member of the exclusive HARM group in San Francisco, which introduced start-ups from the Valley to Wall Street funding sources. The business was so lucrative that Robertson along with the three other HARM members—initials taken from the first letter of Hambrecht & Quist, Alex. Brown & Sons, Robertson, and Montgomery Securities—all negotiated the ultimate deal in which they were bought out by bigger commercial banks seeking to get into the underwriting of hot IPOs. In June 1997 both Robertson and Montgomery were snapped up by the Bank of America and Nationsbank, respectively, with the former boutique going for $400 million and the latter for $1.2 billion. These costly acquisitions begged the question of why financial institutions of such heft as BankAmerica would buy an outside investment banker when it clearly had the resources to develop the business on its own. There was also the failed acquisition of Charles Schwab to raise further doubts about whether the entrepreneurial talent of a Robertson would thrive in the unstable environment of the large San Francisco bank. The maneuvering increased, and within a year BankAmerica merged with Nationsbank and was forced to place Robertson up for sale, with the combined banks keeping only Montgomery. Robertson fell into the hands of BankBoston, another institution about to lose its independence, and the small investment bank was rocked again when BankBoston was acquired by Fleet. FleetBoston would then be acquired by Bank of America in 2004.

The rapid-fire ownership changes for Robertson contrasted with its earlier rise to prominence when the IPO market reached a fevered pitch in 2000 and increased Robertson's annual revenues by over $600 million. Getting in on some hot IPO issues was at the center of the Wall

Street craze, with underwriters in the catbird seat apportioning start-up shares among themselves and favored investors. With many fly-by-night companies being offered, it was imperative to obtain any hot issue before it was publicly traded in order to dump the shares during any price spike caused by the initial euphoria. This generally occurred during the first trading days as stock analysts and the media flooded the Street with ecstatic "buy" recommendations, tempting investors with the possibility of hefty profits. After a few weeks or even days, the issue's price faltered as the spotlight shifted to a new batch of IPOs. The market merry-go-round inevitably crashed as naive speculators emptied their wallets chasing worthless securities. Responsible news sources also began reporting egregious examples of investment bankers benefiting at the expense of their customers. Robertson Stephens was a prime participant in the moneymaking charade, which ensured its downfall when the markets collapsed and its duplicity was exposed.

Its scheming can be illustrated with the Corvis Corporation IPO of July 2000, which Robertson comanaged. This high-tech start-up purportedly dealt with optical fiber switching equipment of dubious technology that was sold to communications carriers on the basis of light's speed and greater carrying capacity over electrical transmissions. The superior performance of light waves traveling through glass fibers, however, could not undo the massive investment already made in electrical systems and networks. This basic infrastructure moreover was adequate for most purposes and, at any rate, poor areas could not afford the sizable amounts needed to convert from electronic to optically based systems. Even in the United States, where heavy Internet usage led to bottlenecks in transmission, the introduction of optical fiber equipment was undertaken in bits and pieces, necessitating hybrid connections between optical fibers and existing copper wiring. Businesses and homes moreover could not be persuaded to subscribe to and finance the new technology because high-speed alternatives like cable were already in place.

A start-up like Corvis consequently faced a precarious future and needed powerful endorsements in order to raise money. As an experienced, high-tech underwriter, Robertson Stephens understood perfectly the shaky underpinnings of Corvis, but handled the company's IPO after analysts and executives at the boutique bank received Corvis shares that could not be sold for six months, a typical length of time known as the lockup period. The holding period was also imposed on Corvis's founders and executives by institutional investors to prevent these insiders from cashing out and jeopardizing the IPO. Any sell-off would leave big investors like mutual and pension funds holding shares in a nondescript company, and to prevent such an occurrence, lockups were instituted that virtually guaranteed that the price would be supported until the institutions cashed out. Other enticements offered big investors by the underwriter included IPO shares sold at a discount to the offering price, which for Corvis was $36 a share, and a chance for more allotments of hot new issues. With major investors brought on board, the Corvis IPO met with tremendous success as shares jumped from the offering price to $108 in a matter of days—heights it would never again see as the funds that were not restricted by holding periods began to dump their shares. Other investors, bound by the lockup period, promptly began ranting about the merits of Corvis to keep its price from collapsing. Media attention was maintained by the IPO's price spike, to which was added a self-serving "buy" recommendation by an analyst at Robertson Stephens who held restricted stock in the start-up. Executives at the investment bank had also purchased such restricted shares and they included the founder of the bank, its president, a managing director, and a head of equity research. By the end of Corvis's lockup period in January 2001, interest in the stock was definitely waning with the price falling to $26. It was now a stale issue and furthermore was about to announce a $90 million quarterly loss that would send its share price below $7.00. Probably spurred by inside information, a stampede out began, led not only by Robertson executives but by the analyst who continued his buy recommendation even as he was exiting the issue.[12] For the bank, such shady practices were not without swift retribution. Business evaporated after 2000, forcing the bank to cut over five hundred employees. By the middle of 2002 its parent, FleetBoston Financial, determined that its interests would be better served in closing the once-sought-after underwriter and take a write-off of $659 million rather than sell the boutique to a buyout partnership of Robertson managers. It would be a fitting end to a minor player—it controlled only 4.6 percent of the IPO market—which at the time of its demise was facing a civil investigation by the National Association of Securities Dealers (NASD) for taking kickbacks from investors seeking bigger allotments of IPO shares.

Scandal Ensnares a Bulge-Bracket Bank

While Robertson was fading, the probe targeting IPO abuses was growing, fueled by complaints by even institutional money managers who were frozen out of IPO shares after refusing to pay high commission fees of $3 a share compared with the usual 5 cents a share. Such charges were usually ignored because the free-for-all markets of IPO sales and equity private placements had always produced disgruntled investors who had lost sizable amounts after these securities became worthless. Outlandish commissions as a quid pro quo for IPO shares, however, were a violation of federal securities laws, and because of the credibility and clout of institutional complainants, both the NASD and the Securities and Exchange Commission were compelled to investigate the accusations. The twin probes resulted in a $100 million penalty levied against the major investment house of Credit Suisse First Boston, which managed 15.9 percent of the underwriting business during the dot-com boom years of 1999–2000. It trailed only Goldman Sachs, with 23.1 percent and Morgan Stanley with 16 percent. For its role, CSFB received $700 million in fees, largely attributable to the efforts and reputation of its powerful managing director, Frank Quattrone, who led the bank's technology unit. Quattrone had been lured to CSFB in 1998 by its chief executive Allen Wheat, who like everyone else on the Street was intent on getting a bigger share of the dot-com underwriting frenzy. CSFB stood in the front ranks of major, or bulge-bracket, investment banks, with backing from its parent commercial bank, Credit Suisse of Zurich, but it lacked the heft of front-runners Goldman Sachs and Morgan Stanley, where Quattrone had made his reputation. To get him to move, Wheat was forced to offer him considerable financial and operating incentives, which meant giving him control over his own group of brokers, a public relations staff, and stock analysts covering technology issues. CSFB also agreed to pay Quattrone a percentage of the revenues generated by his unit. As with most deals for star performers, the huge marginal costs were barely covered by the additional business brought in, and Wheat had to flog other parts of CSFB for profits that would satisfy its parent. He did not have far to look. Right under Wheat's nose was the torrid IPO market in high-tech issues for which investors paid an arm and a leg for large share allotments from the underwriter. Since many of these issues tripled or quadrupled in price on the first day of trading, customers that were given huge blocs at the opening price sold during the opening hours, reaping enormous capital gains, with the cycle then repeated with succeeding IPOs. At the center of this massive wealth creation were underwriters like CSFB, which allocated shares and inherently felt that they should share in the good times. Since a simple cash kickback from the

customer smacked too closely of moblike racketeering, CSFB camouflaged its nefarious cut of the profits by charging its customers exorbitant commissions. Unfortunately for Credit Suisse, the SEC required
brokers to break out commissions, fees, and taxes they collected for
handling trades, and thus a surreptitious trail existed waiting to be noticed and questioned by regulatory bodies.

Getting in on VA Linux

In more placid times, federal authorities maintained a slumbering oversight of Wall Street dealmakers, being outgunned by the legal expertise
and financial resources of the banks. As the IPO madness reached a
deafening crescendo, however, the media, through its headline accounts,
coerced regulators into paying more attention to double-dealing investors and bankers who were raking in profits in amounts never before
seen. Egregious deals were being uncovered by journalists who simply
examined those IPOs that experienced the largest price movements. Most
notorious of these was "the December 1999 VA Linux deal [that] was
just about the zaniest of the IPO frenzy."[13] Using the Linux operating
system that competed against Microsoft's Windows, VA Linux in its
public debut generated a huge amount of buzz because the start-up had
the potential for dethroning the software kingpin. This was possible because Linux was freely offering its open-source program over the Internet
while Microsoft sold packages of its operating system over the retail
counter and through original equipment makers. Microsoft moreover
was being bedeviled by the Justice Department's antitrust investigation
as well as Bill Gates's misreading of the Internet's potential. As a result,
analysts were already calling the start-up "the next Microsoft," and its
underwriter, CSFB, was busily allocating its IPO shares to customers
willing to share in the anticipated rewards. Offered at $30 a share, the
stock's price soared to a close of $239, making it the biggest first-day
mover, up 697.5 percent, of the dot-com boom. The ecstatic rise had
been fully anticipated by investors, and Credit Suisse bankers now went
into overdrive to get favored customers to cough up some of their easily
won gains. The record price swing naturally made it into the headlines
and became the principal discussion topic of innumerable talk shows, in
the process searing December 9, 1999, the IPO's appointed date, onto
the usually vacuous memories of government oversight officials. In addition, responsible journalists had already uncovered unseemly dealings

in prior IPO offerings, with the *Wall Street Journal* leading off its November 12, 1997, front page with how Robertson Stephens used "spin" shares to milk the IPO phenomenon. The scheme was not as gross as the overcharging of sales commissions for bigger IPO allotments, but the quid pro quo was equally obvious in enriching underwriters and their favored clients. Spin shares in red-hot IPOs were simply allocated to important investors like Joseph Coyne, founder and head of a software firm, who could return the favor by awarding investment-banking business to the underwriter. In this case, one hundred thousand IPO shares in a firm called Pixar were demanded and allotted to Coyne at the offering price. As Pixar soared 77 percent on its first day of trading, Coyne cashed in or "flipped" his spin shares for a reported $2 million gain. While such activity violated securities rules, no investigation was started by the NASD or SEC. The latter agency pleaded ignorance of the occurrence even though flipping had become rampant at the time of the 1995 Pixar IPO, with numerous underwriters establishing "spin desks" for allocating sought-after issues.[14] Robertson Stephens eventually got a warning from securities regulators in April 2002 in a belated response that became moot after the boutique bank was closed. Credit Suisse First Boston on the other hand would be ensnared by the slow-moving SEC, particularly for its egregious behavior in the more spectacular VA Linux IPO.

The Securities and Exchange Commission, which could not help but remember the fireworks surrounding the VA Linux debut, stumbled upon records of large trading fees paid CSFB at the time of the IPO. The inflated commissions moreover were paid by seasoned institutional traders like Ascent Capital and Back Bay Management, and each firm had received inordinately large allocations of 17,950 shares apiece in the much-sought issue. A 1,000-share allotment would have been more normal. The extenuating commission payments involved trades in Compaq, Citigroup, Kmart, Kroger, and AT&T, for which Ascent or its chief executive forked over $502,000 while Back Bay incurred commission costs of $387,550. Using such transactions, CSFB made sure "that as some customers' IPO profits grew, so did the stock-trading commissions they paid."[15] Furthermore, when the SEC uncovered the unseemly profit-sharing process, the dot-com mania suddenly collapsed, leaving investors with massive losses and no longer beholden to bankers for IPO issues that had turned dead cold. VA Linux, which had closed at $239 its opening day, fell to $4 a share in March 2001. Trading evaporated in lockstep with underwriting, leading to a falloff in profits at CSFB, an occurrence that raised serious concerns at its parent bank in Zurich. The taint of financial scandal also colored the disposition of Swiss executives toward their Wall Street subsidiary, and this was not helped when CSFB, just as U.S. markets crashed, acquired the investment-banking house of Donaldson, Lufkin & Jenrette for $13.5 billion. The huge outlay compelled Standard & Poor's to lower the credit rating of both CSFB and its Swiss parent in May 2001. Prior to this, the embattled top executive of CSFB, Allen Wheat, was summarily dismissed in a sure sign that severe penalties would be meted out for those involved in the Wild West IPO process. New management immediately cut two thousand jobs at the investment bank and reduced by about $300 million the compensation paid to top-flight employees like Frank Quattrone. At the start of 2002, CSFB agreed to pay $100 million to settle charges resulting from the SEC and NASD investigations, the fifth-largest payment of its kind by a Wall Street operative. While the broker maintained that it had followed industry norms in distributing IPO shares during the bull market, the SEC determined otherwise and demanded the $100 million in order to cover $70 million of "ill-gotten gains." These arose from the scheme to share 35 to 65 percent of IPO winnings, which CSFB told its customers should be kicked back to it in the form of commission payments on unrelated trades.[16] The settlement in addition to restructuring costs associated with the downsizing resulted in a quarterly loss of $1 billion, with more red ink about to spill due to CSFB's involvement in Argentina's debt crisis and the bankruptcy of the Enron Corporation. Akin to other roadrunners during the go-go 1990s, Credit Suisse First Boston veered off the fast track as markets sold off in the new millenium and careened into a brick wall, leaving its flummoxed parent bank in Switzerland to sweep up the mess.

More Denouements

Among *Fortune*'s billion-dollar losers' club,[17] no one lost more than Michael Saylor, founder of Microstrategy, who like other lucky entrepreneurs arrived at the dot-com gala at exactly the start of the gold rush that lifted his holdings to $13.5 billion. The charmed prince unfortunately forgot to leave the ball when the clock struck midnight, from which time he and his golden company began ebbing into oblivion. His downfall contrasts with billion-dollar loser number two, Jeff Bezos of Amazon.com, who saw his worth plunge by $10.8 billion. Despite the debacle, however, Bezos and his viable e-retailing operations remain in the Internet game. Saylor's management of his jerry-built enterprise in contrast was too slipshod to withstand the pummeling forces when the music stopped, at which time Microstrategy's accounting maneuvers attracted the scrutiny of the Securities and Exchange Commission. Apparently Saylor fudged his start-up's bottom line to get the attention and money of investors. This illicit activity was repeated ad nauseam by Global Crossing, Enron, and WorldCom, erupting into a major crisis of confidence enveloping the executive suite. Million, even billion-dollar scams were uncovered in the artificial reporting of revenues as well as the use of swaps and off-book partnerships to enhance profits and reduce expenses. Froth from the Internet bubble shielded these phony schemes, but the ensuing crash revealed that faux emperors wore no clothes and furthermore had built corporate castles on the sand. Saylor's castle may have been one of the biggest, and it crumbled quickly when the first wave hit.

How his fraudulently managed company attracted billions in start-up money is truly indicative of the intense greed that gripped the financial world when it became spellbound by the incorrectly assumed Internet's exponential growth of 100 percent every three months. To be sure, Saylor had all the right attributes to propel him to the front ranks of software development, an arcane field paced by billionaire Bill Gates of Microsoft and Larry Ellison of Oracle. He was young, handsome, and obviously intelligent—having attended MIT on an ROTC scholarship—and he realized that computer programs that promised much but delivered little could be peddled to gullible corporate officers. After all, most information-tech managers possessed only a superficial knowledge of software's capabilities and could hardly own up to their shallow expertise, for which they were well paid. Besides, their colleagues were investing in corporate infrastructure and software tools to enhance operations, making it mandatory for lagging IT chieftains to follow in step. Glimpsing such a scene, Saylor realized that his data-mining software was too esoteric to explain to these dullards, and he shrewdly adopted the messianic sales pitch that using his services would spread information and unleash the intelligent decision-making lying dormant in all corporate systems. This gospel-speak got his company's sales personnel into the executive suite, where they advanced their cure-all data-mining applications programs. No less than the *Washington Post* was impressed:

> In 1992 Microstrategy developed an early version of the product that
> would become its franchise: software that allowed companies to extract
> useful bits of information from their unwieldy corporate databases. . . .
> While seemingly trivial, such data would prove vital to the companies,
> and even as other software companies were developing similar "data min-
> ing" products, as they were called, Saylor and Bansal [a Microstrategy
> co-founder] were able to impress and attract an early array of *Fortune*
> 500 customers.[18]

The *Post's* jejune backing was of course key to getting sales from an
ignorant corporate America, but even Saylor's messianic message about
unleashing intelligence could not hide the fact that his software was
simply a me-too product of few overwhelming capabilities. In short order, financial scandal and the market's flameout would curb repeat sales
and turn the company into a has-been by April 2000.

During the prior year's liftoff, however, Saylor had uncovered the
golden mother lode that could be mined on Wall Street, where he promptly
brought his song-and-dance routine. Software firms Microsoft and Oracle
were flying high—not to forget VA Linux—and like the better-known
founders, Microstrategy's CEO held a large 73.1 percent of his company's
shares. The share price languished in the low $20s, but if the price were
to double, his holdings would be worth a billion dollars. The increase
would also benefit a planned $2 billion secondary stock offering. Such
calculations prompted the CEO to court the New York media even as a
developing storm began dissipating his sound bites. The tempest was set
in motion by the company's dubious way of calculating its 1999 profits,
with earnings during the latter half of 1999 apparently boosted by recording, up front, revenues from deals that spanned several years. This
allowed the company to report a strong earnings growth of 20 percent as
opposed to a loss of fourteen cents a share. The latter would have immediately sent the stock to the roadkill dumping ground, in the process
grounding Saylor's dreams of running for president of the United States,
launching a $100-million, tuition-free online university, and erecting
his own palatial mansion on the Potomac River. Unfortunately, his sophomoric accounting tricks were easily spotted because they had frequently
been used by other earnings-starved start-up companies. Here, Saylor's
expensive lifestyle worked against him, as conservative auditors at the
SEC began to question where the money was coming from to finance
the CEO's leased Gulfstream jet, chauffeured limousine, and spectacular soirees, with one taking place at the Washington Redskins' stadium

to celebrate the New Year. An examination of the financial books uncovered the fictitious earnings, and on March 20, 2000, Microstrategy was forced to restate its bottom line and report a large loss for 1999. The stock price plunged from $226 to $86 a share and continued downward. Within a year it reached $4 a share and was all but forgotten by Wall Street and the media, which had once pumped up its price to $313. A chastened Michael Saylor now worries about being remembered for being the biggest loser—$15 billion—of the millennium.

In addition to the huge drop in wealth and status suffered by Saylor, Microstrategy's plunging stock price took many of the company's faithful investors down with it. Ordinarily shrewd in their financial dealings, the market-savvy bunch was suckered not only by the fast-talking CEO but by the professional henchmen he had employed to perpetrate his accounting and public relations charade. These promoters were abetted by a laid-back board of directors that chose to ignore all the warning signs. Included in this cast of characters was Saylor's chief of staff Mark Bisnow, who was once an aide to presidential candidate Bob Dole. He was hired to be Saylor's "personal publicist" and "put him in front of the right people."[19] One of the ways Bisnow used to do this was to allocate the company's sought-after IPO shares to corporate leaders at top U.S. companies who were only too willing to cash in as soon as the stock went public. Favorable press and public relations were easily garnered as the stock price hurtled upward, but Bisnow failed miserably when the shares fell. Furthermore, his advice to Saylor to take responsibility for the accounting missteps fell on deaf ears as the now highly brash billionaire began blaming his chief financial officer Mark Lynch for the overreporting of income. Lynch together with Saylor and co-founder Sanju Bansal formed Microstrategy's inner circle and in the end were deemed responsible by the SEC for the company's misleading financial statements. All were charged with civil accounting fraud and forced to pay $350,000 in fines. Because of "ill-gotten gains" resulting from the fraud, the three executives were also compelled to pay back a total of $10 million, and Lynch "was barred from practicing accounting before the SEC for at least three years."[20] The principal deal that aborted the rise of these executives rested on a $52.7 million transaction with NCR, the computer equipment and cash register manufacturer. It turned out to be a circular movement of funds in which Microstrategy sold $27.5 million worth of software and services to NCR and at the same time bought $25 million worth of products from the same company. Minimal if any cash changed hands, yet both companies booked higher sales revenues. Microstrategy recorded $17.5 million in sales for the quarter during a critical time when the firm was attempting to raise $2 billion in a secondary offering of its then-high-flying stock. The additional revenues enabled the company to report a quarterly profit whereas without them, a loss would have resulted, placing the stock sale in jeopardy.[21] This unfortunately for Saylor was what transpired when revenues for the quarter had to be restated.

As overseer of the scandal-plagued company, Microstrategy's board of directors (having no less than its own auditing committee) was in a position to nip the incipient fraud in the bud before it consumed top management and then the entire firm. But the board's vice chairman was John Sidgmore, who was recruited simply because he also held the same position at WorldCom, the second-largest telecommunications carrier. A figurehead adornment, Sidgmore lacked the experience needed to protect the fiduciary interests of the shareholders. He had been asked onto the board to make it easier for the Internet start-up to peddle its shares on Wall Street. The vice chairman in turn was eager to join because he would get access to the company's surging stock at cut-rate prices. A small fortune could be quickly made. Moreover, because Sidgmore had joined Microstrategy only in the last six months, he could easily evade blame for the financial irregularities that were slowly coming to light. Such were the opportunistic maneuverings of board members during the bubble years, when the most perfunctory examination would have uncovered gross corporate malfeasance. It was, however, in their self-interest that directors "see no evil, hear no evil, and speak no evil." Such laying low moreover gave cover to Microstrategy's vice chairman as it hurtled through its stormy scandals and Sidgmore escaped the tar-and-feathering that hit both Saylor and Lynch. He was not so fortunate when scandal hit WorldCom and brought down its CEO and CFO. As in the Microstrategy debacle, Sidgmore was a board vice chairman, and he again pleaded ignorance of the massive accounting fraud that forced WorldCom into the largest corporate bankruptcy in history. Months before the denouement, Sidgmore had succeeded the discredited Bernie Ebbers as chief executive, and immediately upon this elevation sought a $10 million retention bonus. He confidently promised to keep the company out of bankruptcy—a promise, as well as his bonus, that were eviscerated by the fury of investors whose security holdings were plummeting in value. Upon filing for bankruptcy court protection, Sidgmore was forced to step down by his board and newly appointed creditors who wanted "to avoid the appearance of tainted management still at the helm."[22]

The Wild Ride of Mr. Pitt

Harvey Pitt's rise and fall at the Securities and Exchange Commission shows how close the interlocking relationships were among U.S. regulators, high-level government officials, corporate executives, and the lawyers and accountants who practiced before the SEC. Pitt failed to graduate from an Ivy League law school, but this was not a liability when Richard M. Nixon was president. With assistance from an in-house lawyer, Pitt became a staff attorney at the agency and rose to become chief counsel of one of its divisions. In the tumultuous final years of the Nixon administration—then embroiled in the Watergate scandal—Pitt was chosen to be the top assistant to the agency's chairman. He himself would be appointed chairman by President George W. Bush. In the interim, Pitt used his earlier SEC experience to become a Beltway (after the highway circling Washington, D.C.) securities lawyer, when in 2000 one of his clients was Michael Saylor, the embattled CEO and founder of Microstrategy, who was being investigated by the commission. Sidgmore, vice chairman of the software firm, was also embroiled but was being represented by a law firm retained by his company.

Sidgmore during his brief tenure as CEO would again square off against Pitt, who now chaired the SEC. It was not a friendly encounter. In the commission's civil fraud suit against the teetering telecom giant, Pitt was particularly disturbed by the way the company stubbornly refused to acknowledge many of the questionable accounting practices that would lead ultimately to its bankruptcy. In particular, the accounting for reserves and depreciation charges appeared manipulated in order to meet earnings projections and boost the company's stock price. In 2001 and the first quarter of 2002, for example, $3.8 billion in operating costs were listed as capital expenditures, resulting in profits for the period instead of losses. Customarily capital expenditures are depreciated and spread over several years, in the process reducing up-front costs. Reserves—set aside for contingency payments like lost lawsuits—also appeared to be arbitrarily used to boost profits. Pitt expressed outrage at these practices and suggested criminal prosecution for those involved. The harsh criticism moreover may have been expressed to camouflage his own self-serving moves to elevate his SEC position to the level of a cabinet official. The audacious effort surprised even the White House, which had appointed him agency head. The incident together with another blunder would lead to Pitt's resignation in November 2002.

Events leading to Pitt's final days began on July 30 of the same year, when, pressed by headlines about corporate malfeasance, President Bush created a new oversight accounting board to crack down on the fraud and abuse occurring at such places as WorldCom, Enron, and Global Crossing. It was a political ploy to quell the public's growing anger because the president's own party had "tried to eviscerate the S.E.C.'s budget" when it "took power in the House in 1994. The commission has become an 'expensive regulatory burden for investors,'" remarked a Republican House member assigned to the task of reviewing the SEC.[23] In the new regulatory setup the oversight board and the SEC shared in the unenviable jobs of overseeing very powerful Wall Street and accounting firms that had always resisted any meddling from Washington, D.C. In the charged atmosphere, Pitt attempted to choose a head of the new board who would resolve the financial mess while appeasing congressional Republicans and professional interests. Pitt's first choice was the chairman of TIAA-CREF, a large pension fund, who stood for strict accounting rules to curb the abuse. There was an immediate negative reaction from the profession as well as an endorsement of the nominee by Arthur Levitt, Pitt's Democratic predecessor chairman at the SEC. Both responses convinced Pitt to flip-flop and instead name William H. Webster. The action opened Pitt up to charges that he had caved in to political interests and pressures from the accounting profession. The chairman would have survived the accusations, given that Webster was a notable Washington insider who had been a director at both the CIA and FBI. The turmoil of the accounting and corporate scandals, however, turned Webster's approval process at the SEC into a rancorous debate, which Webster survived by a split 3–2 vote. Within five days the approval was torn asunder when Webster revealed that he had headed the audit committee of a company accused of the fraudulent practices he was now supposed to end. Moreover, the admission had been told to Pitt before the vote, who failed to communicate it to other SEC commissioners. Rebuke and scorn rained down on the chairman and he promptly resigned.

Crash Consumes Excite@Home

For the most part, the SEC was merely an onlooker with respect to the Internet bubble, neither comprehending much of the underlying technology or the dynamics of the financial froth. Its bureaucrats along with the politically appointed commissioners simply hoped that the bubble would not pop during their tenure. In such a regulatory environment, executives at dot-com start-ups as well as the venture capitalists that backed them subscribed to the notion that there were no restraints in their fast-track quest for the gold at the end of the Internet rainbow. Moving quickly was what counted, especially when it involved a dot-com connection, as in the merger between Excite and @Home: "[In January 1999] Excite, the troubled yet promising Web portal, merged with @Home, the promising yet troubled high-speed Internet service provider. Hailed at the time by @Home's CEO as the 'new media network for the 21st century,' Excite@Home has ended up instead as digital roadkill, its assets picked over by bondholders and AT&T, its stock trading for pennies, its customers and creditors at the mercy of bankruptcy court."[24]

With 20–20 hindsight, it is easy to see what went wrong, but at the time it was impossible to foresee the tragedy awaiting these offspring of both Silicon Valley and the Internet Age. Excite, the older sibling, offered its stock to the public on April 4, 1996, backed by the leading venture firm Kleiner Perkins, which held a 23 percent equity position. Its portal business developed so rapidly that by 1998 it was third behind Yahoo! and AOL in number of Web site visitors. Annual Yahoo! traffic came to 31.4 million visitors, while AOL and Excite followed with 22.9 million and 19.4 million; Netscape and Microsoft rounded out the top five. Like Yahoo! moreover, Excite was the brainchild of Stanford students who had sufficient programming expertise to develop software tools to aid neophyte Web surfers. Media giant Walt Disney was so impressed with its lineage and growth trajectory that it offered to take a stake in Excite in order to make its own cyberspace domain more attractive. Excite managers dismissed the idea under the assumption that the purchase price for the buy-in was too steep for Disney. Excite shares at the time commanded a market capitalization of $18.1 billion, while old-media Disney's stock value stood at $76.3 billion. In a more realistic move, Disney settled for the smaller Web guide, Infoseek, in which it invested $900 million for a 43 percent stake. It was still a goodly amount, reflecting the considerable success cyberspace had generated in terms of offering news, stock prices, sports, weather, cartoons, and films to millions of fee-paying viewers in addition to placing paid ads on their Web sites, which added to revenues.

Months following its rejection of Disney, Excite flip-flopped and agreed to be taken over by its Silicon Valley neighbor @Home. It was a match made in virtual heaven, with @Home, a swiftly growing Internet service provider, second only to America Online, offering faster connections than the slow-paced AOL dial-up system. Moreover, interactive and large data transmissions were clogging AOL's telephone lines while @Home's network used the greater bandwidth-carrying capacity of cable TV systems. As in Excite's launching, @Home had the powerful backing of Kleiner Perkins, together with the formidable technical abilities of Milo Medin, a former NASA engineer. Medin quickly came up with the design that allowed @Home to build a high-speed Internet access ramp on top of the cable TV infrastructure operated by AT&T, Cox, Comcast, TCI, and others. Using extant cable systems meant a superfast start-up for @Home, with 4 million residential customers quickly enrolling in its broadband connection service. These were mostly existing users of the private cable TV systems, and to corral the customer base, @Home was forced into some debilitating contracts.

For one thing, most of the revenues for its service went to the cable companies, which also received equity positions and seats on the board of the small ISP. TCI, for example, ended up with 40 percent of @Home's shares. Moreover, @Home could not back its service with the programming content of the cable TV companies, which would have solidified the loyalty of its 4 million subscribers. As cheaper competitors began to erode its business, @Home realized how gaping a hole the lack of content was, especially when the cable companies began developing their own high-speed ISP networks. Some operators like Time Warner moreover were planning to merge with large Internet service providers like AOL, with the entire media giant's content expected to be distributed over the latter's huge network. Tiny @Home was further rocked in 1998 when AT&T acquired TCI and, realizing that ten-ton Ma Bell was about to take control of the board, @Home frantically arranged for a shotgun marriage with Excite. The maneuver was buoyed by the red-hot, dot-com stock market, which valued the all-stock deal at $6.7 billion. Unfortunately for the merging partners, the Wall Street bloom was withering in January 1999 when the merger was announced. The stock of the combined company would continue to move upward for another three months before being swallowed by the market's crash.

As the stock price of Excite@Home plunged from $60 a share to 13 cents, Ma Bell heavy-handedly took control of E@H's board, then bought out the interests of Cox and Comcast. By the end of 2000, with hope of a stock market rebound fading and its shares trading below $10 a share, Excite@Home was forced to call off its $5.1 billion merger with Chello Broadband. A $4.6 billion write-down of assets followed at the beginning of 2001, as did a Chapter 11 bankruptcy filing in September. In the bankrupt firm's subsequent dismemberment, AT&T grabbed the @Home high-speed service for $307 million, leaving the Excite portal for others. The fission would dash the once-breathless hopes of marrying the portal's content to @Home's broadband Internet service. It also cast a dark cloud on the later and larger merger between AOL and Time Warner, which was predicated on similar synergistic goals. In the end, such megamergers, at least in the Internet Age, were doomed not by the hubris of high-tech executives or even by the difference in corporate cultures of the combining companies, as management gurus are apt to say, but by the simple lack of financing. The money dried up, and the start-up's stock price, its surrogate currency, nose-dived. Lacking retained earnings as well as ad and subscription revenues, the dot-com high flier sees the end of the road only too late. Thus, made-in-heaven mergers are foreordained to burn in hell because today's "fat" years were followed by harrowing lean times. Furthermore, even with billions in the bank and strong revenue sources, survivors of the bust years may not emerge to lead a rebound. Microsoft, Oracle, and Cisco Systems have enormous reserves as well as steady income from operations, but their shares are lagging in the current Nasdaq and tech recovery. These behemoths are finding it difficult to get on a growth trajectory that again attracts Wall Street's attention and are falling behind Amazon, eBay, Yahoo! and others that with minor or major course corrections are seeing their shares touch new highs. Such is life on IT's fast track, with front-runners being constantly created and destroyed.

—— Chapter 6 ——
Microsoft Curbed

On June 7, 2000, Microsoft Corporation was found to have repeatedly violated the Sherman Antitrust Act by decision of a federal district court, which ordered the breakup of the software company. A year later, an appeals court vacated the order even though it upheld that the company had abused its monopoly "in its entirety" in the desktop computer business. Thus the epic encounter between the U.S. government and the house that Bill Gates built appeared to reach a zero-sum conclusion, further diluted by the myriad claims of victory in an industry that was rapidly reshaping the world. What did go forward, however, was the black stain of monopoly power abuser indelibly stamped on Microsoft that would give it pause should it attempt to extend its strong-arm tactics to other markets. Big Brother was now watching to ensure that a small Internet company like Netscape would never be bludgeoned by the arrogant bully. In addition, "There is some worry [that] even though [the company] would retain an effective monopoly it would be so hamstrung by government oversight that its profit margins would inevitably erode."[1] So forcefully had the monopolist label been fixed that an exhausted Bill Gates stepped down as CEO and refrained from antagonizing the court with such descriptions of its ruling as an "unwarranted and unjustified intrusion into the software marketplace; a marketplace that has been an engine of economic growth for America."[2] Such officious remarks had prompted nineteen state attorneys general to join with the federal government in the courtroom battle. With Gates sidelined as board chairman, the new CEO, Steven A. Ballmer, is attempting to turn the company away from its freewheeling, survival-of-the-fittest mentality to one of building alliances and cooperating with other high-tech enterprises. It was an acknowledgment that the environment had inexorably changed following the bursting of the Internet bubble, and although revenues and profits continued strong at Microsoft, a skeptical Wall Street was concerned about its growth prospects, especially since it was now seen as a lumbering brute that preferred to smash competitors with its monopolistic power rather than challenge them with innovative products. This loutish image was furthermore cultivated by Gates during the antitrust case and delineated by Judge Thomas Penfield Jackson in his breakup order:

1. "Microsoft as it is presently organized and led is unwilling to accept the notion that it broke the law or accede to an order amending its conduct."
2. Microsoft "may yet do to other markets what it has already done in the PC operating system and browser markets."
3. The company "has announced its intention to appeal even the imposition of the modest conduct remedies it has itself proposed as an alternative to the nonstructural remedies sought by the plaintiffs."
4. "Microsoft has proved untrustworthy in the past. In earlier [1994] proceedings in which a preliminary injunction was entered, Microsoft's purported compliance with that injunction while it was on appeal was illusory and its explanation disingenuous."
5. "Moreover, plaintiffs' proposed final judgment is the collective work product of senior law enforcement officials of the United States Department of Justice and the attorneys general of 19 states, in conjunction with multiple consultants. These officials are by reason of office obliged and expected to consider—and to act in—the public interest; Microsoft is not."[3]

These conclusions by Judge Jackson, appointed to the court by the conservative president Ronald Reagan, were totally at odds with what business and legal specialists had expected. Microsoft's defense team furthermore appeared well-matched against the government since the company's rise to preeminence in high-tech industries was grounded in its software capabilities that were respected and used everywhere. Also, the company had bested the competition with technical innovations as well as marketing brilliance to give it its exalted status, and the judge overseeing the case was expecting the company to defend itself along the lines of its exemplary past. So why did the case reach such a wretched split-up result? A critical turning point came before the opening of the trial when U.S. prosecutors went to Microsoft's headquarters to depose Bill Gates. He was expected to be "articulate, passionate, tough, direct, intelligent and very, very knowledgeable about everything relating to the case." Instead, the deposition tapes, when shown in court, depicted a mumbling company chairman and co-founder who was "uninformed, obdurate, and unaware of anything related to the government's charges." The judge was forced to admit that "here is the guy who is the head of the organization, and his testimony is inherently without credibility."[4] The deposition was shown at the trial's start, and it would be downhill for the company, concluding with the breakup order. Beyond the court-room, the public came to see Microsoft as a corporate bully—as claimed by its competitors—that was nearly torn asunder by the stonewalling testimony of Gates who, until then, could do no wrong.

On June 28, 2001, the U.S. Court of Appeals for the District of Co-lumbia Circuit, where the antitrust case was heard, affirmed part of the lower court's ruling and reversed in part the judgment "that Microsoft violated Sec. 2 of the Sherman Act by employing anticompetitive means to maintain a monopoly in the operating system market."[5] The determi-nation that the company illegally attempted to monopolize the Internet browser market was also reversed. The appeals court instead ruled that Microsoft violated the Sherman Act by:

1. Imposing licensing agreements with computer equipment mak-ers that restricted their pre-installment of the Netscape or any rival browser instead of Microsoft's own Internet Explorer browser.
2. "Threatening Apple Computer that it would cancel work on a suite of Office applications for Apple's own operating system unless Apple made greater use of the Microsoft browser."[6]
3. Deceiving two independent software vendors into believing that they were developing software for Java technologies with cross-platform capabilities—able to run on an operating system other than Windows. Instead, they "ended up producing applications that could only run on Windows [in the process preempting Java's] potential threat to Windows' position as the ubiquitous platform for software development."[7]

An essential element of the case centered on Microsoft's successful launching of the IE browser by tying or bundling it with Windows, which held 95 percent of the PC market. By such an arrangement the district court had determined that the company had per se violated Section 1 of the Sherman Act. The appeals court found "that integration of the new functionality into platform software is a common practice and that wooden per se rules in this litigation may cast a cloud over platform innovation in the market for PCs, network computers and information appliances."[8] The court stated that the rule of reason should have instead been applied to the tying arrangement and remanded the finding to the lower court.

The maddening struggle to unwind the complexity of software integration that extends monopolistic power consequently remains on the judicial merry-go-round. Resolution of the problem, moreover, is made more difficult, if not impossible, by:

1. The fast-paced nature of software innovation that makes moot efforts to adjudicate disputes when the business outcome has already been determined.
2. A lengthy appeals process that overturns earlier decisions and muddies the waters by applying legal opinions to a complicated technical situation. In this case, for example, it was impossible to say where the boundaries were between browser and operating system code. Whether the tying of IE to Windows technically enhanced the browser was thus difficult to determine.
3. Political change at the White House, with new appointments at the Justice Department having a different outlook from preceding officials.

The greatest impact of the appeals process was the voiding of the order to break up Microsoft: "Divestiture is a remedy that is imposed only with great caution, in part because its long-term efficiency is rarely certain."[9] Such a remedy furthermore required stronger evidence of Microsoft's actions leading to monopolistic power in the browser market. Absent such connections, any of the company's unlawful behavior could be restricted with less-severe injunctions. The significance of the court's go-slow approach on divestiture was further accompanied by the presidential election of George W. Bush, who was less inclined than Bill Clinton to pursue a breakup of the innovative software company. The appeals court also removed Judge Jackson from the case because of flagrant violations, and this gave impetus to the Bush administration's decision to drop the effort to dismember Microsoft. The government also shelved plans to prevent Microsoft from tying only its programs like IE to Windows. A settlement was reached on November 2, 2001, on the anticompetitive practices found by the court in Microsoft's intimidation of third parties. It ended restrictions on PC makers, enabling them to install competing programs without fear of retaliation from the software giant. Uniform licensing terms for PC makers were also mandated for Windows, and discounts could not be given to computer manufacturers that favored the company's software.

Technical aspects were more difficult to address, although the settlement required Microsoft to disclose more information about its systems software's application programming interface (API). This would give independent software vendors an easier time in developing middleware programs like browsers and media players that would run smoothly on Windows. Specific to middleware developers only, the disclosure did not apply to other business applications such as personal finance software, which Microsoft sells. Since the company always has new versions of its operating systems in progress, it can still withhold valuable API information from most vendors while it develops or upgrades competing products that interface well with its Windows OS. Rivals were particularly dismayed that nothing in the settlement restricted the company from adding products such as Web services and media-playing software to Windows, which could extend its monopolistic power in PC operating systems to the Internet. This would give it an advantage that was demonstrated when it linked its Internet Explorer browser to Windows. In addition, the agreement did not force Microsoft into admitting that it had violated antitrust laws as found by the two federal courts. The epic case consequently ended with the defendant still a high-tech leviathan that turned back a surprising verdict to break it into two parts to stop the spread of its Windows monopoly. But not all was as it was before the litigation. The PC market had matured, and the searing stock market crash had permanently altered the IT environment to the extent that even the software giant had to make strategic adjustments as it sought to keep its leadership role and corporate growth intact.

Beyond the PC

Microsoft may have held more than 90 percent of the market in both desktop operating systems and office applications software, but growth in these aging areas had slowed to less than 10 percent per year. New markets away from its PC-based monopolies consequently had to be entered quickly, and they were approached without the business leverage that Windows could confer. Large competitors like AOL Time Warner, IBM, and Sony were not bullied so easily, since Microsoft was attempting to catch up to leaders that had distinct technical, production, and marketing capabilities. Moreover, the dot-com flameout devastated numerous high-tech start-ups that were current or potential customers of the company's services. Online music and video distribution was also in disarray, but it represented a new arena that Microsoft entered with its Media Player software, competing against rival players from RealNetworks and Apple Computer. Microsoft bundled the new product with Windows XP, the latest version of its desktop operating system, resurrecting the specter of an unrepentant recidivist forgetting the gruesome spectacle of almost being cleaved in two by the U.S. government. Its nearly successful opponents, however, had not forgotten and filed a legal complaint with the European Union, alleging that the company was again extending its Windows monopoly to conquer new territory. While the legal action centers on the Windows XP operating system, a prior complaint focused on an earlier OS version that was bundled with the Media Player. The tying was determined to be illegal by the staff of the European Commission, which also found that Microsoft had abused its monopolistic power by restricting access to its Windows API code by competitors. The staff findings were forwarded to the commission, which could force the company to unbundle programs tied to Windows.

The advantages given Microsoft by its OS monopoly also helped it end a long-running battle that the company had with AOL Time Warner, the large Internet service provider. AOL, now the parent of Netscape, had charged Microsoft with antitrust violations in the browser war, and the issue was settled with a $750 million payment to a cash-starved AOL. Microsoft, flush with revenues from its desktop monopoly, could easily afford to pay such a large amount and even threw into the deal better access to Windows that would improve AOL's online service. Microsoft also agreed to license its Media Player software to AOL for the distribution of the latter's audio and video products over the Internet. To prevent piracy of Time Warner's music and movies, Microsoft began work designed to thwart online theft of media property. Finally, the agreement between the adversaries was a potential blow to RealNetworks, whose software was used by AOL subscribers to download films and music.

Database Battle

Although it possesses $46 billion in reserves as well as demonstrated market power to beat back smaller rivals, Microsoft has not been so triumphant in other hotly contested areas. Its MSN service, for example, trails AOL's by millions of visitors, and the same is true for instant messaging, with the field being joined by a reinvigorated Yahoo! In terms of advertising fees, America Online—in spite of depressed markets—still garners 44 percent of all ad dollars, with MSN getting 10 percent and Yahoo! 9 percent. The small percentage in addition to heavy marketing expenses to gain subscribers adversely affects MSN's bottom line, especially as e-commerce slows. It is also forced to charge lower monthly rates than AOL, and its pricing is being undercut by smaller, cheaper providers. In travel agency bookings done on the Web, Microsoft's Expedia service has a 25 percent market share, behind front-runner Travelocity at 35 percent and ahead of Priceline.com with 17 percent. Entrenched competition has also been encountered in software for enterprise servers, high-powered computers that run major business systems. In this corporate setting, Windows, which was developed for the home computer, does not carry as much clout as competing products from IBM, Oracle, Sun Microsystems, and Linux, which established recognized franchises while Microsoft focused on the PC market and on antitrust litigation. It is therefore not surprising to see that in May 2000, at the height of the dot-com boom, Oracle and IBM were locked in battle for the $10.9 billion relational database market, with Oracle leading with a 40 percent share. IBM had only 18 percent but closed the gap by acquiring Informix, which had a 5.7 percent share that bested Microsoft's at 5.1 percent. In a prior era, IBM, then the industry kingpin, held the lion's share of the database business because of its stranglehold, which it still has on mainframe computers. A nimble Oracle sprinted into the lead by selling 50 percent of the software used on Unix servers, which it accomplished by harnessing IBM's database technology to Unix systems.

By the turn of the century, other companies had developed enterprise application programs that used databases for managing core activities in accounting, customer service, human resources, and supply management. These firms included Germany-based SAP AG, PeopleSoft, and Siebel Systems. For the most part their application software extended Oracle's territory because they were linked to information stored in its databases. In the slowdown following the dot-com bust, sales for the older database programs were to plateau while growth in applications continued strong. This prompted Oracle to launch eBusiness Suite, which, like Microsoft's Office suite for the PC, integrated various application programs that together interacted with the Oracle database.

and business applications software spiraled upward at torrid rates of 50 to 100 percent per year while older products plodded along at noticeably slower speeds. This induced established software makers to take profits from successful operations to underwrite development in the growth areas. The movement was furthermore prompted by Microsoft's victory over Netscape, illustrating that the leap to new software fields could be done with sufficient technical, marketing, management, and financial resources. The antitrust case against the Redmond, Washington, monopolist also abetted the transition because it gave pause to Microsoft's marauding and allowed competitors to proceed without fear of being thrust into mortal combat with Bill Gates's empire.

The dot-com bust also made new market planning and development imperative as revenues from established product lines slowed to a trickle. In addition, numerous markets had only recently sprung to life, with no dominating player. The $20.1 billion enterprise software market, for example, was led by SAP with a 32 percent share at the beginning of 2002 even as the Walldorf, Germany, company was having difficulty securing business in North America. For one thing, the company was forced to allocate considerable public relations sums to differentiate itself from another widely known SAP that translated TV programs from English to Spanish for the large U.S. Latin American audience. Such problems impelled the German firm to shift its marketing operations to Manhattan in order to get better coverage from the New York media.

An entirely different set of problems faced Oracle, which was second in sales with 15 percent of the corporate software market. Its CEO, Larry Ellison, had already attracted too much negative attention with his controversial remarks, and industry leaders were quick to deride anything he said or did. Thus Conway, upon hearing of Oracle's bid for his company, labeled such action as "diabolical," intended merely to undermine PeopleSoft's acquisition of JD Edwards. The competitive strategy behind the takeovers is understandable because PeopleSoft had 10 percent of the market, and with the 4 percent from JD Edwards would achieve near parity with Oracle's 15 percent. Moreover, PeopleSoft was taking market share away from Oracle, especially with the failure of its 11i application suite. Ellison also needed PeopleSoft in its own efforts to counter SAP's U.S. campaign. Such verbal backstabbing and strategic maneuvering, while appearing sophomoric, attested to the high degree of competition at the commercial frontiers of software development. In the current imbroglio, PeopleSoft's top management inadvertently pointed the way to its possible takeover by suggesting that it purchase Oracle's enterprise application division when the latter encountered a lukewarm response to the 11i introduction. Taking umbrage at the suggestion, Oracle countered by suggesting that it take over PeopleSoft instead, especially since it could offer cash and not its downtrodden stock. Upon further examination, Oracle learned that Conway had been successful in turning PeopleSoft around and speeded up plans to bid for the company when the latter reported that 2002 net income had risen to $182.6 million. Meanwhile, it shelved plans to buy Siebel Systems, which had remained in the red. In such a manner, Oracle could be selective in acquiring those companies whose customer base and products meshed with its game plan, particularly since its 2002 net income totaled $2.2 billion, giving it a solid financial base. The strong earnings stream also allowed the company to increase its cash bid for a recalcitrant PeopleSoft by more than $1 billion.

Impact on the Titans

Microsoft, archenemy of Oracle and many of its neighbors in Silicon Valley, looked upon the hostile bid with some consternation because it impinged on its own plans to enter applications. The West Coast giant, however, demurred when asked if it would come to PeopleSoft's rescue by countering with its own bid. It preferred to "let sleeping dogs lie" given the legal wrangling that nearly split the company in two. In addition, at the time of the settlement the federal judge admonished Microsoft to "change its predatory practices which have been part of its competitive strategy. [Otherwise] this court will exercise its full panoply of power to ensure the letter and spirit of this decree are carried out."[12]

PeopleSoft furthermore already maintained that the Oracle takeover violated antitrust statutes, and this was seconded by the Connecticut attorney general, acting on behalf of the state, which was a user of the company's software. Information systems would be in limbo if the takeover went through, and consequently the attorney general described Oracle's action as "a classic antitrust violation, going from three competitors in a market to two, and leaving those two with more than 50% of the market."[13] In the charge, the state of Connecticut narrowly defined the application market as limited to SAP, Oracle, and PeopleSoft, purposefully leaving out the Big Enchilada, Microsoft, in order to more vividly paint Oracle as a monopolist. And indeed the inclusion of because of difficult times. Even with the opposition's disarray, soft has not been terribly successful in staking out much in pace. For example, it has not "clearly articulated the .NET vision or technologically savvy users and IT managers who have been g Microsoft applications for years. And the two-to-five year time-Microsoft has outlined has left a lot of users skeptical that such an aking can be achieved at all."[14]

ther area where Microsoft appears to have stumbled is in video , where its Xbox console was expected to compete against Sony's ation 2. Xbox is planned as an entry point and platform to the entertainment market, with the Internet used to download games gage players from around the world. Microsoft expended billions video game player, and even with its credible debut and satisfac-pressed by Gates on its commercial progress, rumors keep flying e company might exit the field. Xbox remains a distant second to nd competitive pressures are building in more important areas. In)03, "International Business Machines Corp., in a bid to win more mall-business market, [made] a direct attack on Microsoft Corp., ating what has been a veiled conflict."[15] In opening the new front, no longer the hardware goliath that was brought down by MS-out a marketing heavyweight that successfully used its mainframe oly to transform itself into a software and services powerhouse. the company moreover that launched the IT era, and its main-and minicomputers still power the Internet and proprietary net-Its moves into software were discretely planned, with the rmation going unnoticed by a myopic media transfixed by the oft antitrust case and the criminal activity on Wall Street. Even Stewart received greater coverage, and at any rate IT gurus like tes had relegated IBM to the roadkill heap along the information ghway. The cavalier dismissal by the software chairman seemed d as Big Blue backed the puny platform efforts of Java and Linux thermore anointed Louis Gerstner, an industry nobody, as the ho would lead the company out of its money-losing morass. As umnist remarked, "How the heck can some guy who knows squat omputers save what was once the world's greatest technology y?"[16] The jury is still out on whether the company was saved Gerstner's tenure (1993–2003), but few will dispute that at the his retirement it was a remarkably different company and fit e to take on Microsoft after the latter had been bloodied by the

Microsoft, which already is in applications, would determine if the Oracle takeover is approved by regulatory bodies in the United States and Europe. Oracle is already rebutting the antitrust argument by insisting that the market is in flux and that it is merging with PeopleSoft to compete against SAP and Microsoft. While the inclusion of Microsoft might aid Oracle in Washington, D.C., where the Justice Department is expected to review the case, the addition of SAP might not help with regulators at the European Commission. They may be more inclined to view Oracle as a smaller Microsoft-type bully using its strong position in databases to keep SAP out of North America. The drawn-out arguments of the Microsoft case may thus have a replay in judicial and regulatory settings, ultimately reaching a whimpering end, like its predecessor, long after innovations in software bypass the plodding proceedings. And companies like Oracle, SAP, and IBM will rise and fall and perhaps rise again in reaction to internal forces as well as predatory blasts from the Microsoft "death star."

SAP

Founded far from the madding U.S. crowd, SAP AG was nevertheless forced to work and compete with the Americans in a pre-Microsoft, IBM-centric world. Its top executive Hasso Plattner was even an employee of the computer company, although he shrewdly gravitated toward writing applications for the mainframe instead of concentrating on hardware. Decades before Big Blue realized that its obsession with machinery would bring it to the brink of ruin, Plattner developed software packages for the company but failed to interest his IBM superiors in their commercial development. He left the company and established SAP, which produced and retailed shrink-wrapped financial programs that ran on corporate mainframe computers. At about the same time, Bill Gates was similarly dealing with IBM, offering his operating system for the new personal computer. Oracle in the early 1970s was also beginning its database business—again with IBM assistance—with the three fledgling companies never anticipating that their paths would cross. In the era of the mainframe, the Internet was a surreal concept that offered little to the start-ups and even established companies like IBM. It galvanized attention twenty years later, however, as growth slowed in traditional areas and the dash began to get into enterprise, corporate portal, and Web services and software.

Enterprise programs based on corporate functions like customer and supplier management became a natural extension for SAP when the Internet began connecting companies with customers and suppliers. Customers could be monitored and inventory and supply chains automated to increase efficiency and facilitate decision-making. Portal software in contrast allowed employees to access their company's in-house databases and use available programs when away from their offices. With Web services, tools and building-block software could be downloaded from the Internet to create and operate intercorporate networks. As these developments occurred, the early promise of the Internet as a distributor of knowledge-management software was realized, prompting Microsoft to enter the field with its .NET initiative and IBM with its WebSphere software and consultants. The rival systems each ran on different platforms, with IBM using the open-source Java technology from Sun Microsystems and .NET based on Windows and other Microsoft proprietary products like its SQL (database) Server software. Users were large corporations that, in the older era, constituted IBM's mainframe customer base and with which it still retained considerable rapport. In the new competition for small and midsize companies, IBM and SAP are jointly marketing Big Blue's services with the latter's industry-specific software solutions.

SAP in addition acquired the firm Top Tier for the development of corporate portal software that competes against Microsoft. The German firm had earlier, in 2001, attempted to launch its own portal, but the computer engineers who constituted its sales force had little of the experience needed for marketing the complicated technology. Hence the job was turned over to its acquisition, the more nimble and customer-oriented Top Tier. During the salad days of the Information Revolution, SAP's software in the absence of competitors was simply snapped up by eager corporate customers hoping to gain an operating advantage over rivals. Such a dreamlike existence came to a shattering end when SAP began facing competition from both Oracle and Microsoft. Reacting to the new realities, CEO Plattner hired marketing whiz Marty Homlish from Sony to head the division, which was moved from Europe to New York. A $100 million advertising budget was allotted to enhance the company's image, a difficult task given the company's name. The new executive also worked with Plattner to make its software user-friendly and as a result easier to market. A third member of the high-level team was Henry Kagerman, who would replace Plattner as CEO in May 2003.

The trio decided to streamline product offerin[g] programs into applications suites which, of cours[e] very successful desktop Office suite. SAP alre[ady] programs for production control, customer man[agement] terprise activities, and therefore putting them int[o] a difficult job. Its users moreover could now be i[n] plete set and forgo the buying of individual prog[rams] one at a time, increased the system's downtime that glitches had not been introduced. Developm[ent] lated initiatives enabled SAP to take an early lea[d] ware market with a 20 percent share compared wi[th] and 5 percent for PeopleSoft. Its percentage furth[er] ing 54 percent in 2002, with earnings rising 15 year. Such results present an optimistic outlook, [...] ist. As a leading vendor, SAP has become emb[...] wars between Microsoft's .NET and IBM's Java-[...] that wins will become the standard-bearer for We[b] new CEO, Kagerman, has the highly risky task of on the winning side.

Platform Wars

Although one standard will eventually emerge fr[om] confrontation, such a result will hardly mean that to the trash heap. The Internet is too huge a com[mon] entity, even as powerful as Microsoft or IBM, to gains in one area will be offset by losses elsewhe[re] proaches the platform rivalry with its own strengt[h] top operating systems and IBM in high-end corp[orate] former company's competitors are, furthermore, and acquisitions to ensure that Microsoft does not monopoly to the Internet. They have also made eff[ort] Java's "open source" platform as an alternative to been disorganized because IBM, which works wit[h] fronts, has no desire to lead the Java forces becaus[e] in such a role. In a similar vein, Sun Microsystems preoccupied with saving itself in the aftermath of sion, when its stock price fell to less than $3 a sh[are] open-source advocate, VA Linux Systems, has al[ready] federal government. The Armonk, New York, computer giant preferred to watch from the sidelines, however, as brasher combatants spawned in the IT revolution were only too eager to take on the empire of Bill Gates.

In addition to Ellison of Oracle, Scott McNealy of Sun Microsystems was a leader in the anti-Microsoft trenches and sallied forth in 1995 with the Java programming language that in combination with the Netscape Navigator browser and a virtual machine program represented a direct assault on the Windows platform. At the time, the personal computer was the principal entrée to the Internet, and because it was controlled by Windows, opponents were fearful that Microsoft would monopolistically expand into Internet commerce and computing. This was technically achievable because software that enabled e-commerce had to be built on the Windows platform for seamless interaction between client and server computers. These were frequently low-end corporate desktop computers that ran on Windows and its predecessor, MS-DOS. Their proprietary code was often shared with independent software developers, bringing them into the Microsoft orbit. The OS furthermore exerted a stronger gravitational pull as more computers used Windows and as newer versions with enhanced capabilities were launched. Windows in fact was developed primarily to facilitate Internet transactions, which the older DOS could not do. Its introduction thus became a clarion call to its many foes that if left unchallenged, Microsoft would gain significant control of the Web.

Sun's Java was expected to thwart this game plan because, with the use of a browser and virtual machine, it was capable of accessing the Internet without going through Windows. Sun was also a major player in the server computer market for large corporations, and its hardware and software were familiar to information managers. Eventually Java's code was released and, with its use, enabled software engineers and developers to run their applications or enterprise programs on different platforms, even proprietary ones like Windows and the OS for Apple's computers. Modifications to debug and better adapt Java to various needs could also be undertaken by its users, and it became an open-source language when the upgraded software code was posted on the Internet for use by other parties. By August 1997, Sun estimated that four hundred thousand programmers were improving Java. The effort included start-up firms that were financially backed by the $100 million Java Fund, which had been set up by the venture capitalist Kleiner Perkins Caulfield & Byers along with IBM and Compaq Computer. An agreement was also signed between IBM and Sun to develop a Java operating system for consumer appliances, and the technology was licensed by Ericsson for possible use in its cellular phones. Java's introduction was furthermore a response to the Internet's siren call, and it seized the attention of corporate chieftains and information managers when the *Wall Street Journal* christened Java as the World Wide Web's lingua franca.

Heralded as it was, Java failed to blunt Microsoft's drive onto the information superhighway. Sun lacked the deep pockets and technical depth to support a sustained challenge to Windows because it never secured a steady stream of income from Java users the way Microsoft did with its proprietary systems. It would be the same quandary for Yahoo! whose Web sites and information were accessed without charge, sending the portal into a deep financial hole when the dot-com ads evaporated. Java's setback on the other hand was not related to the stock market collapse, which in due time wreaked havoc everywhere, but on the individualized manner in which the language was developed. McNealy had planned it as a platform that would rival Windows, but independent users and licensees found that software running on Java did not execute as well as programs written for Windows. And why should developers spend time and money enhancing Java's performance when suitable platforms based on Windows, Unix, and Macintosh were available? Users thus selectively made improvements that advanced their own Web programming or ignored Java altogether. Another deficiency was its slower performance compared to other platforms, and on the information network, not being up to speed had debilitating consequences. Two years after its emergence, Java was being used to operate only 1 percent of online Web pages.[17]

Microsoft furthermore was routing the Netscape browser—an integral part of Java's operating paradigm—and with its monopolistic largesse, had formed new initiatives in Web services based on open industry standards. One of the most important of these was XML, or extensible markup language, which numerically categorizes information on diverse formats and databases to allow its exchange between different computers and programs. Software from different platforms can also be shared using the simple object access protocol, which permitted Web services or sites to autonomously initiate requests of other Internet services. Applicable services could be found with the standard UDDI Web directory, and documents were retrieved and routed using the WEBDAV protocol. Microsoft developed these standards because its .NET initiative had to interact with other platforms in order to be of use to software developers.

The company was also demonstrating to regulators and the federal court that it was not attempting to take over the Internet and merely following existing standards.

.NET was introduced in June 2000 under the clumsy name Next Generation Windows Services, which was soon shortened to Windows.Net and then again to simply .NET. The change was part of Microsoft's campaign to attract developers into using and paying for .NET tools and services instead of those from Java. Subscription fees would also be imposed to help the company recoup its $2 billion investment. Plans are furthermore underway to generate additional income with linkages to Windows. The proprietary operating system is expected to be upgraded to better work with programs built with .NET tools, with the new OS version debuting as Windows Server 2003. Its big Office moneymaker in desktop computing will also become available over the Internet on a subscription fee basis and, with the use of XML, its programs could ostensibly run on non-Windows platforms. Extending the reach of the popular Office suite was an important reason why Microsoft has embraced industry standards that enabled cross-platform exchanges. The company had to accept the reality that the Internet was hardly Windows-exclusive territory with only PCs as entry points, but was instead a polyglot of mainframe and server computers connected to handheld and notebook-size devices using a variety of platforms based on Linux, Unix, Java, and Sun's Solaris OS as well as Windows. Microsoft, however, insists that its Web services and tools perform better with Windows.

In corporate computing, Java—because it arrived first—has more programmers and information officers in its camp than Microsoft's .NET. Java is also recognized as being an industrial-strength technology that can handle enterprise programming while the untested .NET may lack such capability. To overcome this perception and buttress .NET, Microsoft developed the Visual Studio.Net programming tool to assist independent software vendors who build Web products and services. It has been successful in gaining their attention, and .NET is now used by 40 percent of developers while 51 percent remain with Java. Microsoft is also handicapped in cyberspace because few high-end servers of large corporations run on Windows. Linux moreover has staked its claim as an open-source operating system for these servers that can be downloaded from the Internet and licensed at low cost, which increases its use by hard-pressed companies. The Linux platform is also supported by IBM, making it a formidable entity in high-end corporate computing.

Web Software, Services, and Servers

As the complexity, intensity, and speed of Internet computing advanced, specialized computers called portal and directory servers developed that connected corporate computers to the Internet and searched myriad databases for relevant information. In the last decade, moreover, the nature of information changed from text-based data processed by file servers to graphical representations run on Web servers. Multimedia content was also sent in real time over networks that had considerable carrying capacity. These developments were accelerated by strong consumer demand for audio-visual entertainment that could be accessed by the home computer. Media companies stampeded into the new market by upgrading servers to handle broadband exchanges. Web advertisers similarly incorporated graphic and multimedia experiences to attract customers with Web sites crafted using services and tools downloaded from the Internet. This helped in the development of programs that ran the Web servers. Similar innovation also occurred in application software and servers that manipulated data and presented results in a format that aided decision-making. Output from one query could prompt additional searches and analysis to yield a more comprehensive report. For these jobs, servers had to have the requisite software, in addition to an operating system. The term server thus designated either hardware or software, and platforms encompassed the computer and its operating system upon which application programs were built.

In contrast to Microsoft and Oracle, Sun Microsystems produced both server hardware and software but its emphasis on the former placed it in a precarious position when PC maker Dell entered the competition. Although Dell kept to the low-cost end of the market, Sun was simultaneously squeezed at the high end by IBM, which had migrated from its base in mainframes. Sun's corporate computers moreover used the company's proprietary Solaris operating system while the open-source Linux OS ran competing machines from IBM. In hardware systems sold by Sun, a large corporate computer, running Solaris, controlled applications and Web servers, and even though these were built on the Java platform, information managers were leery of going with the proprietary Solaris software because it was not compatible with other platforms. IBM's use of the versatile and powerful Linux operating system, moreover, enabled a single mainframe to control and even replace large numbers of servers, which helped Big Blue take market share away from competing high-end Sun servers. To regain lost revenue, Sun was forced into low-end servers, where there were smaller profit margins and where Dell was solidly entrenched. As large bites were being taken out of its main source of income, Sun's quarterly net fell into the red at the end of 2001. Like Big Blue, McNealy had relied too long and too much on hardware, and the downturn following the dot-com collapse made it difficult to shift the company's efforts to software and Web services, where profit margins were robust.

Hardly touched by the dot-com boom and bust, a reorganizing IBM used the 1990s to become a major competitor in software and services for corporate computing. Its software ran its mainframe and application servers in competition with BEA Systems, Sun, and Oracle, but the company remained above the fray in enterprise applications that engulfed Oracle, PeopleSoft, and SAP AG. With WebSphere on the other hand, it was first in offering Web services and software tools over the Internet, getting 30 percent of the fledgling market, including a large job from the auctioneer eBay. Grossly underestimated by the competition, IBM grabbed the account from Microsoft and BEA Systems by offering a system built on open-source technology. The package included the Linux OS and the Java programming language, which, because of their nonproprietary nature, were not only available but had low licensing costs. Linux and Java also did not lock a customer into a contractor's proprietary system, thus alleviating the fear that a breakthrough originating elsewhere would be difficult to incorporate in an up-and-running system. The eBay victory highlighted two other trump cards integral to IBM's open-source strategy. Its 160,000-person worldwide consulting force could integrate the various software and hardware parts and oversee start-up, scale-up, and system maintenance. Such support was unavailable from other high-tech vendors, where arrogant posturing was the norm, promising much but delivering little. These advantages made corporate information officers more inclined to turn to IBM's quiet professionalism. Its understated corporate ambience further enabled Louis Gerstner to substantively transform the company even as the din from Wall Street and Silicon Valley reached a fevered pitch in the dot-com mania.

On his first day as CEO, "Lou Gerstner arrived at IBM on April Fools Day in 1993 and found himself at a company that had become in many ways a sad joke."[18] Its $16 billion loss in the early part of the decade ended any thoughts of greatness that Big Blue had held, and its rank-and-file employees were ready to swallow the prescription plan put out by the new chief or lose their jobs. Many were sent flying out the door anyway, along with cherished strategic underpinnings like Big Blue's singular reliance on proprietary technology, which it had developed. Its turn to open-source systems was prompted by a lagging expertise, particularly in conducting business on the Internet, which Gerstner stipulated as the main path to growth. The new game plan required immediate decisions, especially in choosing either a closed, proprietary platform like Windows or positioning hardware and software systems on Linux and Java technology. Having suffered at the hands of Microsoft, IBM could have become one of its major opponents, blaming it for the morass it was trying to get out of. But because Gerstner had not gone through the PC wars, he never experienced Microsoft's "mad-dog Mensa"[19] culture and therefore had no vindictive feelings about the company. He instead sought the advice of customers and found that they were in need of services and software that would enable them to take part in the Internet Revolution. They were also fearful of being locked into the Windows platform while innovation was leaping forward, but lacked the expertise for implementing their own open-source system. This uncertainty enabled a reputable enterprise like IBM to step into the breach and assist clients as they made major e-business investments. In these jobs, IBM adopted a middle-of-the-road approach in which it did not champion one standard over another but instead pulled parts from rival producers that met its customer's needs. For them it would also be a minimal headache solution with a lot of handholding by Big Blue in putting the system together and making it work. This resulted in a big payoff as "revenues from services such as systems integration, product support, consulting, and website hosting surpassed computer hardware revenues for the first time."[20] When Gerstner arrived in 1993, services accounted for 27 percent of total revenues, and the percentage increased to 41 percent on 2001 revenues of $86 billion and rose again in 2002 to 45 percent of sales, to yield 48 percent of the company's pretax profits. In addition, the Global Services unit, which grew to number 160,000 consultants, was integral to IBM's major offensive in software that accounted for 15 percent of 2002 revenues and 29 percent of pretax profit. The success in services and software was achieved because customers were not interested in connecting the individual parts but in purchasing the proper functioning of an entire package. Company consultants could consequently freely bundle IBM's services, software, and hardware, and boost sales across numerous product lines. Alliances were also formed with enterprise software producers like SAP, PeopleSoft, and even Microsoft, since their programs were frequently chosen to satisfy order requirements.

Microsoft Curbed

The principal impact of a resurgent IBM has been on the Internet expansion plans of Microsoft as the two behemoths staked out Web services and software. The competition has already provoked price-cutting in the market for small and medium-size business. IBM is offering a 24 percent discount on its WebSphere Commerce Express as a way of undercutting Microsoft's price for its competing Internet infrastructure software. This aggressive move was part of a strategy for countering the Windows.Net initiative for large corporate accounts. It also demonstrated that Big Blue would not stand aside as it did in PCs and let Microsoft take over the market for smaller firms. This has slowed growth for both companies, but the effect is more telling for the software giant because it was such a recent high flier until the PC market matured. Profit growth slowed, forcing Microsoft to acknowledge the new reality by paying its first cash dividend in order to boost its lagging stock price. Stock options were also eliminated because those that had been issued became worthless. And in paying a dividend, Microsoft was admitting that it could no longer increase growth by investing more of its $46 billion cash reserve and therefore was returning some of it to investors. The incentive for using options to attract the "best and the brightest" employees was also dead, killed by the moribund stock price. Realizing this, both Bill Gates and Steve Ballmer sold hundreds of millions of dollars of their Microsoft shares in 2003, giving up on hopes that their price would quickly rise.

—— Chapter 7 ——

The Bubble Bursts

Arrival of the third millennium was accompanied by the $183 billion merger of America Online with Time Warner, which *Business Week* hailed as "a new kind of conglomerate whose very existence will likely change the contours of information and entertainment media—digital and otherwise."[1] The magazine's cover featured New Economy titans Bob Pittman and Steve Case—both from AOL—who had created the "colossus" that would "redefine the future." It was not to be. Within four months, fissures in the dot-com boom appeared that implosively led to its $7 trillion collapse. This scarred newly born AOL Time Warner, causing $223 billion of shareholder value to go up in smoke—$8 billion of which was suffered by Ted Turner, its largest shareholder. *Business Week,* quickly forgetting the lavish superlatives, dubbed it the "the worst deal in the history of misbegotten megamergers."[2] In the flip-flop, the magazine replaced the cover photos of Case and Pittman—who were no longer in charge—with the face of Dick Parsons, the demure, surviving CEO charged with rescuing this poster child of the dot-com boom and bust. The prior titans unceremoniously exited as their jerry-built merger fell apart.

First to go was Bob Pittman, tin god of the Internet, who was scratched when online ad revenues evaporated. Second was Gerald Levin, who believed that AOL's technology would transform Time Warner into a New Media company. Third went Steve Case, who had convinced Levin that AOL would lead its partner to the digital promised land. Fourth was Ted Turner, who swallowed the hype from Wall Street and Silicon Valley and consequently lost the most. He would personify the inexorable psychological forces operating on these big shots—he was vice chairman of AOL Time Warner—during this torrid boom and bust period, and like the squirts who lost a million or two, he would call himself "the stupidest person in the world not to have sold earlier."[3] The billionaire lamented his inaction while his 60 million shares went from a peak price of $100 to $20, selling them on May 5, 2003, near the market's bottom.

Turner really had nothing to gripe about because he had received the shares in late 1996 for selling his broadcasting and film properties to Time Warner. At the time Time Warner's stock, because the company was not participating in the Internet Revolution, was bumping along at $20 a share, and it would zoom to its $100 peak in 2000 when the merger was announced. As such, the paper profit earned on the markets up leg (1996–2000) was lost on the down leg (2000–2003). In addition, he no longer controlled the media empire that he had formed around CNN, TNT, Turner Classic Movies, New Line Cinema, and other holdings, but this was due to his decision to sell them for a large amount of risky securities in first Time Warner and then AOL Time Warner. The loss is particularly bitter because at sixty-four, Turner—except for leftover billion-or-two dollars—has little to show for what took him a lifetime to build. This was his first major setback, and thus the lesson of selling at the top was never learned. Strategies of being extremely cautious during any boom and taking profits before the panic selling begins have generally been adopted by seasoned investors who survived prior market downturns. Ups and downs have always characterized equity investing, but for first-timers like Turner it was easy to believe that not only was he born under a lucky star, but his capitalist skills and daring had transformed him into a "master of the universe." How else could he interpret his good fortune? The Internet was eclipsing the automobile as the greatest invention, and its expansion had spawned the biggest bull market ever. Less ebullient chroniclers like the *New York Times* and the *Economist* urged caution, but these Cassandras were ignored by the swashbucklers who were charging into the New Economy. They furthermore bet their billions on a phenomenon that they knew little about, ignoring the market risk and believing the dubious accounting numbers released at headquarters and hyped by Wall Street analysts. But Turner, as the largest shareholder at both Time Warner and the combined AOL Time Warner, was an insider, sitting on both boards as vice chairman. How could one in his position be suckered in by the deal and its dealmakers?

Greed Blinds All

Mercury, Roman messenger god of commerce, delivered a $2.5 billion blessing on Turner in January 2000 when the surprise announcement of the merger sent Time Warner stock up by $25 a share. In one bewildering day, Turner's 100 million shares—which dwarfed the 876,000 shares held by Gerald M. Levin, Time Warner's chairman and CEO—skyrocketed in value by $2.5 billion. The action convinced Turner to vote for the merger "because we have a stronger company that will create value. It's not so easy to go out and recreate AOL."⁴ It would be a remarkable comment from a business tycoon who rarely if ever surfed the Internet and consequently had very little understanding of AOL's business. In such ignorant bliss, Turner gave no thought to selling a portion of his $10 billion stake in the new company even as shrewd investors began to take profits and hedge their bets. Instead, the glib words of AOL's Steve Case were taken to heart when he said: "Traditional media and assets have a vibrant future if they can be catapulted into the Internet age."⁵ Case was implying that the merger with AOL would send Time Warner's stock price into the stratosphere just when Turner and the older Gerald Levin were looking for a stunning climax to careers that had built the nation's largest media company. There were also the humanitarian projects in conservation, international peace, and nuclear disarmament that Turner could now fund with his gift from the gods, allowing him to stay in the media's spotlight during his golden years. In truth, the craving for attention drove all corporate moguls, and with the merger Levin and Turner were once again front and center, besieged by questions on how to create synergy in the union of such disparate entities as AOL and Time Warner. Flippant answers were readily given by technically illiterate executives at both companies, and as in a true Greek tragedy, they would live to see their tenuous synergies come undone even before the merger was finalized.

Merger of the Millennium

Rationale for the marriage of old and new-age companies hinged on the marketing of Time Warner's entertainment productions, including movies, magazines, music, television programs, and books, over AOL's Internet service. It followed the similar reasoning behind Sony's purchase of Columbia Pictures and CBS Records and Matsushita's takeover of MCA and its recording unit and Universal Pictures film studios. Both Japanese electronic giants were intent on fostering synergy between the producers of entertainment software (films, music) and the hardware (TV sets, film projectors) that delivered programming to viewers. The strategy failed because the Hollywood star power embodied by temperamental actors, writers, singers, and directors often left when their firms were acquired to form competing companies. Sony's efforts also stumbled as inept producers, since dismissed, shot extravagantly expensive movies that bombed at the box office. Matsushita sold most of its entertainment properties to Seagram's of Canada, which then dealt them to Vivendi of France, with all three owners suffering financially by first overpaying for the glamorous Hollywood units and then failing miserably to effectively manage them.

Despite such earlier setbacks, the electronic transmission of Time Warner's entertainment and published titles remained a recurrent dream of Gerald Levin, who in 1989 was climbing to the pinnacle of the media world. That year Levin engineered the $14 billion merger between the Time-Life empire of Henry R. Luce with Warner Communications. Becoming CEO of Time Warner in 1992, Levin could now actualize his ambitious plan to enter the digital age using the cable network, started with HBO, which was growing under his control. In 1995 his company's cable system increased substantially with the purchase of Turner Broadcasting, making Time Warner the second-largest cable operator by the time of the AOL merger. Cable networks had the carrying capacity to handle audio and video transmissions and were already bringing in substantial subscriber fees for the delivery of television programming. The technology furthermore had been enhanced three years earlier when Time Warner embedded thin optical fibers in the cable strand, permitting two-way communications between viewers and program producers. Video on demand—the industry's Holy Grail—was now potentially in reach, with Time Warner able to charge premium rates for transmitting specific movies or TV programs to viewer sets at requested times. With strong backing from Levin, the company launched Full Service Network, with tens of millions of dollars budgeted to lay the optical fiber-cable system and develop the TV set-top box needed by viewers to place video requests. Unfortunately for Levin's ambitious plans, the two tasks were difficult to complete, with consumer interest waning as the system remained daunting to users. It was easier instead for them to buy a VCR player and rent a few titles. Based on lackluster results, Levin closed the Full Service Network in 1997. By then, too, the Internet was evolving into a competing entertainment, information, communication, and e-commerce medium, and AOL was raking in subscriber and ad revenues for its popular, user-friendly, connecting service to the World Wide Web.

Before the merger, Pathfinder had been another Levin attempt to go digital, this time with an online Web site featuring an extensive list of

Time Warner's most popular magazines. Articles from *Time, Sports Illustrated, People, Fortune, Money, Entertainment Weekly,* and others could be downloaded to lure readers into placing subscriptions. Revenues for the portal would also come from advertising fees paid by the company's film, book, and music divisions, which would make the Web site an upbeat directory of pop culture. It would be directed at the free-spending audience of teenagers and young adults with their nonstop social binges, now catered to by a virtual shopping mall that was always open. Pathfinder complemented Full Service Network and together, at least in Levin's mind, united Time Warner's disparate parts into a marketing media juggernaut. Even Steve Case at AOL was impressed with the concept since his Internet service always needed entertaining and informative content that would retain and attract subscribers. Building an entertainment production empire on the scale of Time Warner, however, was beyond the reach of the company, leaving Case with the sole option of enticing Levin into a merger. This could be done if Levin's digital initiatives failed and if the stock market propelled AOL's stock to heavenly heights while keeping Time Warner's at the bottom. Unfortunately for both CEOs, those wishes were fulfilled.

The demise of Pathfinder was a glaring premonition of what was in store for the megamerger because it demonstrated that the various units of Time Warner by itself could not work together even with generous funding from Levin of $100 million. Time-Life's old guard saw no reason to participate in a project that undermined the established order, and film and music division heads saw no marketing advantage in advertising on something as nebulous as cyberspace. For the latter group, moreover, the company lacked the means for forcing them to do its bidding, because, like the disastrous Hollywood foray by Matsushita, division heads could leave with their recording and movie stars. Thus, five years after the merger of Warner Communication with Time Inc., the two sides were still separate operating entities interested only in their business niches and not concerned for the bottom line of the parent company. The shortsightedness even prevailed at the magazine level. As summarized by the managing editor of Pathfinder: "It was all such a struggle. They all wanted to have their own titles and own look and feel, so it was clearly a hodgepodge of stuff."[6] In the end Pathfinder splintered, with film and magazine heads building their own Web sites using their own resources with little if any coordination from headquarters. It was akin to a president declaring war with none of his generals showing up for battle. Indeed, Old Media had evolved as a loose collection of fiefdoms, each nurturing pet projects and cultivating powerful outside contacts in case of a major failure or loss of power. Pathfinder's managing editor, for example, became president of MSNRx.com after Time Warner killed the portal. Despite the departure and recalcitrance of his corporate bureaucracy, Levin—although exasperated—did not give up on the Internet, and his ambition was heightened by an unexpected call in October 1999 from AOL's CEO, who suggested a merger.

By then, the white-hot IPO market was funding the wildest dot-com schemes with start-ups spending with abandon to attract media attention. Advertising on AOL's Web sites and in Time Warner's publications soared as Amazon's credo of "getting big, fast" ruled the day. Operating profits were no longer necessary because Wall Street was willingly showering billions of dollars on front-runners in the Internet sweepstakes. The mania enveloped both Levin and Case, but had a markedly different impact on their company's stock price. As the largest Internet service, AOL's stock rocketed upward 59,000 percent from its public debut in March 1992 to the beginning of 2000. Most of the rise occurred in frenzied trading over the two years 1998–2000, as shown in Figure 7.1. In contrast, Time Warner's stock price remained flat at the bottom of the chart, ignored by institutional investors and day traders even though its revenues were five times those of its acquirer, America Online. AOL's market capitalization of $164 billion—versus $97 billion for Time Warner—was furthermore not the only yardstick by which the deal would be structured. Although a smaller company in revenues, AOL's profits dwarfed those of its merger partner, resulting in its stockholders receiving 55 percent of the merged company's stock. Even with the greater share, some of these investors were disappointed in the deal, and the stock fell from its peak 1999 price. They reasoned that combining with an old-line media company that failed to get two major online initiatives off the ground would impede the growth of AOL and saddle the Internet high flier with people like Ted Turner, who had never sent an e-mail message. To overcome the resistance, Case reassured his stockholders, who were mainly interested in seeing their shares go up another 59,000 percent, that synergistic billions would come from peddling Time Warner's programming and published content over the Internet. As to why such sums had not been achieved by Pathfinder? The CEO ascribed it to "poor execution. I thought they had a great opportunity, but for them at the time the Internet was a curious peripheral. For us, it was the

Figure 7.1   **Percent Gain in AOL and Time Warner Shares**

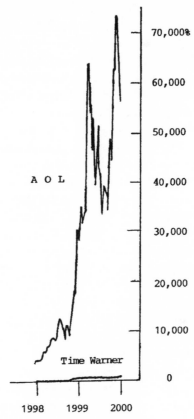

Source: Adapted from "The Online Generation Courts the Old Guard," *New York Times*, January 11, 2001, p. C1.

be-all, end-all."[7] The implication was that AOL had the wherewithal to bring Time Warner's marketing into the digital age. Case neglected to mention, however, that old-line entertainment and media chieftains might drag their feet and undermine his online efforts just as surely as they did with Levin's Pathfinder and Full Service Network.

Voodoo Goodwill

At the frothy heights of the bubble boom, Case and Levin received re-sounding support from Wall Street hype creators such as Mary Meeker of Morgan Stanley and Henry Blodget of Merrill Lynch, who were only too willing to bless the era's biggest merger. Their enthusiastic endorsements drowned out naysayers like Jessica Reif Cohen, Merrill Lynch's media analyst who didn't "see a desperate need to make a deal."[8] Even Ted Turner ruefully noted that the "strong personalities" who would lead AOL Time Warner inevitably meant that there was "potential for some friction."[9] These were readily countered by Blodget's perfunctory forecast of the merged company's stock price based on estimated earnings before interest, taxes, depreciation and amortization (EBITA) of $11 billion and earnings-per-share of $2.30. A billion dollars was added to future EBITA that would come from synergistic gains despite Turner's concern for problems in the executive suite. The EBITA number did not include $150 billion of goodwill that the merger would have to write off in annual increments, or have amortized, over the next ten years. The huge amount represented the difference in the purchase price of Time Warner, paid for in high-flying AOL stock, and the fair value of its net assets and was overlooked at the time because:

1. The merger was completed with an exchange of stock in which one AOL share would be exchanged for one AOL Time Warner share and one Time Warner share exchanged for 1.5 new shares in the merged company. The new shares were expected to climb in the continuing bull market and thereby maintain the premium paid for the old shares. Investors moreover were only interested in seeing their holdings rise in price and were unconcerned with any write-off as long as the share price did not fall. Besides, amortization and goodwill were obscure points that no one could be bothered with in the frenzied trading of high-tech stocks.
2. The $15 billion annual write-off was a noncash outlay and hence would not be a drain on the company like an expense payout. In addition, promised gains in synergy were expected to cover the goodwill write-offs as the merger got up to speed.
3. Goodwill also bridged the enormous difference in market capitalization between Time Warner and AOL stock, in effect making the merger possible.

After calculating an EBITA of $11 billion, Blodget divided it by the 4.8 billion shares that would be issued by AOL Time Warner, resulting in per share earnings of $2.30. A conservative multiple of 25 was then estimated based on Time Warner's slower growth while a higher one of

40 resulted if the merger were to follow AOL's faster growth. Applying the multiples, a $55 to $90 price range for the new shares resulted. AOL's stock price then stood at $60 a share and because it was to be converted, one-to-one, into AOL Time Warner stock, the implicit recommendation was that investors should hold on to their shares or buy even more because of the greater potential for an upward movement to $90 and the smaller downside risk of the stock falling to $55.[10] Of course, all bets were off if the stock market tanked—which it did—and if synergies never materialized. Also waiting in the wings was the full $150 billion of goodwill that haunted the company when operating revenues nosedived. Why were these and other huge negative aspects that crippled the merger overlooked by the media and Wall Street? Because the deal was expected to produce a major player in a New Economy, in which use of the Internet and digital technology would produce productivity gains and earnings growth without end. A stock market bonanza would result that would turn the latest stock run-up into a nickel-and-dime affair. The economy would run on Internet time, and all believers would be vindicated, especially investors, financial institutions, media pundits, Wall Street analysts, and visionary corporate leaders like Ted Turner, who had already been declared *Time*'s Man of the Year. It was enough to spin the head of any billionaire. But wait. The megadeal did not usher in a new age but, in hindsight, was the death knell of the dot-com bubble, and the celebrants—who had thrown all caution to the wind—were dancing on the decks of a sinking Titanic. In the aftermath, doomed merrymakers were forced to mull over the neglected questions that hastened the merger's downfall such as: Who would digitally transform Time Warner? When the old-media executive Levin became CEO of the new company, a red-light signal should have gone off. After all, Levin had toiled mightily to move Time Warner onto the Internet and failed. Why didn't AOL shareholders, who saw their stock fall when the merger was announced, question the appointment? Why did Case and Turner wait until too late to move against Levin? How could analysts like Blodget assign $1 billion worth of synergy gains that were to be achieved under Levin's leadership? True, the euphoric period and the general ignorance about the Web cowed most onlookers, and there was a distinct lack of analysis in the media's coverage of this mammoth merger.

As proof that more open discussion and transparency was possible and needed, another major deal appeared on the table at about the same time, between Hewlett-Packard and Compaq Computer. It provoked a gut-wrenching, down-to-the-wire battle between top management who were for the merger and large HP shareholders who were against it. Opponents of the merger elicited specific action plans from management on how the deal would contribute to shareholder value and not result in massive layoffs that demoralized employees. Answers were needed to win approval for the merger and counter the criticism directed primarily at Carly Fiorina, the recently appointed CEO at HP who spearheaded the deal with Compaq. In one blistering attack, the editors of *Red Herring* noted that "the merger will only increase your [HP's] dependence on commodity PCs with their increasingly slender profit margins, while diluting the strength of your successful businesses like printers." As a result, the magazine called on Fiorina to resign.[11] Instead she forged ahead, forming committees of management representatives from both sides that brought the companies together after the merger was approved.

Little of this type of planning and action occurred at AOL and Time Warner because of the lack of opposition to the merger. The new management team was simply proclaimed, with Case from AOL the chairman and Levin from Time Warner the chief executive. Two co-chief operating officers reported to Levin: Robert Pittman from AOL and Richard Parsons from Time Warner. The breakdown of responsibilities between these two had Pittman in charge of most of the growth areas like the AOL online service with its 29 million subscribers, Time Warner Cable (the second-largest cable network, which reached 21 percent of the U.S. home market), and HBO, a cable TV system with 37 million subscribers. Parsons controlled the film and music businesses and tradebook publications, which accounted for $13.4 billion in 2001 revenues compared with the $30.2 billion brought in by operations overseen by Pittman.[12] The lopsided assignments indicated that Pittman would run most of the show and that Levin and Parsons had been given top jobs to placate Time Warner shareholders like Ted Turner, whose approval was needed especially as the stock market began to fall. Pittman moreover had held executive positions at both companies, which would supposedly help him bridge old and new media cultures. Unfortunately, the gap proved too wide to bridge because the resulting setup retained the distinct boundaries of Time Warner's entertainment fiefdoms, preventing the cross-pollination that Pittman and Levin before him had needed. Resistance to any cooperation further deepened when AOL storm troopers marched into the New York offices of Time Warner demanding round-the-clock efforts at bringing the old establishment online. By then, however, the earthquake started by the dot-com bust had shifted the ground beneath the quartet of pro-merger executives, causing their careers to implode. The wolf was at the door and no one had planned for its arrival.

Naturally, all cheering stopped, from investors who had benefited immensely from AOL's rising fortunes to the stockholders of old media companies who were hoping to partake of the Internet feast that had lavished such goodies on their online counterparts. Moreover, the AOL Time Warner merger was expected to be only the beginning, in which Web-savvy firms like Amazon.com, Microsoft, Yahoo! and eBay would transform old standbys like Walt Disney, owner of ABC and ESPN; Viacom, owner of CBS and MTV; and News Corporation, owner of Fox broadcasting and cable units, and bring them into the digital age. Jubilant about the business possibilities were a whole gaggle of stock analysts, investment bankers, and run-of-the-mill consultants who made their living on mergers and acquisitions, public offerings, and forging intercorporate alliances in which old-line companies could stake claims on the Internet and reach those hundreds of millions of eyeballs that were searching the Web for things to buy. Marketing departments generally sought what Case had successfully pitched to Levin: "an [online] integrated consumer space"[13] that would make their CEOs media moguls and send their shares into cyberspace. And already, cable channels like CNN were calling to book airtime for executives who could give their take on such timely topics as how to cash in on the new mass market reached by the Internet or the need for high-speed, broadband networks for procuring parts and services and even trading securities online. The media business, which never quite understood cyberspace, now glimpsed the opportunities that Levin had seized by merging with an Internet provider capable of distributing its information and entertainment programs over vast electronic networks. Pundits applauded the Levin move, and investors, alerted by their stock brokers, began buying in on the ground floor before prices of lagging media stocks took off like Time Warner's had done. Investment bankers searched for merger candidates and salivated over the fees that would roll in from anticipated megadeals. Telecom companies offered their cable systems and laid optical fiber networks in anticipation of heightened demand for high-speed transmission of music and video titles. Enron of natural gas origins became an energy trader and broadband broker with funny money from off-book partnerships that eluded the oversight of its rubber-stamping board and less-concerned bureaucratic regulators.

In the giddy atmosphere, an insatiable greed for power and Bill Gates–sized fortunes developed among executives, leading many to deceive their own shareholders by withholding information on the deteriorating condition of their companies. Even the chiefs at AOL were not above the feathering of personal nests, clandestinely dumping their shares when the stock began to sink. For example, as co-COO of the combined AOL Time Warner, Pittman was charged with achieving revenue growth of 12 to 15 percent and a 30 percent increase in cash flow. He reiterated his promise to attain these goals even as the downturn sent ad revenues tumbling, and rationalized his confident expectations by saying that major advertisers gravitated in bad times to media outlets with the largest number of affluent readers and viewers. And no company matched the reach of newly formed AOL Time Warner. As Pittman proclaimed on CNN, "At times when people cut back media expenditures, they're not cutting everybody back, they're cutting the tertiary and secondary guys out. They tend to consolidate into their big players and the people who really give them the horsepower. The good news is, this company has those kinds of TV networks, those kinds of magazines."[14]

To grab and hold onto these big ad accounts, Pittman set up an advertising council where division heads discussed ways of selling cross-platform ads that would run on the company's TV programs, AOL's Web site, and Time, Inc. magazines. It was also a means of bringing the disparate parts of the new conglomerate together, even though Levin before him had failed at a similar gambit. It was never to be: The collapsing stock market shifted the balance of power back to the Old Media division heads, and once ads slowed at the AOL online unit, these crusty veterans were no longer interested in cooperating with Pittman and his New Media upstarts. Ramifications of the resurging recalcitrance were immediately clear to Case and Pittman. Financial goals were in jeopardy of not being met, and the marauding bear market on Wall Street would proceed to maul the company's stock price. It was time to cash in some of their stock and options. From 1999 through May 2002, the duo, while expressing ebullience at AOL's and subsequently the merger's prospects, dumped holdings worth $475 million for Case and $225 million for Pittman.[15] The action is made more shocking because Levin, who was taking most of the blame for the merger's fumbling start, did not sell any of his shares before retiring at the end of 2001 to escape the vitriolic charges being leveled at him. Earlier in April and May, Case unloaded 1 million shares worth $49.1 million, Pittman sold 500,000 shares for $24.75 million, and Parsons, the other co-COO, cashed in 420,000 shares for $20.58 million at high prices of $48 to $51 a share without the public knowing.[16] The problems kept coming, the stock price kept falling, and Case and Pittman resigned, passing the mantle of leadership without a word of dissent to the quiet and unassuming Richard Parsons. Perhaps they were too busy selling their stock to fight over the remains of the badly listing merger. At any rate, their failure to meet financial numbers was released in April 2002, when first-quarter results revealed a record loss of $54.24 billion. The new CEO, Parsons, explained that the red ink was due to a write-off of goodwill, but also conceded that online advertising was falling more than had been anticipated. Pittman was dispatched to the Internet unit to get a handle on the problem, only to come up empty-handed again. He resigned from the company in July 2002, a few months after Levin departed.

Broadband Dispute

According to Levin, the internecine battle between merger partners extended all the way to the top, leading to a confrontation with Case that prompted Levin to leave. The final dispute centered on broadband or high-speed Web access for the AOL service using AT&T's cable network, the largest system in the United States, which the long-distance giant was planning to sell. Levin wanted to purchase AT&T Broadband and combine it with his company's own extensive cable properties in order to achieve a lifelong goal of online music and video delivery to individual homes. He attempted the feat with Time Warner Cable prior to the merger with AOL and having failed, struck the deal with Case. Both agreed that the merger's success hinged on the broadband delivery of Time Warner's entertainment content using AOL's technical and managerial expertise. Cable and Internet divisions were consequently placed under Pittman, assuming that he would succeed in what had become media's Holy Grail. With Pittman's efforts going nowhere, Levin's attention turned to AT&T Broadband, which was up for sale. Plans were initiated for a competitive bid from AOL Time Warner, but these were placed on hold by Case, who felt that such a large undertaking was financially risky in light of the enormous debt—approaching $25 billion—

that the company had accumulated. Levin to the contrary, felt that access to broadband was essential for the survival of the AOL online unit, which was already frustrating subscribers·with its slow dial-up or narrow-band service. The confrontation between company CEO and chairman probably would have torn asunder the already fragile merger if it had reached the board, which was split equally between AOL and Time Warner factions. Vilified by shareholders, especially Ted Turner, Levin realized that it was best to leave, and as a final act got the board to approve Richard Parsons as his successor. In May 2003, Parsons also became chairman when Case stepped down; Turner similarly gave up the vice chairmanship, leaving Parsons in sole command.

Alone at the top, Parsons was faced with irate investors who wanted him to fix the myriad problems, especially at a crumbling America Online. Broadband was thus thrust high on the new CEO's agenda, much as it had been in Levin's waning days. Time was also of the essence because AT&T Broadband was about to change hands, making it imperative for Parsons that AOL have access to the largest cable operation in the nation. In addition, the increase in subscriptions to the company's dial-up service slowed noticeably as some users began switching to a faster service. Already in mid-2002, AOL had 500,000 broadband users, behind MSN and Earthlink with 600,000 apiece. If this continued, the trend would be ominous for AOL as more students and employees became attached to high-speed access at school or the office and followed up with broadband connections to their homes. AOL had banked on its slower service remaining competitive because it was less costly at $23.95 a month compared to $40 to $50 a month for the faster connection. But once Microsoft's MSN began offering broadband, AOL was forced to respond and began offering high-speed connections through the Time Warner cable system. Interestingly enough, Time Warner Cable was offering its own Road Runner broadband service, which was $10 cheaper per month than the exact same service, using the same cable system as AOL's. Road Runner was started in 1996, prior to the merger, and remained independent of AOL as problems like falling ad revenues began to plague the online service. In addition, AOL was reluctant to push broadband because most users were not interested in paying the additional charges. Those that did switch still kept the online service at a discounted rate of $4.95 a month in order to use their e-mail account.[17] Another consideration for AOL in distancing itself from Time Warner Cable included the possibility of using other cable carriers like AT&T

Broadband to expand its reach. Its marketing power as the largest Internet service could also be brought in to negotiate lower access charges and improve profit margins, which were about 27 percent for broadband and a much higher 67 percent for the slower-speed, dial-up service. The greater margin primarily resulted from the lower dial-up telephone charges of $8 a month compared to $40 for broadband cable connections, with the difference in profit rates another reason why AOL was reluctant to pursue broadband.[18]

In the deal that transferred AT&T Broadband to Comcast Communications, the 27 percent minority stake held by the phone giant in Time Warner Entertainment (TWE), which controlled Time Warner Cable, also went to Comcast. As the largest cable operator, AT&T-Comcast had to divest its ownership in Time Warner Cable and began negotiations to sell its TWE stake to majority owner AOL Time Warner. An agreement to that effect was reached with Parsons in July 2002, who wanted total control of both TWE and Time Warner Cable in order to offer high-speed Internet service to the latter's 22 million TV subscribers. Parsons also sought and received broadband access on AT&T-Comcast's cable system. In the agreement, Comcast sold its TWE shares for $2.1 billion in cash, $1.5 billion worth of AOL Time Warner stock, and a 21 percent stake in a new Time Warner cable company. AOL also received permission to sell its online service to about 30 percent of AT&T-Comcast's television customers. With complete ownership of Time Warner Cable, AOL Time Warner now planned to sell the cable company's shares to the public after it had transferred $8.1 billion of debt to a new Time Warner Cable to improve its balance sheet. The IPO, if successful, would also recoup the $2.1 billion cash payment to Comcast. In the postbubble doldrums, however, the cable issue was not expected to be enthusiastically received, particularly since AT&T-Comcast would be concurrently unloading its 21 percent stake. Bad times moreover had descended on the cable industry, which throughout the 1990s added capacity in a fevered race with telecom companies for the high-speed Internet connection market. In addition, cable operators were upgrading systems to accommodate digital television, incurring onerous debt loads that threatened their credit ratings. Bankruptcies at WorldCom and Enron only added to the tense situation as regulators and the media examined financial reports at go-go companies like AOL and found irregularities. Some of these were uncovered by Alec Klein, who splashed his story on the front pages of the *Washington Post* and in a follow-up book *Stealing Time: Steve Case, Jerry Levin and the Collapse of AOL Time Warner.*

AOL Unmasked

Klein's exposé, unfortunately, was too late for beleaguered investors, who had lost $7 trillion in speculative purchases of former high fliers. Many were suckered in at the peak of the bull market in anticipation of retiring with million-dollar portfolios, only to be outwitted by corporate insiders who were selling their shares. Why wasn't such action uncovered before individual retirement plans went down the drain? In the speculative fervor, neophyte investors giddily pursued quick and easy money, betting on the hot tip, and consequently got caught with fly-by-night securities touted by CEO hucksters and glib commentators that became worthless in the dot-com bust. The smart-money crowd, in contrast, exercised due diligence and purchased shares in quality issues such as Microsoft and eBay that would survive a lengthy downturn and prosper in a subsequent business cycle. Investments in lower-quality securities like Amazon.com and Yahoo! that were battered by the bust were also profitable if purchased near their bear-market lows and patiently held for the current recovery to take hold. Those closer to retirement should have turned to intermediate-term AAA investment-grade bonds, provided they had a basic knowledge of interest rate cycles. Unfortunately, small investors are rarely advised to buy high-grade bonds because brokers make much less in trading commissions than when they handle equity transactions, especially in a speculative environment with torrid in-and-out activity. There is thus none of the hoopla surrounding bonds as there is with riskier securities like stocks, options, and futures, which have burned even highly experienced traders and financial managers. Moreover, following tips and advice from "informed" sources is frequently disastrous and should never be a shortcut for doing careful analysis and research prior to making investments. An understanding of the capabilities of top management is furthermore extremely important and would have gone a long way in rescuing portfolios from the stock market bloodletting. Asset diversification, especially in fixed-income securities like investment-rated preferred stock and bonds, would also have protected many retirement plans. These commonsense approaches moreover are particularly necessary when dabbling in risky issues like AOL and other

Internet high fliers. Informed evaluations are accessible on the Web with desktop and mobile computers, where familiarity with all the media hype can be gained, compared with unbiased research, and discarded.

AOL is an apt case for investment analysis because from its beginning, the online service was constantly scrutinized. Aspersions were often cast on its networking and software capabilities and, in truth, its service was directed at the technically impaired user and cobbled together by mass peddlers who had at best only a flimsy idea of the Web. Evidence of this occurs in a remark and background of its top executive, Steve Case: "I don't care where the technology is; we just have to be where the action is."[19] The action in Case's teenage and later years centered on pop music, attending concerts, interviewing rock stars, and singing the lead in his own band. These activities took precedence over computer science courses, which at the time tediously entailed the punching out and precise assembling of computer card decks. Naturally Case's first choice for college was one based in Los Angeles, a center of rock music as well as film. Following college, Case attempted to land a job in an advertising firm in New York, where singing and dancing were the loudest, and more than not, the wildest. Pursuing similar interests, Pittman headed for the Big Apple and caught the attention of Case after co-founding MTV, the music cable channel of ear-blasting singers, bands, and fans. He would become president of AOL, reporting to Case as CEO, even though both executives were singularly devoid of any technical or business accounting skills. Pittman's appointment to head AOL Networks moreover was made after the online service had gone dead for eighteen hours. Millions of new customers became disgusted with their first-ever experience with the Internet and when they eventually got online, proceeded to torch AOL with unprintable language. Equally significant, the severity of the outage gave Microsoft additional incentive for launching the IE browser and then the competing MSN service. AOL, weighed down by problems, would be easily coerced into using IE and aiding Microsoft in its browser war with Netscape. And after it was nearly crushed by Microsoft, Netscape ironically would be taken over by AOL.

With MSN, Microsoft promptly marched onto AOL's turf by initiating an unlimited access plan for a flat fee of $19.95 a month. AOL was forced to meet this threat by abandoning its lucrative hourly usage fee and initiate a flat fee, in effect letting MSN dictate the commercial terms of Internet access even though AOL had the much larger market share. The sudden move to unlimited use clogged AOL's circuits, with daily user hours jumping from 1.5 million to 4.5 million. All that a techni-cally hapless Case could do was exhort his subscribers not to spend so much time on the Internet and promise again that more capacity was being added to enable unlimited service. The costs of additional capac-ity furthermore mushroomed into the hundreds of millions of dollars because network-challenged AOL was forced to pay outside contractors premium rates to do the work at the height of the dot-com boom. Mean-while, under the flat rate user plan, revenues were dropping and sub-scribers—fed up with the busy signal at AOL—were moving to other services. What was cash-strained headquarters to do? Go to Wall Street, of course, and use its rising stock price to effect mind-boggling mergers and acquisitions that would knock the socks off the digirati business community. And in Case, Pittman, and an abrasive, driven lawyer, David M. Colburn, AOL had the requisite wheeler-dealers who could do just that. Arriving in 1995, Colburn was put in charge of the business affairs division by Pittman to form alliances that would shore up AOL both industrially and financially. Fortunately for Colburn, it was the go-go years of the boom, and partners willingly negotiated all types of in-volved, even questionable deals that would attract media attention and send their stock price soaring. Rising equity prices translated into: over-whelmingly enthusiastic support from large shareholders like Ted Turner and mutual funds, backing from pliant boards, more stock options that mind-numbingly-enriched executives like Case and Pittman, and geegaws for the henchmen who handled the details and sometimes dirty work. Colburn, for example, got many of the advertising deals for Pittman, and in return AOL paid to have rock bands perform at his children's birthday parties. At the end, when questions surfaced about the legality of his deals, Colburn, known as a maverick, was promptly dismissed.[20] The company's upper echelon quickly dissociated itself from the dis-credited underling even though many benefited from his work. Case, for example, took in $158 million from exercising a part of his stock op-tions and received $475 million from the later sale of stock. With such windfalls to account for to the IRS and SEC, he understandably chose to be a laid-back chairman as opposed to chief executive of AOL Time Warner. Time was needed to cash out his vast portfolio before its paper wealth vanished, especially since Colburn's deals were coming to light. The same vibrations were felt by the CEO, Gerald Levin, who exercised stock options worth $152 million even though he, unlike Case and Pittman, refrained from dumping his shares.[21]

Revenue Enhancements

In 1998, AOL entered into two major deals that brought in Compuserve
and Netscape to place the Internet service provider at the front ranks of
e-commerce. They also set the stage for the Time Warner bid in 2000.
All were convoluted in nature, necessitated by the need to make the
transactions using stock or services as payment with little if any outlay
of cash. Complicated advertising agreements were hammered out that
exchanged ads on the AOL Web site for services, products, or other
tangible assets. These became questionable revenue-enhancing deals that
were investigated by the SEC and involved other dubious, fast-growing
entities like WorldCom, which had a role in the Compuserve acquisition. The dealing began in 1996 when AOL, with 8 million users, had
bested rival Compuserve convincing its parent company H&R Block to
sell the money-losing business. Although the purchase price was steep,
AOL had to act to prevent Microsoft, which had entered the access market with MSN, from securing a dominant position through its own buyout
of Compuserve. Microsoft moreover could easily afford the $1.2 billion
price tag while AOL had to use its rising stock price to make a creditable
bid. The stock deals furthermore had become commonplace and allowed
AOL to purchase the network systems of ANS Communication in 1995
for $35 million in stock and cash to help alleviate its busy-signal prob-
lem. Prior to that it contemplated purchasing UUNet, a much smaller
competitor, but instead decided to take over the ANS network. Meanwhile, UUNet, under its CEO, John Sidgmore, was taken over by the
long-distance telecommunications carrier WorldCom. Sidgmore and Case
then hammered out a tripartite agreement for Compuserve that ran along
the following lines:

1. WorldCom purchased Compuserve from H&R Block for $1.2
   billion in stock.
2. Compuserve was then traded to AOL for its ANS subsidiary. In
   addition, WorldCom paid AOL $175 million and gave AOL a
   seat on its board.
3. AOL agreed to use the ANS network, which it just sold to
   WorldCom, for the next five years with usage costs remaining
   unchanged over the life of the contract.[22]

In the end the deal would have hellish consequences for the participants.

Overjoyed at receiving turbocharged WorldCom stock, H&R Block saw its holdings become worthless when WorldCom went bankrupt. Sidgmore succeeded Bernie Ebbers as CEO of WorldCom but was forced out in a matter of months, tainted by the alleged corporate malfeasance of his predecessor. AOL barely survived the Internet implosion, and its failed merger with Time Warner forced Case to resign as board chairman. In the midst of the dot-com boom, however, no thoughts of these impending disasters marred the celebration of the Compuserve acquisition, with AOL already planning to buy Netscape, which it did three months later in November 1998.

The media, barely noticing the Compuserve deal, went agog over the $4.2 billion purchase of Netscape Communication Corporation because it set the stage for an anticipated battle between AOL and Microsoft. The media frenzy was further heightened by the federal government's antitrust court case, which floored the software giant even as AOL was shoring its ranks with the 9 million users of Netscape's portal. With its own 13 million subscribers and now with the programming expertise of Marc Andreeson and his cohort from the University of Illinois, who developed the Navigator browser, AOL appeared to have the marketing and technical prowess that could punch gaping holes in Microsoft's Windows monopoly. Or so it seemed at the time. The alliance against Microsoft was bolstered by another Internet powerhouse, Sun Microsystems, which had made pioneering advances in desktop and server computer hardware, the Java programming language, and Solaris operating system that ran Web sites and processed e-transactions. In the three-way pact, Sun also had the virtually impossible task of bringing the rock-and-roll aficionados at AOL together with the geeky-nerdy Netscape types to form a united front against Microsoft's Internet expansionism. The Netscape Navigator browser could now have a chance against Microsoft's IE competitor since it would be bolstered by AOL, which dominated MSN in Internet service, and by Sun, which had developed Java to undermine the Windows monopoly. The agreement forging the three-way pact rested on an exchange of AOL for Netscape stock, which made the latter an AOL subsidiary. With Sun, AOL formed the iPlanet partnership that took control of Netscape operations and sold its software using Sun's sales force. Sun paid AOL $310 million a year, and when the partnership ended in 2002, kept control of iPlanet. In addition, AOL purchased $500 million in hardware and services from Sun, which paid $350 million in advertising, marketing, and licensing fees to AOL.

The deal was generally applauded by the business press because it appeared that finally Microsoft would be stopped from barreling its way onto the Internet by stomping on smaller competitors like Netscape. AOL appeared capable of stopping such a charge, but the deal nevertheless exposed two of its notable shortcomings. Most obvious was its slim cash reserves compared to Microsoft's deep pockets and its attendant reliance on the booming stock market to make acquisitions using its high-priced shares. AOL also lacked managers who could integrate Netscape and its potent technical staff into the parent company. The brief tenure of Marc Andreeson, Netscape's star programmer and co-founder, at AOL highlighted how intractable the problem was of uniting the two disparate corporate cultures. Appointed chief technology officer at AOL, Andreeson was enthusiastic about the merger, saying: "These two companies have been moving in the same direction, and the fit is a good one."[23] He personally gained a windfall by receiving close to a million shares in rapidly climbing AOL stock in exchange for his holdings in Netscape, which were being hammered by the introduction of Microsoft's Internet Explorer browser. His enthusiasm for his new employer, however, quickly faded as AOL continued to keep its icon on Windows and use IE as the default browser on its Web site, even though it now owned the competing Netscape Navigator. The schizoid behavior confirmed that Netscape was of little strategic value for AOL except to possibly bulk up its asset base and give it a more solid image. Under this benign neglect, Netscape's market share deteriorated markedly as Microsoft enhanced IE with new features and kept on bundling the browser with its Windows operating system. It also used its superior technical and financial resources to develop and support its MSN Internet service with powerful ad campaigns during an economic slump that brought AOL and Sun to their knees. These events led Andreeson to resign after only seven months at AOL and profit handsomely by selling his AOL shares in the waning days of the bull market. AOL executives hardly noticed his departure, as they were preoccupied with the challenges from Microsoft, which was overcoming the legal assault from the Justice Department and gaining on all virtual fronts in the Internet competition. Also distracting was the continuing SEC investigation of those revenue-enhancing deals made by AOL's Case, Pittman, and Colburn, even as the trio pursued their giddiest acquisition plan, to take over the media giant Time Warner.

Pulling Off the Big One

To consummate the megadeal, shareholders at Time Warner had to be convinced that AOL's management would take charge of their moribund company and drive it into the twenty-first century. Any hint of slowing growth would doom the merger. Pittman was thus hired to increase ad revenues or form deals such as the one with Sun that would inflate revenues, cut costs, increase profits, and give the illusion of sustained growth. Such action was needed to keep AOL's stock price up because the stock market was beginning to falter, producing frightening price swings in market averages. In pooh-poohing the wild trading, AOL's management was assisted by an army of upbeat stock analysts who never uttered "sell" or "crash" and who loudly shouted down those who did with frothy statistics and facts that supposedly would send the Dow Jones industrial average—then crossing 11,000—to 36,000. Backing for the numbers came from top executives at Enron, Qwest, which became a major regional telephone company by merging with USWest, WorldCom, and Global Crossing, who reassuringly told investors that all was well even as they printed funny money to support their dubious claims. AOL's chiefs joined the motley chorus, especially in the three years, 1999 to 2001, leading up to the merger when Time Warner's managers and investors were balking at the deal. The more analytical among them suspected that the Internet business had become fundamentally precarious, especially with the entrance of Microsoft, and that AOL's market capitalization would tumble if and when the boom faltered. To calm their nerves, Case and Pittman reported as recurring revenues the $310 million that AOL was receiving from Sun for the iPlanet partnership to camouflage lagging ad sales and subscriptions. The move reassured investors for a while that the macroeconomic downturn was not adversely impacting AOL. When the merger was finalized in 2001, the partnership and payment from Sun ended, making it disingenuous for the company to list the $310 million as recurring revenue instead of a onetime asset sale. The accounting brought on an SEC investigation of this and another part of the Sun deal that was suspected of inflating revenues by round-tripping funds between the two companies. In the first leg, AOL paid $500 million to Sun for what was suspected as overly priced products and services, with the money coming back to AOL mainly as advertising fees. The high prices paid to Sun were the quid pro quo in getting Sun to place ads on AOL's Web sites amounting to $350 million, which was immediately booked as revenues. As accounted for in AOL's statements, the $500 million of purchases was depreciated equally over five years, producing paper profits of $250 million a year. The round-tripping moreover was occurring even as AOL was settling SEC charges of improperly booking operating as capital costs in order to spread the costs over a number of years. This artifice enabled the company to report quarterly profits instead of actual losses during 1995 and 1996. In the settlement, AOL assured the SEC that it had discontinued such practices even as top management was working feverishly to maintain revenues in 2000, when the merger was receiving approval from shareholders and regulatory bodies. Such desperation was also rampant on Wall Street as sell-offs on equity markets were followed by massive layoffs. Hoping to stave off what was looking like a flat-out crash, investment bankers, brokerage houses, and the media cheered the remaining big deals in order to keep alive their commissions, news stories, and jobs.

Like its Internet ally, the rapidly expanding telecommunications giant WorldCom, which had taken over MCI, was now pursuing another major deal, with GTE. It too was attempting to mask faltering revenues with what had become customary, convoluted accounting maneuvers. With both companies desperate for revenues to pull off their wheeling and dealing, it would be no coincidence that each would find additional income from their ongoing relationships. With AOL's service running on WorldCom's network, why not, so the thinking went, round-trip the $900 million a year payment to increase revenues and profits at both companies? Besides, no one would know. Unfortunately, everyone was doing nearly the same thing, and the painful uncovering of such practices would lead to troublesome consequences. WorldCom collapsed into the largest bankruptcy in U.S. history, and while the amount of reciprocal or "wash" sales with AOL was not large, the latter's accounting is being investigated by the SEC and Justice Department. In October 2002, after Pittman and Coburn had departed, AOL restated two years of financial results when an internal review uncovered questionable revenues of $190 million booked from not only deals with Sun and WorldCom but with eBay and smaller firms as well. Examples of such activity are listed below:

1. With eBay, AOL sold ad space on the auctioneer's Web site, and instead of claiming just commission fees it recognized the gross amount of the ad sales as revenues. This boosted income by $80 million in 2000 and $15 million in the first quarter of 2001.[24]

2. Following the Time Warner merger, business affairs head Colburn negotiated deals with WorldCom that increased ad revenues at both Internet and media divisions. WorldCom placed the ads after being assured that AOL would continue to use its telecom network, thus round-tripping millions of dollars between the two companies.

3. A similar arrangement with Oxygen Media was made in which AOL Time Warner invested at least $30 million in the women's cable channel, which in turn used Time Warner's cable system and paid $100 million for online ads.[25]

4. An arbitration award won by an AOL subsidiary was paid with the purchase of online ads. The unusual arrangement was made to enhance AOL ad revenues, which were falling short for the quarter ending September 2000. The merger with Time Warner was pending, and questions were being asked about a revenue shortfall as dot-com advertisers began to fail. The shifting of funds allowed Case to report in October that "AOL's advertising growth is right on target." In the same month Pittman answered questions about an ad shortfall with the terse: "I don't see it, and I don't buy it." Wall Street analysts, including Mary Meeker of Morgan Stanley Dean Witter seconded both comments even as capital markets and dot-com startups were loudly imploding.[26]

AOL's frenetic activity extended to discounted rates in order to inflate subscriptions to its online service, which, like the ad account, was falling as the economy stalled. These efforts amounted to offering employees at large retailers like Target, Sears, and JC Penney limited-usage online service for as little as $1 a month. At the time the usual rate would have been closer to $10, with $20 being charged for full service. Using deep discounting, AOL boosted its new subscriber rolls by at least 830,000 and by possibly more of the phenomenal 5 million it claimed to have garnered during 2001 and 2002. As the heavy discounting was uncovered in July 2003, the SEC—already investigating the inflating of ad revenues—quickly sought more information to determine if this too had been used to deceive investors.[27] Unfortunately, even as the probe continued, large and small investors had given up on the company and bailed out of its stock following substantial losses. Currently, as the economy and the stock market begin to recover, AOL

Time Warner, after dropping the AOL prefix in its name, remains stuck in damage control necessitated by questionable business practices and wondering what to do about the merger in general and a diminished Internet service in particular.

Elevated COO

In the aftermath of the meltdown, Dick Parsons—because he was the most reserved executive of a glib ruling quartet—picked up the reins of what was now a synergistic mess and tiresomely vowed to lead the company out of the wilderness. He was also the least tainted in the company's upper echelon, which was vitally important given that the Justice Department was now sniffing at those nefarious deals. There was also growing apprehension in executive ranks as colleagues at Enron, WorldCom, and Adelphia, the nation's fifth-largest cable company, were handcuffed and criminally charged. Parsons was also a lawyer and had been handpicked by Levin, another lawyer and his mentor, not for his leadership skills—which were few and far apart—but for his government contacts and legal abilities to work with federal authorities. The new CEO had been deputy counsel to Vice President Nelson Rockefeller and domestic policy adviser in the Gerald Ford White House. With another Republican, George W. Bush, as president, it was deemed best for an investigated company to have a credentialed member of the GOP as head, and Parsons was given the additional title of chairman when Case stepped down. This took place after board members at Enron and WorldCom were viewed as culpable by regulators for enriching themselves when their rogue executives used the company treasury as personal piggy banks. In such an intimidating environment, it is easy to see why Pittman, Levin, and Case would cash in their chips and make a fast exit, leaving Parsons, who never waxed fervently about synergy or the World Wide Web, as the man in charge.

From the beginning of his tenure, Parsons maintained that the AOL Internet service, which he knew very little about, would remain in the fold despite its unseemly problems. Fortunately for this approach, the scheming at AOL was child's play compared to the grosser dealings elsewhere, and if Parsons laid low, his company would escape retribution except for the occasional restatement of earnings and some fines, which the profitable enterprise readily paid. There was, however, that enormous debt load of $28 billion, which could not be supported by the company's falling revenues. Credit-rating agencies moreover were well aware of the problem, and to prevent further downgrades because of its shaky financial situation, Parsons turned to the plethora of media properties that could be sold to pare debt. Additionally, in most large mergers top management could cut costs by eliminating redundancies such as duplicate payroll, human resources, and public relations areas. In his typically efficient way, the new CEO achieved meaningful progress on these fronts and was immeasurably assisted by a rousing turnaround on Wall Street that sent the stock up by 26.6 percent in the first nine months of 2003.

As commander in chief, Parsons's first major restructuring victory occurred in August 2002 when the company bought out AT&T's minority interest in Time Warner's cable and entertainment properties. The buyout permitted the company as sole owner of Time Warner Entertainment (TWE) to plan a spinoff of the unit in order to raise $2 billion in cash for debt reduction. With this in mind, Parsons seized the moment when AT&T made plain its willingness to deal after selling its main cable service to Comcast. Ma Bell had lost a ton of money on the cable investments and in its own desperate restructuring efforts was moving to unload the Time Warner minority interest. When it was bought by AOL Time Warner, the company's stock price rose by 7.3 percent, a clear endorsement from the capital markets of the track that Parsons was taking. While the price rise was encouraging, Parsons was still a long way from getting a handle on the debt mess. The AT&T deal, in fact, added to his woes because AOL Time Warner paid $1.2 billion in cash to get all of TWE, and only after it had been spun off would the public offering bring in $2.1 billion. The company's financial situation was further aggravated in March 2003 when the SEC questioned $400 million that AOL had booked as ad revenues. Parsons again ducked responsibility by noting that the alleged impropriety had occurred under his predecessor. He also made the usual reassuring remarks that the company was cooperating fully with the government agency to resolve the matter.

In the following month the financial picture brightened considerably. On April 22 the company sold its 50 percent ownership in the Comedy Central cable channel to Viacom for $1.23 billion and a day later reported a profitable first quarter of $396 million. This compared to the massive $54.2 billion loss in the same quarter of the prior year caused by the write-down of goodwill for the merger. The results led Parsons to say, "We are very comfortable with where we are on the debt-reduction program."[28] At the time Parsons was also negotiating with longtime nemesis Microsoft to settle the antitrust suit AOL had initiated on behalf of Netscape, its browser subsidiary. Executive shifts at both companies had removed the principal protagonists in the case, namely, AOL's Case and Microsoft's Gates, from their CEO positions, giving the less-combative Parsons an opportunity to resolve the issue and receive a badly needed $750 million cash settlement. The dilemma of what to do with the browser subsidiary was also resolved when the Netscape brand name was affixed to a new discounted Internet service to help stem the serious erosion of subscribers at the dial-up low end of the market. The monthly rate of $9.95 matched those of other discounters, whose futures suddenly appeared shakier given the competitive force of the AOL Time Warner goliath arrayed against these small upstarts. With Netscape identifying the discount service, the premium end that charged $23.95 a month and the high-speed broadband service would carry the AOL moniker. With such moves, Parsons attempted to rebuild the troubled Internet service, particularly after it suffered a stunning 2.2 million subscriber drop in 2002. Even with the setback, the unit generated $6.77 billion in revenues and $1.32 billion in cash flow, specifically earnings before interest, taxes, depreciation, and amortization.[29] AOL furthermore still had the greatest growth potential among the company's polyglot divisions, with the rebounding stock market placing a higher valuation on the Internet service. It would thus behoove top management to sell other lackluster profit centers such as its sports teams like the Atlanta Braves and in its book and music business divisions and hold on to AOL until the recovery and forward march of the Internet economy produces an attractive deal.

—— Chapter 8 ——
The Enron Debacle

In March 2000 the dot-com bubble peaked, and then the finger pointing began as market capitalization losses would reach $7 trillion. Financing evaporated for money-losing start-ups concocted by inept and criminally bent founders, and their corporate launching pads quickly folded. Enron, which had built an online empire trading energy and broadband contracts, became a huge casualty, seeking court protection from creditors in December 2001. It was followed by Global Crossing and WorldCom, which had also staked their future on broadband transmission by building and buying optical fiber networks to serve the exponential growth of high-speed Internet traffic. Like colleagues at Amazon.com and AOL, top management at the three bankrupt companies were intent on becoming big—fast!—in order to stake monopolistic claims on the World Wide Web and aggrandize Bill Gates–sized personal fortunes. The wannabes had Caesarian ambitions, but lacked both technical and financial abilities for sustaining bona fide business plans. With the unprecedented use of easy money from Wall Street, Ponzi schemes instead were promoted that bilked billions of dollars from investors, employees, creditors, and business partners. In this they were abetted by cronies in Washington, D.C., Wall Street analysts, investment banks, outside auditors, and law firms that received lucrative fees for their not entirely professional services. Carefully selected members of the boards of directors were also in on the take. Greed of this insatiable, personal variety was, as is often the case, a principal factor in the corporate debacles. As an integral part of human nature, it always watched patiently for an opportune time to strike in wood-paneled executive suites. And the Internet Revolution, with its ethereal promise of continuous productivity gains, became a perfect time for fabricating arcane and fraudulent schemes that grandly conned the media, investors, and oversight bodies. Even *Fortune* magazine was duped into naming Enron as the nation's most innovative company for five years in a row. This occurred at the height of the bull market, when its competitor *Business Week* was dubbing the AOL Time Warner merger the deal of the century.

Journalists at such publications needlessly hopped on the bandwagon to cheer the new digital age while glossing over convoluted business prospectuses on, for example, broadband contract trading. Individuals, in contrast, who understood the involved dynamics of such transactions were busily starting up or at least investing in high-flying Internet companies that yielded spectacular returns, as opposed to merely writing columns on Microsoft, Amazon.com, or eBay and lumping them with such disastrous cases as Enron, Global Crossing, and WorldCom. The managerial abilities behind the successful franchises moreover were readily observable, since these businesses were built from the ground up while the likes of Enron were cobbled together based on jerry-built schemes and ill-fated plans. Such comparisons may have been difficult to perceive in the frothy boom times, but stand out clearly after the Sound and the Fury of the late 1990s dissipated. And for the benefit of a new generation of investors, the Enron stories and their lessons bear repeating in the probably futile hope that another $7 trillion will not go up in smoke.

Ken Lay

Ken Lay was a gentleman and a scholar who, like other executives in the dot-com era, built a corporate empire on financial quicksand and saw it sink under a ton of debt. A loyal follower in his climb to the top, "Kenny Boy," as he was affectionately called by George W. Bush, ingratiated himself to power brokers with lavish gifts and political contributions. To aid Bush's 2000 presidential campaign, Lay gave $275,000 to the Republican National Committee as his part of the $1.1 million in soft money that came from his company.[1] Lay also possessed a presentable executive demeanor that helped him quickly climb corporate ladders in the staid energy industry becoming in turn, president of Florida Gas, Transco Energy, and then CEO of HNG, the former Houston Natural Gas. In 1985, HNG was acquired by Internorth and Lay became CEO of the combined companies, thereafter known as Enron. It was an exploration, production, and pipeline company carrying natural gas, and although the business lacked the greasy clout and wheeling and dealing of its cousin the oil industry, profits were steady as usage of the clean-burning gas inexorably climbed in a pollution-conscious world. Natural gas moreover was not lorded over by giant companies like Exxon, and with deregulation the business presented interesting opportunities to climbers like Lay and younger, ambitious MBA degree holders like

...lion cashing in stock options in the two years prior to the ...y's collapse."[5]

...g Resigns

...old $100 million of Enron stock in 2001 even as he recommended ...ares to his employees as "an incredible bargain [because] the third ...ter is looking great."[6] The misleading comments came on Septem-...21, less than a month before he announced the $618 million loss for ...third quarter. By then most of Lay's energies were geared toward ...etly cashing in the fortune he had accumulated at the world's greatest ...mpany. Skilling was also beating a hasty retreat. Elevated to CEO on ...bruary 12, the chief resigned on August 14, ostensibly to spend more ...me with his family even though in June "the No. 1 CEO in the entire ...ountry"—as he was introduced at a Las Vegas cyberspace conference—...gave a rousing endorsement of Enron Broadband's new online trading.[7] "Making markets," according to the visionary CEO, was his company's new business model, which took advantage of the reduction in "transac-tion costs" wrought by the Internet revolution.[8] In reality, runaway trans-action and other costs were toppling the huge trader, with Enron Broadband Services posting losses on July 12 of $102 million on a scant $16 million in revenues. The next day Skilling informed Lay that he wanted to resign in August. It would mark a whimpering end to the CEO's madcap ride to the summit and brisk exit before the bust. He subsequently explained to a congressional investigating committee that "I wasn't there when it came unstuck," and when he departed from Enron, "I believed the company was in a strong financial condition." It failed, he presumed, because of a "classic run on the bank" and therefore it was none of his doing.[9] The CEO forgot to mention that even more than Lay, he had set up and approved the deals and trades that led the company to financial ruin.

Skilling is placed squarely at the center of the mess because he had arrived at Enron not only in the midst of the information technology upheaval that was revamping the company's business, but in the throes of energy deregulation that freed natural gas markets from heavy-handed government intervention. In such turmoil the opportunistic Skilling en-tered the sleepy Texas pipeline company with his guns firing and trans-formed the place with wild-eyed schemes that enhanced his career and pocketbook, even making himself into a global energy and commodities

Jeffrey Skilling and Andrew Fastow. The information technology revolu-tion was also making headlines as Microsoft and Dell Computer became overnight success stories based on innovative technology in conjunction with shrewd marketing and management. These leaders were furthermore charging onto the Internet, with their every move covered by a fawning media, and attracted imitators in slower-moving enterprises like Enron, where Lay and Company were eager to plug into the action.

While Lay may have wanted in on the Internet boom, his career in the overregulated natural gas sector had ill prepared him for the fast-paced, free-for-all nature of e-commerce. He further lacked project develop-ment and management skills, never having started so much as a corner grocery store, and the absence of meaningful entrepreneurial experi-ence made him reliant on younger, glib executives who willy-nilly pro-moted projects that increased their bonuses but doomed the company. Lay, masking his ignorance in futures contracts and broadband trading, hired and promoted these movers and shakers because they looked and acted like his fellow Houstonian Michael Dell, chief of Dell Computer, who was on his way to dethroning IBM in the PC market. Of course, they had none of Dell's abilities, but for Lay, appearance, big ideas, and fast talk trumped substantive planning and successful execution.

Skilling Becomes CEO

Fortunately, for Lay, a capable Rich Kinder was second in command after Enron was formed by the acquisition of HNG by Internorth. Under Kinder's watchful eye, revenues climbed to $13.3 billion in 1996 from $5.3 billion in 1990, while profits, mainly from natural gas and petro-leum operations, rose to $584 million in 1996 from $202 million in 1990. Kinder accomplished the steady growth by controlling costs and setting reasonable targets, which his division heads, with some effort, generally met. Progress came despite the hands-off stewardship of Lay, the company's CEO, and a laid-back board that Lay controlled by using perquisites like travel on corporate planes, outlandish directors' stipends, and pay for unnecessary consulting work. "Enron Board members were compensated with cash, restricted stock, phantom stock units, and stock options. The total cash and equity compensation of Enron Board mem-bers in 2000 was valued by Enron at about $350,000 or more than twice the national average for Board compensation at a U.S. publicly traded corporation."[2]

Despite the nurturing of its board, Enron's performance increasingly resembled a nickel-and-dime affair, especially when compared to high-tech companies in PCs, software, and networking. Kinder's 17 percent profit increases were, in Lay's eyes, becoming stale news compared to the exponential growth at such high fliers as Dell, Cisco, and Yahoo! In 1996, Lay replaced the steady but lackluster Kinder with the younger, ambitious, and energetic Jeff Skilling, who not only had an MBA from Harvard—Kinder and Lay went to the University of Missouri—but worked under John Sawhill, a former head of the Federal Energy Administration. Fastidious cash management, budget targets, and cost control—mainstays under Kinder—went flying out the door, replaced by Skilling's mantra: "Cash doesn't matter. All that matters is earnings."[3] Cooking the books to sustain earnings growth had arrived at Enron as it had at AOL Time Warner and WorldCom, where major mergers, acquisitions, and entry into high-tech and high-finance businesses were predicated on keeping the company's stock price climbing in response to higher earnings. To spur growth, revenues and profits on multiyear deals were booked up front and major costs were capitalized, diluting their impact on a given year. In the New Economy, the currency that counted was the company's share price. If cash to pay expenses or close deals was needed, all a CEO had to order was the printing of more shares, provided of course that the stock was a high flier and sought after by investors. A meeting with the underwriters would set a date for the new offering, and Wall Street analysts, relying on company-written press releases, would start recommending the issue to buyers. It was best if the shares had a strong dot-com connection, and to forge such a linkage, Skilling repositioned Enron's activities from dry-as-Texas-dust natural gas operations to the flashy online trading of energy futures contracts.

In the new go-go trading arena, moreover, Skilling found that he could circumvent accounting cost controls by dealing in contracts whose time horizons extended beyond ten years. Because of the high risk of projecting asset prices so far into the future, most contracts expired within a year. In uncharted waters, Skilling could do much as he pleased, in effect placing arbitrary future valuations on long-term contracts with no one willing to contest the numbers because they were coming from the biggest energy trader that presumably had the most expertise on the matter. A $1 million contract, for example, could be valued at $10 million ten years from now, and the generation of the $9 million gain would be recognized up front to enhance the year's profits. Arthur Andersen,

Enron's independent auditors, refrained fror have jeopardized the $152 million in fees it wa: pany headed by Skilling. Corporate executives line since earnings and not cash flow were used nuses, promotions, and the amount of stock opti was rosy as long as the stock market and Enron's s company simply imploded when equity prices head

> At the time of Enron's collapse in December 2001, En as the seventh largest company in the United States, lion in gross revenues and more than 20,000 employ had received widespread recognition for its transition energy company with pipelines and power plants, to a h enterprise that traded energy contracts like commodities, new industries like broadband communications, and ove billion dollar international investment portfolio.[4]

Enron's downfall began in the fall of 2000, six months after market and its shares had topped out with the latter peaking share. Interestingly enough, the stock did not drop precipitou many of the burnt-out dot-com issues because its finances were boosted by accounting gimmicks and expressions of confidence vincingly parlayed by top management. These tactics attracted s buying from desperate investors who were locked into huge and gr ing losses and were making last-minute investments in issues that mig rescue their portfolios. The continued fall in Enron's stock price, how ever, began to unravel the partnerships that were concocted to conceal an enormous debt load as well as artificially enhance revenues and prof its. This led to the bombshell announcement on October 16, 2001, of a $618 million quarterly loss, and the following day the company reval ued its assets downward by $1 billion. The stock, already trading below $50, tanked toward zero. Bankruptcy quickly followed, on December 2. The world's greatest company, in the words of its once illustrious chairman Ken Lay, was now a financial basket case. With its stock trading for less than fifty cents a share, former SEC chairman Arthur Levitt looked on in dismay as the accounting abuses he had worked against had, despite his efforts, brought on an implosion in which: "Investors lost more than $60 billion. Some five thousand Enron employees lost their jobs, and many also lost their retirement savings because their 401(k) plans held mostly worthless Enron stock. Enron executives, meanwhile, made trader in the same league as those found on Wall Street or in the Chicago trading pits. To accomplish this, quick, enormous profits were needed to attract the attention of the media and markets, prompting the wunderkind to adopt mark-to-market accounting, in which an asset's value is based on the latest market price for long-term contracts. The method was used in a $1.3 billion, twenty-three-year contract that Enron Gas Services Group, under Skilling, signed with the New York Power Authority to supply natural gas to the authority's power generating plants. While prices were fixed for the first ten years, they could subsequently be adjusted to reflect changing conditions. Because of the inherent risk of the lengthy time horizon, other gas suppliers were reluctant to negotiate such long-term deals. These fuddy-duddy concerns, however, were brushed aside by the New Age Master of the Universe, who was intent on making his mark and moving on if the markets turned against him. Even if he were still at Enron when things fell apart, Skilling could easily place any blame on one or more of his subservient underlings. After all, he had hired most of them, increasing employment at the company from 7,500 in 1996 to 20,600 in 2000 and gaining the loyalty of these associates and analysts by giving them fat salaries and bonuses. Operating moreover with nonexistent oversight from a lethargic board and boss, Ken Lay, Skilling audaciously booked most of the $1.3 billion from the power authority contract up front as proof that he was a big-bucks player. The highly risky move was submitted to and received approval from Enron's board as well as from its outside auditing firm Arthur Andersen, and even the SEC. He then extended the same mark-to-market accounting method to other areas under his expanding control, including the online trading of gas, electricity, and broadband futures contracts.

More Risky Business

Prior to Skilling's appointment as chief operating officer, the corporation engaged in what were typical activities like exploring, producing, and supplying natural gas and oil to major industrial users like electricity generating power plants. Short-term futures contracts were bought and sold on mercantile exchanges like the NYMEX to hedge or ensure against losses caused by price fluctuations. If, for example, the price of natural gas was expected to drop in the next six months, Enron as a producer would sell a futures contract committing itself to the delivery of a given quantity of gas in six months that locked in today's higher price. In general, buyers of these futures agreements would be users of the item, such as power generating plants that wanted to insure against supply problems that could disrupt their operations and were satisfied with the purchase price on the contract. Users buying the contract would also be protected against unexpected price increases that could gravely impact the financial health of the company. Regulated utilities were especially vulnerable of being squeezed because increases in costs, such as higher natural gas prices, could not be readily passed on to customers. Instead, approvals for higher rates had to be requested from state commissions, a slow and cumbersome process. As a producer, Enron covered its part of a hedge contract with its own considerable supply sources. Having these under its control minimized the possibility of not being able to fulfill its part of any futures deal. More speculative, uncovered trading also pervaded futures trading, and this was characterized by the sale of an item for delivery that the seller does not own or produce. Known as shorting an item, the seller would be betting on a fall in price, at which time it would purchase the item on the spot market with his gain being the difference in price between the lower purchase price and the earlier, higher contract price. Such "naked" trades could lead to considerable loss if prices were to suddenly rise instead of fall, forcing the seller to make good on his promise to deliver by buying the item at a higher price. Akin to gambling because of the large risks involved in forecasting future price movements, this aspect of the market invariably received much media attention with its shouting and cryptic hand-signaling in commodity trading pits making excellent film footage on TV news programs. The prospect for large gains earned on risky trades naturally attracted Skilling, and he resolved to turn Enron into an online market maker of contracts, where he had little expertise, and on commodities like metal and paper, which the company did not produce.

Derivatives

Dealing in naked futures, Enron entered the little understood and lightly regulated world of negotiating and trading derivatives. It was where big money could be made overnight because these contracts often involved huge monetary amounts, and small price movements in the right direction produced enormous gains. Moreover, 90 percent of the face value of a contract could be secured with borrowed funds. The speculative nature of derivatives arose because their values derived from price or interest rate differences in underlying assets or liabilities. Derivatives trading, like the trading of futures contracts on commodities such as oil and natural gas, grew out of the need to hedge against adverse price, foreign exchange, or interest rate movements by buyers and sellers of such contracts. Because of the chance for hefty gains, speculators entered the market, trading uncovered positions in not only the usual commodities like soybeans, gold, and crude oil, but in more esoteric items like broadband, foreign currencies, and air-quality rights. Swaps were also considered derivatives, with these contracts generally being negotiated between private parties and not traded on monetary exchanges. Swaps were entered to reduce borrowing costs or to hedge against foreign exchange movements and were so abstruse that a swap arrangement doomed Bankers Trust, one of the largest and supposedly sophisticated New York banks, resulting in its takeover by the foreign Deutsche Bank.

Enron's Exemption

"One of Enron's key corporate achievements during the 1990s was creation of an online trading business that bought and sold contracts to deliver energy products like natural gas, oil or electricity. Enron treated these contracts as marketable commodities comparable to securities or commodity futures, but was able *to develop and run the business outside of existing controls on investment commodities and commodity brokers*"[10] (emphasis added). How was Enron able to operate this way, particularly when the U.S. Commodity Futures Trading Commission (CFTC) was established to provide such specific oversight? Enter Dr. Wendy Gramm, the commission's chairperson under the first President Bush and who in November 1992 was looking for a position elsewhere after Bill Clinton won the presidency. A director's seat on the Enron board was where she landed, and to ensure the appointment, she secured a highly favorable exemption for the company in her waning days at the CFTC. "She pushed through an exemption that not only prevented federal oversight but also exempted the companies from the CFTC's authority—even amazingly, if the contracts they were selling were designed to defraud or mislead buyers."[11] The exemption was then codified into law with the passage of the Commodity Futures Modernization Act of 2000. The measure moreover had the endorsement of Gramm's husband, who chaired the U.S. Senate Banking Committee, which had oversight jurisdiction of the CFTC. In truth, neither congressional committees nor government agencies possessed the expertise or capability for monitoring the derivatives business—much of it being in the form of privately negotiated contracts—as it grew to an estimated $60 trillion in 2000. Coinciding with the massive growth of such financial engineering, markets worldwide were being deregulated. In the altered environment, productivity would be unleashed to give rise to a higher standard of living—or so the theory went. Enron, of course, would be at the forefront of the New Economy, and with the CFTC off its back and Skilling at the helm it was charging online where it had never been before.

EnronOnline (EOL)

The unregulated EnronOnline exchange began trading in November 1999 at or near the peak of the dot-com boom, and quickly expanded its business to cover eight hundred commodities. Volume on the exchange skyrocketed, which typically happened during any euphoric period as traders attempted to cash in on the good times. Those that brazenly took long positions (buying and holding) profited handsomely because shortages were occurring in the U.S. economy resulting from the country's longest economic expansion. California particularly benefited from the sustained growth—in part due to Silicon Valley's role in high technology—but even in the Golden State, the heightened consumption and production as well as its burgeoning population were taxing energy supply systems. Deregulation of electrical power markets also impacted the supply-demand equation, with temporary or perceived shortages causing spikes in rates that were no longer capped. The volatility fueled trading profits on EOL, and the hefty gains accelerated the frenzied activity. In the first five months of 2000, its virtual trading desk handled more transactions than any other Web site, arranging 110,000 trades worth $45 billion. Unfortunately, the huge volume did not translate into bottom-line profits because, as the market maker in so many commodities, EOL was forced, when there was little activity, to buy or sell contracts in order to sustain continuous trading and keep clients from using other trading venues. An inventory of contracts each costing millions of dollars had to be held, and these were bought using funds borrowed at high interest rates. At the time the Federal Reserve was restricting the money supply in an effort to curb "irrationally exuberant" markets. EOL, which had borrowed $3.4 billion in the first six months of 2000 to build its inventory, consequently was paying $2 million a day in interest charges. To minimize these costs, the trading desk attempted to close (sell) its positions and repay lenders, and as long as it received a higher price for its contracts, a profit resulted. But even in bull markets, prices move down as well as up, and when rising interest expenses compelled Enron to sell holdings, it would at times result in a loss.[12] In addition, losses soon swamped gains when the market peaked in 2000 and prices turned downward with a vengeance. The hundreds of Enron traders who had made ungodly amounts in correctly predicting price movements were now losing on a daily basis.

John D. Arnold experienced such vicissitudes as an Enron trader. In 2000 his natural gas trades resulted in profits of $200 million, which were wiped out by the market's reversal, giving him a $27 million loss for the year. The next year was wilder still. The twenty-seven-year-old trader racked up $750 million in profits, with $600 million resulting from bets on anticipating price movements. The remaining $150 million came from trades that supported the company's role as a market maker. The star trader was rewarded with an $8 million performance bonus even as Mother Enron and its auditing firm Arthur Andersen were hurtling toward bankruptcy. The $2.9 billion in trading profits earned by Arnold and his colleagues set off a money-grabbing binge by corporate bigwigs as investigators and creditors closed in on the financially insolvent company. With Enron now a den of thieves, trading with the firm and on its Web site ended, and Arnold with his $8 million bonus quit to start his own hedge fund.[13]

The California Energy Crisis

Even with all the noise, posturing, and hand-waving, Enron's trades were little noticed outside of energy circles because they were being drowned out by the truly spectacular gains and losses running amok in Wall Street's IPO market. This changed somewhat when power outages gripped California at the end of 2000, thrusting the huge energy trader into the spotlight, where it had always wanted to be. Unfortunately, the glare from the publicity exposed the company to charges of price-fixing and fraudulent trade practices. Together with the imploding U.S. economy and stock markets, it marked the beginning of a swift end as Enron was tarred and feathered for its egregious behavior during the madcap years of the late

1990s. It was not as if it were the sole evil perpetrator during this period. Lay, Skilling, and Fastow's notoriety made headlines because their alleged fraudulent activity brought so much woe to the state of California, and to many of the company's investors and employees whose retirement accounts evaporated as its stock price nose-dived. In the turmoil, all three executives handsomely profited by selling shares and stock options before releasing the bad news that the company was broke. It was a startling denouement. The prior year the company had made a "killing" from the California crisis, leading its governor to seek refunds for windfall profits from the energy trader for causing the blackouts and price spikes in natural gas and electrical power markets. Prices peaked at the end of 2000, coinciding with the power outages, and when Enron reported a 182.4 percent increase in operating income for the year ending June 2001, it would immediately be branded a corporate villain by elected officials, regulatory bodies, the public, and a witch-hunting media.[14] The din goaded the Federal Energy Regulatory Commission (FERC)—which had been listless for most of the period when markets under its control were failing—into investigating and issuing a belated, insipid report, which stated: "EnronOnline (EOL), which gave Enron proprietary knowledge of market conditions not available to other market participants, was a key enabler of wash trading. This created a false sense of market liquidity, which can cause artificial volatility and distort prices. Staff further finds that Enron manipulated thinly traded physical markets to profit in financial markets."[15] By the time that the report was released, Enron had already entered bankruptcy, $80 billion was lost in the California crisis, and billions more went down the drain as the company's stock plummeted. About all the FERC report established was its own inability to properly regulate markets during turbulent times, leaving investors, consumers, and buyers of power like the large Pacific Gas & Electric utility that declared bankruptcy, to fend for themselves.

For those at risk, knowing how Enron churned markets and manipulated prices is a start toward dealing with a future crisis resulting from lax government oversight and trading companies hell-bent on capitalizing on the chaos. At Enron, impetus to pursue fraudulent trades sprang from its myriad money-losing projects that were draining the company of cash and maxing out legitimate credit sources. These had been entered by freewheeling dealers and traders to enhance their bonuses, even if they entailed going after illegal profits.

In October 2002, Timothy Belden, head of Enron's Western energy-trading desk, pled guilty to wire fraud in an attempt to manipulate the electricity market in California. One scheme involved the issuance of a fraudulent supply schedule that could not be met because the power was to be transmitted from Nevada over a line too small to handle the delivery. In addition to overloading the line, the undeliverable power set off a shortage alert in the California computer monitoring system. Belden took advantage of surging rates by rerouting the transmission and selling the power at the higher emergency spot price. This also enabled Enron to get payments from the state for relieving the congestion it had intentionally caused. As a result of such manipulations, revenues in Belden's unit climbed from $50 million in 1999 to $800 million in 2001. Even though it was becoming insolvent, Enron gave the head trader $5.1 million in bonuses, again demonstrating that top management had no inkling of the impending cash crunch. In his guilty plea agreement, Belden was forced to disgorge $2.1 million to pay for his illegal activity and cooperate in the government's case against higher officials like Skilling and Lay. Both have been difficult to implicate because Belden's trading was carried out in the company's West Power Division in Portland, Oregon, far from company headquarters. In addition, the trader had specific expertise and training, having earned a master's degree in public policy from the Berkeley campus of the University of California and worked for five years in modeling energy markets at the adjacent Lawrence Berkeley National Laboratory. With such a background, Belden was in a position to make positive contributions to the deregulation of energy markets. Instead, he hitched up with Enron in 1998 and immediately began to wreak havoc on the electrical grid supplying California. His illegal moves were traceable, and his expertise fingered the trader as the only one capable of carrying them out. As to motivation, the youthful vice president lamely rationalized that he "was trying to maximize profit for Enron."[16]

As for the California energy crisis, it was ended by the stock market crash and attendant economic recession. As business stalled, companies curbed their operations and reduced their demands for high-priced power. Residential demand faltered as workers lost their jobs and even their homes, no longer able to keep up the mortgage payments. On April 6, 2001, Pacific Gas & Electric, the state's largest utility, sought bankruptcy protection, unable to continue buying energy at deregulated prices for sale to price-regulated residential consumers.

Broadband Hopes

With energy trading moribund, Skilling pinned his hopes for growth on a new unit called Enron Broadband Services (EBS), which handled the high-speed transmission of data, video, and voice communication using optical fiber networks. Entry into the telecom business was announced on January 20, 2000, closely following and greatly overshadowed by the AOL Time Warner merger. To attract Wall Street's attention, Skilling made the outrageous claim that EBS would "bring fundamental changes to the Internet [and to the] existing Internet delivery platform" by building a new, national network of optical fibers that would implement video on demand.[17] Selling access to its digital information and entertainment superhighway would bring Enron $22 billion by 2004 while the delivery of programs and other Internet content like sports games, news, and weather to subscribers would grow to $11 billion by 2008. To support these projections, the Enron CEO announced the purchase of eighteen thousand high-end servers from Sun Microsystems that would control the traffic on its optical network. Sun's CEO, Scott McNealy stood shoulder-to-shoulder with Skilling at the time of the announcement and cheerfully endorsed his new partner's plan despite Enron's distinct lack of experience with computers, software, and wide-area networks. To counter such negative perceptions, Skilling introduced the Enron Intelligent Network, which had been developed to ostensibly provide faster and cheaper service than competing systems. Obviously vaporware, the new network was still enough to convince Wall Street analysts and brokers into recommending Enron's stock to their investing clientele. Its price would jump by 25 percent. Company insiders quickly moved to cash out. Ken Lay, who dubbed video delivery service a killer application service akin to e-mail, sold $100 million worth of stock in 2001. Skilling dumped $70 million worth of shares from 1996 to 2001, as would Kenneth Rice, CEO of the broadband unit. Reasons for the mad dash out surfaced after the company fell into bankruptcy and prosecutors began examining the books and deals. It would be too late, however, for investors and employees who had held onto their shares as advised to do by Lay. Their losses would again prove the age-old maxim of following what the head honchos are doing and not what they are merely saying. It would be, however, difficult to see through the vaporware in this case because the optimistic pronouncements about EBS and the intelligent network were designed to keep the stock at elevated prices, thus deceiving investors into holding their shares. To conceal his sales, Lay sold his shares back to the company in a private transaction that was hidden in the small-print footnotes of a cryptic financial statement sent to shareholders. These statements, moreover, are mailed only annually, and being unfathomable because of their leaden prose, they are usually discarded without being opened, much less read. This forces investors to seek more reliable and understandable sources of information to get at what is really happening. And even during the Internet mania of early 2000, portentous signs were flashing, indicating that EBS would likely crash and burn in its attempt to crack the broadband market.

Braking the Exuberance

Most ominous were the remarks by the Federal Reserve chairman Alan Greenspan, who in 1997 had raised the possibility of an irrationally exuberant, overvalued stock market. The Fed cautiously increased interest rates once that year, but backed off as inflation, its principal concern, remained tame. The IPO market subsequently went into overdrive with such issues as TheGlobe.com rocketing from its opening price of $9 a share to $97 on its first day of trading July 28, 1998. The spectacle electrified a mob of wannabes, and the number of new offerings raced upward from 29 in the first quarter of 1999 to 94 in the second quarter. The central bank reacted swiftly raising the federal funds target rate six times in 1999 to 2000, with the last move at 0.5 percent, twice the 0.25 percent increase of the other five. By April 2000 the Nasdaq, where most Internet issues were traded, had suffered through three of its worst days: falling 7.64 percent on April 3, 7.06 percent on April 12, and 9.67 percent on April 14. *Business Week* rhetorically asked on the cover of its April 17 issue, Is the Party Over?

Investors who were still climbing on the EBS bandwagon apparently did not think so. The broadband market, like the Nasdaq, however, had peaked, and numerous signs were appearing of its imminent demise. Plans to install 14 million miles of fiber-optic cable began after release of Netscape's browser, which made e-mail and surfing the Web as easy as watching television. Music and video on demand, instant transactions like stock trading from one's own PC, transmission of voluminous business files, even videoconferencing were now possible, provided that the world's telecommunications infrastructure could be upgraded to carry the volume of traffic that was doubling every three months. This widely quoted statistic set off a stampede by long-distance telecom companies to build capacity that would accommodate the doubling of demand and put them in the lead to operate a global, fee-based network that mimicked Microsoft's monopoly in software systems. Unfortunately for the industry, the exponential growth in Internet usage did not continue, and by 2000, when Enron was set to enter the business, demand for use of fiber-optic lines had fallen behind supply, causing prices to tumble. From the first quarter of 2000 to the first quarter of 2001, the cost of a 150 megabyte-per-second connection between New York and Los Angeles dropped from $1.7 million to $600,000 a year. Between Miami and New York it decreased from $880,000 to $200,000. By the second half of 2002, over 97 percent of the laid fiber lines were dark, most having never transmitted a single photonic packet of information. Supply swamped demand, with the former estimated at 150,000 gigabits per second of both dark and lit carrying capacity, and the latter being 15,000 gigabits per second.[18] The glut was also exacerbated by breakthroughs in transmission technology, with one of the most important arriving with the invention of dense wave division multiplexing. Before this development, data was transmitted over a single wavelength of light; after, the same beam of light could be split into 320 distinct wavelengths, each capable of carrying the same amount of data as the single wavelength. The breakthrough translated into a one-thousandfold increase in the capacity of one optical-fiber strand, all the while Enron and other companies were laying billions of dollars' worth of lines, each containing numerous fiber strands.[19] With most of these never used, is it any wonder that Enron, Global Crossing, and WorldCom entered bankruptcy within months of each other?

Staving Off Bankruptcy

Enron, despite is suicidal expansion into fiber-optics, did not go quietly over the bankruptcy cliffs. Fastow and probably Skilling had known for a long time prior to the final filing that the company and its special entities were running short of cash and credit. Hence the need for altering financial statements to come up with virtual profits that would bolster the stock price and keep creditors and investors in the dark. The late launching of EBS after the market had peaked was part of the charade that led to accusations of fraud brought against corporate officials by the federal government. On March 12, 2002, Kevin Howard, EBS vice president of finance, and Michael Krautz, an accountant in the same unit, were charged with securities and wire fraud in a conspiracy to generate profits by masking actual losses. On May 1 both the Justice Department and the SEC filed charges against the CEO of EBS, Kenneth Rice, for engaging in fraudulent activity and making false and misleading statements about his unit's financial condition and operational capabilities. The deception was invoked not only to maintain investor confidence in the company's stock and cloak Rice's stock sales, but to lure partners into making deals with EBS. The joint venture with Blockbuster, the video retailer, to form a pay-per-view service, was one such hyped deal that Blockbuster would never have entered if it had known that EBS and its parent were flat broke and, furthermore, did not have the technology to deliver video on demand. Roped into the deal by wildly optimistic projections, Blockbuster would have become aware of the true situation, and the possible exposure sent EBS into overdrive for ways to maintain the deception.

The Special Purpose Entity

EBS inevitably fell back on the creation of a special purpose entity (SPE) called Braveheart to boost earnings. The accounting partnership had been in use since Enron entered energy trading to meet its enormous cash needs, especially when the firm became an online market maker for a slew of futures contracts. Outside capital sources could be tapped for much-needed cash provided these had at least a 3 percent stake and exercised control over the venture. Enron could also "record gains and losses on transactions with the SPE and the assets and liabilities of the SPE are not included in the company's balance sheet, even though the company and the SPE are closely related."[20] EBS, for example, had already sold some of its nonperforming dark-fiber assets to another SPE, the LJM2 partnership, which generated $100 million in revenues and $30 million in cash. Braveheart was created, when Enron's reputation with investors and creditors was still intact, to raise funds for the Blockbuster deal. At the time, Enron itself could not add to its debt by simply borrowing from a bank because the added liability would have to be recorded on its balance sheet, and agencies like Moody's and Standard & Poor's would lower its credit rating. The downgrade would have devastated the stock and toppled the company. The SPE route was thus used.

Braveheart

Project Braveheart was incorporated in the state of Delaware at the end of 2000 and capitalized at $124.8 million with financing of $115.2 million provided by the Canadian Imperial Bank of Commerce (CIBC). The CIBC investment was secured by an agreement in which Enron would pay the bank nearly all the cash received from the Blockbuster deal for the ensuing ten years. CIBC never got a penny from the arrangement because Blockbuster was terminated three months after Braveheart began. In effect, the SPE was established as a conduit through which a cash-needy Enron was able to get at the $115.2 million that came from CIBC. In order to do this, Braveheart had to be an independent entity with 3 percent, or $3.74 million of its capitalized base of $124.8 million, derived from sources outside of Enron and the Canadian bank. Two million dollars was raised from nCube, a computer supply company controlled by Larry Ellison, Oracle's CEO. The remaining $1.74 million was scrounged up from another Enron SPE called SE Thunderbird, such action being resorted to because no other independent funds were available. With outsiders having a 28.5 percent ownership of Thunderbird, $7.1 million was transferred under the ruse that $2 million, or 28.5 percent of $7.1 million, represented outside funds that were needed to make Braveheart an independent entity.

As soon as it was established, Enron grabbed $53 million from the SPE, claiming that it was its share of the profits from the Blockbuster deal. Of course, the joint venture was operating at a loss, and even if it were making money, Enron's share should have gone to CIBC. Such technicalities were shoved aside by a desperate Enron, and in the first quarter of 2001, $57.9 million more was siphoned from Braveheart, pretty much eviscerating the $115.2 million from CIBC and making the SPE of little value to Enron. It would be closed in March 2001.[21] Bigger concerns were plaguing headquarters. Wall Street, faced with plummeting stock prices, pulled the plug on broadband investments, sending Enron's shares into a free fall. Creditors and investors began clamoring to get their money out of the SPEs and other Byzantine deals that were now strangling the company. The financial cupboard, however, was bare, with Enron forced to borrow nearly $2 billion to cover a negative cash flow of $1.3 billion. In June its stock fell below $48, perilously close to the $47 trigger that would unravel another SPE called Raptors that had been formed to mask $504 million of losses. Knowing the end was near, CEO Jeffrey Skilling tendered his resignation on July 13.

Fastow at the SPE Helm

This ignominious departure left Andrew Fastow, chief financial officer, at the helm of a sinking ship. It was poetic justice because the young CFO had climbed into the executive suite by developing the infamous special purpose entities that had allowed Skilling to transform Enron into a top-tier securities and commodities trader.

> The nature of the new business required Enron's access to significant lines of credit to ensure that the company had the funds at the end of each business day to settle the energy contracts traded on its online system. This new business also caused Enron to experience large earnings fluctuations from quarter to quarter. Those large fluctuations potentially affected the credit rating Enron received, and its credit rating affected Enron's ability to obtain low-cost financing and attract investment. In order to ensure an investment-grade credit rating, Enron began to emphasize increasing its cash flow, lowering its debt, and smoothing its earnings on its financial statements to meet the criteria set by credit rating agencies like Moody's and Standard & Poor's.[22]

Enter Andrew S. Fastow, CFO and Skilling protégé, who used the SPEs to create bogus profits, hide much of Enron's debt in off-the-book partnerships that he also set up and controlled, and enrich himself by $30 million and his assistant, Michael Kopper, by $10 million. In August 2002, Kopper became the first Enron executive to plead guilty to money laundering and conspiracy to commit fraud, using in particular the Chewco SPE which he controlled. He also agreed to cooperate in the criminal investigation of Enron which two months later ensnared his boss. Fastow was charged and then indicted on seventy-eight counts of federal fraud, money laundering, and conspiracy, which included the destruction of documents vital to the investigation. Pleading not guilty to the charges, Fastow was tied in the indictment to the creation and management of a host of partnerships named LJM1, LJM2, and the Raptors that figured prominently in the demise of Enron and its auditing firm Arthur Andersen. Enron's collapse would be overshadowed by the WorldCom bankruptcy; nevertheless, Fastow's

mind-boggling schemes to keep Enron financially afloat while enhancing his net worth placed him near the top of all-time corporate
sham artists.

Of course, Fastow argued that he was just doing the bidding of higher-
ups or, as his lawyer explained, "Enron hired Andy Fastow to do off-
balance-sheet transactions. The Enron board of directors, the chairman,
the CEO, directed and praised that work. Enron's lawyers, other lawyers, accountants, praised and approved and reviewed that work."[23] The
SPEs, however, were mainly covered with the fingerprints of the
company's CFO since he was the sole executive in a position and with
the expertise to craft them. Their labyrinthine construct also suggests
that Fastow knew he was exceeding legal limits and violating the
company's code of conduct. To rebut claims that he was merely following orders, Enron's board convened an investigation to examine the transactions between the company and the SPEs. It found that:

> What he presented as an arrangement intended to benefit Enron became,
> over time, a means of both enriching himself personally and facilitating
> manipulation of Enron's financial statements. Both of these objectives
> were inconsistent with Fastow's fiduciary duties to Enron and anything
> the board authorized. The evidence suggests that he (1) placed his own
> personal interests and those of the LJM partnerships ahead of Enron's
> interests; (2) used his position in Enron to influence (or attempt to influ-
> ence) Enron employees who were engaging in transactions on Enron's
> behalf with the LJM partnerships; and (3) failed to disclose to Enron's
> Board of Directors important information it was entitled to receive. In
> particular, we have seen no evidence that he disclosed Kopper's role in
> Chewco or LJM2, or the level of profitability of the LJM partnerships
> (and his personal and family interests in those profits), which far exceeded
> what he had led the Board to expect.[24]

LJM1 Partnerships

Begun in 1999 while times were still ebullient, LJM1 was created to
hedge $290 million in gains made by Enron on its $10 million stock
purchase of Rhythms NetConnections. Enron, through its ties with the
underwriter, received an allocation and purchased a large number of
shares of the Internet service provider at its offering price. Going public
in 1998 in the midst of the dot-com boom, Rhythms's stock skyrocketed, giving its investors an immediate windfall. Enron, however, was

bound by a lockup period and could not sell the stock until the end of 1999. By then, investors with huge gains and not constrained by any holding period would have dumped their shares and moved their money into newer, hotter issues. Hence there was a need for the hedge, to protect Enron's gains in the event that the stock nose-dived. Ordinarily Enron would have negotiated a put contract with an independent party that would allow it to sell the shares at prevailing prices thus protecting Enron in the event that they fell in price. Enron in turn would pay the other party if Rhythms' stock went up. This would have been easy to do in a put contract dealing with GM or IBM shares, but for some unknown ISP company with limited or no earnings or assets, the risks were too high as dot-com flameouts were becoming routine on the information superhighway. In the end only a contrived counterparty like LJM1 could be found to hedge the gain. It was furthermore a sham transaction because Enron was one party, and the counterparty was controlled by its CFO. Being on both sides, Fastow early on found it more profitable to work on behalf of his partnerships and use his position at Enron to coerce its managers who were negotiating on behalf of the company into yielding to demands made by the SPEs. The dual roles were also useful in attracting investment funds from large financial institutions such as Citigroup, which invested $15 million to become a limited partner in LJM2. Fastow promised that he "will always be on the LJM side of the transaction,"[25] in effect guaranteeing a solid return on the money invested by partners even if it had to be taken at Enron's expense. Large fees for investment banking services were also used to attract funds from the banks. Citigroup, for example, received $99 million from Enron from 1998 to 2001 for handling some of its investment banking activity.

The Rhythms Hedge

To camouflage the conflict of interest—Fastow calling the shots on both sides of an Enron-LJM deal—the put hedge surrounding the Rhythms NetConnections stock gains was organized around four LJM partnerships. The implementing contract was negotiated between Enron and LJM Swap Sub, LP, which was controlled by LJM SwapCo that had Fastow as its managing director. LJM Swap Sub had one limited partner, LJM1, which capitalized Swap Sub by transferring 1.6 million shares of Enron stock and $3.75 million to Swap Sub. LJM1 had received 3.4 million Enron shares from the company in exchange for a $64 million note out of which the 1.6 million shares were sent to Swap Sub. LJM1 had one general partner, LJM Partners LP, from which it received $1 million, and two limited partners that had each invested $7.5 million in LJM1. Swap Sub consequently had $3.75 million and 1.6 million Enron shares to back its part of the hedge in the event that the Rhythms stock fell in price. At its highest price of $90 a share, the cash value of the Enron stock amounted to $144 million, which could not cover completely the $290 million hedge on the Rhythms gain. Moreover, Enron's stock price fell in tandem with Rhythms, thus placing Swap Sub further in the hole as backer of the hedge. If the hedge had been negotiated and signed by independent parties in an arm's length agreement, Enron, upon realizing that Swap Sub could not meet its contractual obligation, would immediately have sued it in order to salvage as much as it could from the deal. Instead, Enron elected not to exercise the put option of the hedge contract, paid LJM Swap Sub $30 million, and got back 1.6 million of its shares from the SPE. Mitigating circumstances occurred that forced Enron's top management and its board to quietly unwind the lucrative hedge deal in June 2000 and not expose any of the possibly fraudulent practices of the LJM1 partnerships.[26]

The Board Goes Along

One reason why no fuss was raised was that everybody who was anybody in the company had approved the LJM1 partnerships, with Lay, as chairman, presenting the Fastow proposal for board approval on June 28, 1999. At the meeting:

> Enron and Andersen [the company's auditor] personnel explicitly told Board members that the proposed transactions involved innovative uses of derivatives, Enron stock, forward contracts, and off-the-books special purpose entities [and] despite clear conflicts of interest, the Enron Board of Directors approved an unprecedented arrangement allowing Enron's Chief Financial Officer to establish and operate the LJM private equity funds which transacted business with Enron and profited at Enron's expense. The Enron Board's decision to waive the company's code of conduct and allow its Chief Financial Officer (CFO) Andrew Fastow to establish and operate off-the-books entities designed to transact business with Enron was also highly unusual and disturbing. This arrangement allowed inappropriate conflict of interest transactions as well as accounting and related party disclosure problems, due to the dual role of Mr.

Fastow as a senior officer at Enron and an equity holder and general manager of the new entities.[27]

LJM2

Despite the irregularities the board approved LJM1, and three months later approved LJM2, continuing Enron's foray into high-risk accounting and finance in late 1999, at the peak of the dot-com speculative boom. It was a time when all caution had been abandoned in the quest for IPO, derivative, and SPE riches. No one wanted to be left behind, particularly the business elite of Houston who sat on Enron's board and manned its executive suite. Lay, Skilling, and Fastow were consequently merely following the herd in transforming the staid energy company into one of the world's largest trading and investment firms to rival the financial behemoths on Wall Street. As the new game plan sent Enron's stock soaring, no less than Merrill Lynch would be drawn into its SPE constituency, with promised annual returns of 30 percent on the $394 million raised by the brokerage house for LJM2. With such a high-powered player on board, Fastow was emboldened to report superlative results, and in May 2000, trumpeted that the partnership had produced $200 million in earnings and $2 billion in funds flow for Enron. Of the latter amount, $125 million came from six transactions finalized in only eight days in the fourth quarter of 1999. No one questioned such an impossible performance, and why should they? These numbers were being made routinely in the IPO and Nasdaq market on dot-com start-ups that had negative earnings (losses), few assets, and a couple of wild-eyed founders building personal fortunes on flaky business plans. In such an environment, Fastow quickly realized that outlandish results were not only par for the course but, like the start-ups, could yield huge personal profits. When asked by a board member, Fastow replied that he was paid $23 million from LJM1 and $22 million from LJM2 for managing the partnerships. The partnerships, or SPEs, could be set up quickly whenever he desired, and with each deal between Enron and the SPE, Fastow ensured that the company not only capitalized the SPE, usually with its stock, but also guaranteed profits for investing partners. This was done because the CFO browbeat underlings into giving highly favorable terms to the SPEs. With Enron as lead investor and apparent guarantor of munificent returns, limited partners from Wall Street were quick to get on board and JP Morgan Chase, BT/Deutsche Bank, and CIBC together invested $50 million of the total $400 million that went to various LJM2 partnerships.

Fabricating Earnings

The bevy of special purpose entities, in addition to enriching Fastow, became increasingly vital to Enron as its money-losing trading and investment vehicles consumed enormous amounts of cash. With the CFO in charge, Enron-SPE transactions generated virtual funds and earnings that kept the stock price at elevated levels and, during its final days, kept the company itself from going under. One deal illustrating how earnings were created occurred at the end of 1999 as Fastow searched for ways to pad income by $12 million and enhance cash flow by $28 million. A quick sale of three floating power plants would serve his purpose, except no buyer could be found for the specialized assets. With time running out, Fastow contacted colleagues at Merrill Lynch, reminding them that they had received $40 million in fees from Enron in 1999, and in all probability could look forward to doing a similar amount of business in 2000. Realizing that Fastow was engaging the broker in an asset parking scheme designed to produce misleading financial results, Merrill Lynch initially hesitated but then agreed after Fastow promised that the power plants would be repurchased in six months and give Merrill a 22.5 percent rate of return on the deal. Furthermore, the broker would have to put up only $7 million of the $28 million purchase price, with the remaining $21 million coming from Enron. The following year the last leg of the transaction was done when the power plants were sold to LJM2, giving Merrill Lynch a $775,000 profit. While Fastow, mainly alone and in secret, arranged matters at Enron, more bureaucratic maneuvering was taking place at Merrill as memos and e-mails were sent seeking information and approval for the quixotic purchase of three floating power plants. The communications were subpoenaed by prosecutors after Enron collapsed and used in part to charge and then indict Fastow on seventy-eight counts of fraud, conspiracy, and money laundering. He pled guilty to two of the counts at the beginning of 2004 and received a ten-year prison sentence that was conditional on his cooperation in the continuing investigation. Also indicted was Enron vice president Daniel Boyle, who allegedly assisted Merrill in its sale of the power plants. Of equal importance to investigators was the role played by the large Wall Street firm. Was it part of an asset parking scheme to create bogus Enron profits? Initially denying that this was the case and that it had done nothing wrong, Merrill dismissed two of its executives in October 2002 for not cooperating in what the SEC called a fraudulent asset parking arrangement. The two men were subsequently accused of help-ing Enron manufacture profits in the power plant deal. After two more of its managers were similarly charged, Merrill Lynch paid $80 million to the SEC in an attempt to settle the matter without the firm admitting or denying any guilt. This caveat was unacceptable to federal prosecu-tors, however, who believed that Merrill was criminally culpable for its part in the fraud. Moreover, the Justice Department had earlier won a criminal conviction of Arthur Andersen, Enron's auditor, which led to the demise of the accounting firm. Ominously boxed in by the growing scandal and to escape prosecution, Merrill Lynch accepted responsibil-ity for its employees' action in the Enron case in an agreement with the Department of Justice. In addition to eliminating the abusive practices, the firm agreed to hire an outside auditor and lawyer approved by Jus-tice to ensure that it complies with the terms of the settlement.[28]

Prepay Transactions

At about the same time the complicity of two large New York banks was revealed when JP Morgan Chase and Citigroup agreed to pay $300 mil-lion to settle their part in defrauding Enron investors. The banks like Merrill Lynch had skirted the letter of securities laws to obtain invest-ment banking activity from Enron as well as receive quick, guaranteed profits in deals with the SPEs. The greed infecting the IPO market had spread to supposedly, reputable lending and investing firms, allowing a CFO in Houston, albeit at one of the nation's largest companies, to en-gage in the concealment of $20 billion in corporate debt and put his company on the road to financial ruin. Lawmakers, unaware of the se-cret deals, were baffled at the extent of the damage done by the company's bankruptcy, prompting the U.S. Senate to hold investigatory hearings. These uncovered structured financial or prepay transactions entered into by Enron and its banks to disguise loans as commodity sales in order to hide the debt from investors, lenders, and credit-rating agencies. As le-gal transactions, prepays were used by energy companies when they negotiated long-term contracts to supply oil or natural gas. The buyer would pay for the full amount of the deal, allowing the seller to book the sale up front before delivering the fuel. Enron's prepays never resulted in any fuel deliveries, therefore it was receiving the money as a loan and not for a commodity sale. Senator Carl Levin, who chaired the hearings, charged that "U.S. bankers, brokers, accountants and lawyers have an obligation to analyze and understand the consequences of their actions, and they will be held accountable for deceptive transactions."[29] Another Senate panel found "systemic and catastrophic failure" on the part of the SEC and sent a terse reprimand to Harvey Pitt, then its chairman, stating that: "If the SEC had pressed Enron about these and other troubling disclosures when they first appeared in Enron's 1999 annual report, some of the enormous losses suffered by workers and investors might have been prevented. The investing public expects and deserves more meaningful protection from the ultimate market watchdog."[30] Stung by the criticism, the SEC—particularly after its chairman was forced to step down—redoubled its efforts to determine how and why Enron, already in a financially precarious state, obtained $3.8 billion from Citigroup and $2.6 billion from JP Morgan Chase in loans disguised as commodity sales. Using the ruse, Enron did not have to list the loans as liabilities on its balance sheet and furthermore added the amounts to its revenues to boost income.

The Mahonia Prepay involving two special purpose entities of JP Morgan Chase is shown on Figure 8.1 These were based in the Channel Islands off the coast of Scotland and dubbed Mahonia and Stoneville Aegean. They were established offshore because JP Morgan's charter did not allow the bank to engage in commodity deals. To obtain $394 million from Mahonia, Enron negotiated a long-term contract to supply $394 million of natural gas to the SPE. Mahonia prepays the purchase, which is discounted in advance like a bank loan and gives Enron proceeds of $330 million. To repay the loan, Enron purchases $394 million of natural gas from Stoneville Aegean and pays for the gas with monthly payments. For the books, Enron takes delivery from Stoneville, which counterbalances what it ships to Mahonia. There are of course no shipments of natural gas, making the roundabout transaction a loan from Morgan through one of its offshore entities and repayment of the loan to a second SPE.

With such loans to Enron exceeding $2 billion, Morgan became increasingly anxious about being repaid, and months before Enron went under asked its borrower for two assurances that guaranteed repayment if it did not. One was a letter of credit from a large European bank, and the second was the issuance of $1 billion in surety bonds by eleven insurance companies. After Enron defaulted on the loans, the European bank and insurance companies refused to pay and took Morgan to court, in the process venting details about the scheme to mask loans

Figure 8.1 **Prepay Transactions**

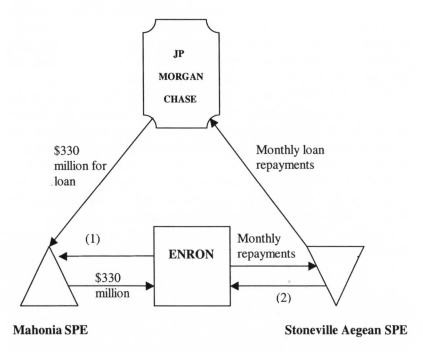

Mahonia SPE   Stoneville Aegean SPE

Sources: Bryce, *Pipe Dreams*, p. 289, and Eichenwald and Atlas, "2 Banks Settle," p. C7.

Notes: (1) Enron contacts to supply $394 million of natural gas to Mahonia and receives $330 million in cash; (2) Enron contracts to buy $394 million of natural gas from Stoneville Aegean and pays with monthly installments.

as commodity contracts. On the day the case with the insurers was to go to the jury, Morgan agreed to a settlement in which it absorbed $400 million in bad loans, and the insurance companies paid it $600 million of the $1 billion surety bond guarantee. The bad-loans charge contributed to a $1.3 billion write-off for the fourth quarter of 2002, which included the setup of a $900 million reserve to pay for lawsuits from shareholders who suffered from not only the collapse of Enron but the financial demise of WorldCom, Global Crossing, and other major borrowers. In the earlier third quarter, Morgan wrote off $500 million because of the Enron bankruptcy. Citigroup meanwhile set aside $1.5 billion as contingency for the same regulatory and litigation cases buffeting JP Morgan Chase.

Finger-pointing also erupted between the bankers and Arthur Andersen, Enron's independent auditor. Morgan charged that it was following guidelines distributed by the auditing firm for setting up legitimate prepays. This contradicted Morgan's memos to Andersen, which attested that the deals were proper accounting transactions and that Mahonia was an entity not controlled by the bank. The latter assertion was difficult to believe because the tiny offshore unit, capitalized at a mere £10, had participated in billion-dollar deals with Enron and Morgan. In the $300 million settlement with the SEC, both Morgan and Citigroup agreed not to engage in these deceptive schemes even if they fell within the letter of the law.[31] The SEC's director of enforcement called the settlement "a reminder that you can't turn a blind eye to the consequences of your actions. Financial institutions may not look the other way when their clients use them to manipulate financial results."[32]

The Raptors Bite

> One important example of Enron's undisclosed, off-the-books activity that had a dramatic, negative impact on the company is the Raptor transactions. The Enron Board knowingly authorized the Raptor transactions, despite their high risk accounting, lack of economic substance, and significant potential claim to Enron stock and stock contracts. In many ways, the Raptors were the accounting gimmick that brought down all of Enron.[33]

The fall also brought down Arthur Andersen, which gamely helped Fastow, Enron's CFO, set up Raptor I, II, III, and IV to skirt accounting rules and received $1.3 million for its assistance. Each Raptor was capitalized at $30 million with the funds transferred from the Fastow-controlled LJM2 partnership. Collectively they were further backed by $1 billion of Enron stock and other company assets. The huge collateral was needed to cover $1 billion in losses that Enron suffered by investing in two shaky companies that collapsed in the stock market crash. In order to move the losses to the SPEs, the Raptors had to be independent entities, financially able to cover the losses, and funded and controlled by external equity sources. The outside money came from LJM2 with a percentage of the $30 million capitalization applied to meet the minimum 3 percent requirement for third-party equity. Fastow again ran the Raptors, even though he was Enron's CFO, and primarily represented the latter in their negotiations of the hedge contract with Enron. The hedge called for the Raptors to take ownership of Enron's money-losing stock investments, thereby removing the billion-dollar loss from Enron's books. Fifty-five million Enron shares worth $1 billion went to the Raptors in exchange for a $1 billion promissory note. The note was collateralized by the Enron shares, and if the price of the stock fell below certain trigger prices, Enron was required to transfer additional shares or assets to the SPEs. Otherwise the hedge contract would dissolve and the stock investments returned to Enron with the $1 billion loss subsequently posted on its financial statement. The highest trigger level was at $57.78, and as Enron stock fell below $60, it was set to go off in the first quarter of 2001. The accountants from Enron and Andersen who had set up the hedge moved to shore up the SPEs by cross-collateralizing threatened Raptors with high trigger prices with those that were still out of danger. This was objected to by Fastow, who did not like the idea of placing some Raptors at risk in order to keep weaker ones viable. He therefore amended the remedy to permit a temporary cross-collateralization for only the first forty-five days of 2001, which allowed Enron to keep the losses off its books when it reported its financial results for 2000. Enron's stock price continued to fall during the first quarter, and since quarterly results had to be reported in April, a new stopgap measure was enacted in which the value of the healthy Raptors was assigned to those that had become impaired. Such an assignment of interest, like temporary cross-collateralization, violated accounting rules, making Andersen an accomplice in the Enron-SPE fraud. In September both the Raptors and Enron were dealt body blows when a separate accounting team from Andersen uncovered a major error in the booking of the $1 billion promissory note that the Raptors had given Enron. Instead of correctly recording it as a liability, the note was booked as an asset, and to rectify the error a $1 billion reduction in shareholder equity had to be taken for the quarter ending in September. Andersen accountants subsequently issued a memo stating that they "had 'changed their opinion of the proper accounting' for the Raptors and no longer supported the capacity of the Raptor SPEs to continue to 'hedge' Enron's investment losses."[34] The revised opinion forced Enron to abort the entire scheme and repurchase the shares it had loaned to the ill-fated Raptors.

Final Implosions

The company was doomed on October 16, when Ken Lay, Enron's chairman, reported a $618 million loss for the prior quarter. The next day Enron publicly acknowledged the $1 billion accounting error on the

Raptors promissory note and reduced shareholder equity by $1.2 billion. The company also froze assets in the Enron Corporation Savings Plan, the 401(k) retirement account for employees, because of scheduled administrative changes. This prevented the cashing out of vested holdings, which were mainly in Enron stock. Two days later the stock fell 10 percent, to $26, and by the end of the month was trading near $10 a share. Not covered by the savings plan, top management quietly unloaded their shares and exercised profitable stock options. On October 22 the SEC began an inquiry into the company's accounting methods, and on October 24, Fastow was replaced as CFO. On December 2 the company filed for bankruptcy protection.

As Enron entered its death throes, Arthur Andersen madly attempted to extricate itself from the clutches of its failing client. One day after the SEC began its inquiry, Andersen's chief auditor at Enron began the wholesale shredding of documents that might implicate the firm. He would subsequently plead guilty to obstruction of justice. On March 14, 2002, the firm was indicted on the same charge and was found guilty on June 15, but not because of the shredding. Instead the jury found that financial statements released by Enron on October 16, 2001, had been deliberately altered by Andersen to mislead the SEC. Following the trial, the eighty-nine-year-old firm closed its doors with a final announcement: "In light of the jury verdict and the underlying events, Andersen has informed the [SEC] that it will cease practicing before the commission by Aug. 31, 2002."[35]

The related implosions produced calls for corporate governance reform, especially with respect to the relationship between top management, the board of directors, and the company's independent auditing firm. These were codified in what came to be called the Sarbanes-Oxley Act, and while impetus for its passage was given by the Enron-Andersen debacle, it would take the bigger WorldCom scandal to get the bill through Congress and signed into law. On June 25, 2002, WorldCom—following the resignation of its tainted CEO, Bernard J. Ebbers—first unveiled details of its own corporate fraud, and within a month lawmakers agreed to pass Sarbanes-Oxley. The legislation requires external auditors to report to the board's audit committee and not to company executives, who could pressure them into concealing negative findings. The chief executive and CFO both have to certify the accuracy of company financial statements and can face up to twenty years in prison if they report information that misleads investors. Accountants are required to keep audit working papers for five years, and destroying these documents can result in prison terms as long as twenty years. These provisions in the act are directly tied to the egregious executive practices at Enron, and even though Jeffrey Skilling and Ken Lay have not been charged with any wrongdoing as of the start of 2004, substantive reforms have been passed. There is also a massive record of the misdeeds, which grows as other officials are charged, such as Richard Causey, Enron's chief accounting officer. If nothing else it will warn investors and employees not to take the integrity and ethics of corporate leaders for granted, and that any equity investments should be made with due caution. The same advice will be extended to corporate bond investing in the next chapter, which focuses on the telecom industry implosion.

—— Chapter 9 ——

The Telecom Crash

In 1984 the venerable Ma Bell system was split in two: AT&T's long lines and the seven geographically separated local telephone companies known as Baby Bells. The government-ordered breakup, while deregulating long-distance operations, kept the local calling areas monopolistically intact. The Federal Communications Commission also weighed in by ruling that data traffic, unlike voice communications, was not subject to access charges by the regional Bells. In doing so, data transmission over the entire telecom network of local and long lines was deregulated, spurring competitors like WorldCom to enter the business. Founded as Long Distance Discount Services (LDDS) in 1983, the tiny start-up that became WorldCom was barely noticed by either AT&T or the local Bell telephone companies, which continued to bureaucratically conduct business as if their nationwide monopoly had never ended. Preoccupied by the Great Breakup, the telecoms also remained aloof of the early Internet, then known as the Arpanet and still under government control. In the mid-1970s, AT&T, as the largest telecommunications company, was even asked to take over the network, but because it carried no commercial traffic, Ma Bell was not interested and declined the offer. The Baby Bells similarly remained uninvolved and, significantly, saw no reason to contest the FCC decision to deregulate data traffic going through their lines, even though they were in a position to block the ruling. They would, however, heatedly complain after the cable industry seized 70 percent of the broadband or high-speed Internet market that carried huge data files between business sites. Such untoward competition had never existed in their formerly tightly regulated and protected environment, and the local telecoms missed a second opportunity to embrace broadband when DSL (digital subscriber line) technology was invented at Bell Labs in 1988. DSL upgraded the capacity of copper telephone wiring, allowing it to carry high-speed digital transmissions, but because Bell executives could see little reason to stray from their profitable analog calling system, the breakthrough was shelved for the next eight years. In 1989, WorldCom went public and began the mergers and acquisitions that made it the largest operator in Internet data traffic. To help attain this position, optical fiber networks were installed by the company to increase transmission speed. Cable companies meanwhile streamlined their systems to handle two-way interactive communications with customers to counteract incursions from satellite operators.

Start-ups, Mergers, and Acquisitions

By the early 1990s the Information Revolution, encompassing advances in desktop computing, software and operating systems, and local and wide-area networking, had made such momentous strides that even the Bells were compelled to take notice. AT&T, more exposed than its progeny to the effects of technological and competitive change, attempted to adapt by acquiring NCR, already a worn-out computer company, for $7.5 billion. Ma Bell had always considered itself a leader in the fast-evolving computer industry and assumed that it could do more, provided it got the government off its back. It was this type of reasoning that prompted the giant to dump the slow-growing Baby Bells in the 1984 breakup and pursue opportunities in more profitable but riskier areas. In the process the company cut itself off from the enormous cash-generating power of local phone markets, only to pump billions of dollars into fruitless acquisitions. NCR, for example, was acquired in 1992 and sold five years later after AT&T had spent $2.8 billion to spruce it up. In 1994, $12.6 billion more was spent for the acquisition of McCaw Cellular. More significantly, AT&T's long-distance business was being seriously eroded by competitors like WorldCom, Sprint, and MCI, with its share falling from 90 percent in 1984 to 40 percent in 1999. This setback as well as the buying euphoria of the dot-com boom energized a still cash-rich Ma Bell to plop down $11 billion for Teleport Communications Group, $52 billion for TCI, and $54 billion for MediaOne, the second- and fourth-largest cable companies. Why the intense interest in cable? Toward the end of the century broadband Internet service had become a huge growth area, with cable companies controlling 70 percent of the market, far ahead of the Baby Bells, which had finally begun offering DSL service. AT&T would make a quick and grand entrance into broadband with its $110 billion worth of cable acquisitions, but hopes for profits from these moves never materialized. Like those at Enron and other telecoms, broadband ambitions were buried by the stock

market crash and the ending of the dot-com era. To cover the debt incurred by its spending spree, AT&T sold most of its high-priced cable
acquisitions to Comcast for $50 billion.

Earlier, in 1993, Bell Atlantic, now part of Verizon, also attempted to
combine with the large cable company TCI, but not because of broadband concerns. Cable operators had succeeded in installing their own
TV connections to homes and businesses and, given their interactive
capabilities, were in a position to offer voice calling service. To thwart
the unwanted intrusion, Bell Atlantic decided to join TCI and together
build a common pipeline for their respective cable and telephone uses.
Estimating that construction costs would exceed $200 billion, Bell
Atlantic's chairman explained that "It is too expensive to build two or
more routes to the household. One lane on the information highway
with multiple channels: That's the only cost effective way to connect the
pipe to every home."[1] The one lane, of course, would be built by the two
companies, which were seeking to become "the dominant monopoly
proprietor of the information highway,"[2] as inferred by Reed E. Hundt,
chairman of the FCC, who also knew that the Clinton-Gore administration was against perpetuation of cable and local telephone monopolies.
Internet access would also be restricted by the merger since residential
users would have to go through the single lane of a local Bell dial-up
service to connect to cyberspace. Adding to this, the Baby Bells were
petitioning to offer long-distance service, in effect, resurrecting the old
Ma Bell monopoly. The FCC chairman also assumed that TCI-Bell
Atlantic's:

> One-pipe monopoly could require government regulation in perpetuity,
> whereas our policy was to introduce competition and then deregulate.
> The 1994 telephone-cable mergers would have created a powerful force
> behind out-of-date technology, in favor of a closed system and against
> the trends of the Internet. It is even possible that the merged entities would
> have had the economic incentive and political muscle to stifle the growth
> of the Internet.[3]

The policy to deregulate furthermore had been behind the 1984 AT&T
breakup, and consequently a Bell-TCI merger would be a major reversal. Residential cable users moreover were already clamoring about onerous rate increases, and the issue was seized by the FCC to promulgate
lower cable charges. The action would have meant lower profit margins
for TCI, which persuaded the partners to call off the merger that would

have been the largest in history. The setback only increased the already intense lobbying in Washington, as the Congress and White House began to rewrite telecommunications law to cover not only the telecom and cable industries but Internet, particularly broadband, services as well.

The Telecommunications Act of 1996

With powerful interests doing battle on Capitol Hill, the probability for enacting a new law would have been close to zero had it not been for the unrelenting technical advances that threatened the Baby Bell monopolies. Voice over Internet Protocol, VoIP, was on the distant horizon, which could be used to carry telephone calls over the Internet using cable connections. Such digitized transmissions moreover were not subject to access charges even if they did go through the local lines of the Bells. Cable companies also had or were building their own pipelines to users and were spending $65 billion to upgrade their high-speed Internet and phone service. AT&T was also in the midst of acquiring the largest cable system, and even though it stumbled in the endeavor, it would pass the assembled network to an experienced cable operator that eagerly sought to enter telecommunications. Wireless and satellite companies too were capable of or developing phone service and did not need to use the pipelines of either Bell or cable networks.

Facing such threats, the regional Bells decided, as far as the new act was concerned, to relinquish monopolistic control of their calling areas and in return be allowed to expand into long-distance service. Ceding such valuable territory did not come easy for the Bells, and they made it particularly difficult for competitors seeking to provide voice and broadband service even after they had been granted access to local Bell lines by the new law. The stalling came naturally because the Bell network was developed by one operator, AT&T, which guarded against its use by outsiders who could compromise the system or invade the privacy of telephone callers. These concerns resulted in an analog, circuit-switched network that dedicated a secure line to users until their call had ended. It was moreover incompatible with the digitized, packet-switching technology used for communicating on the Internet and therefore required considerable upgrading and modifications by the Bell companies before outsiders could connect to their local lines. The regional phone companies subsequently dragged their feet on the system revamping while they developed their own Internet service using DSL technology. The 1996 act also allowed the incumbent Bell carriers to charge a reasonable rate for the use of their lines and could even undercut competitors since the market was now deregulated. As an example, Pacific Bell charged a local DSL provider $30 per monthly connection, forcing the small company to offer subscribers a rate of $60 a month in order to cover costs and make a profit. Pac Bell then charged its own customers $50 a month for the same service, and with its marketing muscle grabbed 50 percent of the competitor's customers and drove it out of the market. Even after competitors were connected, the ensuing service based on Bell-DSL technology was often poor and occasionally unavailable with little explanation or assistance from the phone company. Frustrated customers, when they could, switched to high-speed access offered by cable operators, giving them nearly twice the market share of DSL. In the first quarter of 2001, cable had 7.4 percent of the market and DSL 3.5 percent. The percentages are numerically small because 88.9 percent of residential Internet access subscribers still used the cheaper, slower dial-up service. Cable and DSL broadband service accounted for the remainder except for a 0.3 percent share held by satellite and wireless companies.[4]

Broadband Challenges

With so many dial-up users, the Bells assumed that broadband investments would not pan out, particularly when e-commerce and surfing the Web appeared to stall when the dot-com bubble collapsed. Big cable operators like AT&T and AOL Time Warner were also hurting from ill-conceived mergers and acquisitions. In addition, the regional phone companies were preoccupied with moves to offer long-distance calling service, and to assist this effort they merged with each other and bought smaller, local carriers. The seven Baby Bells consequently became four: Verizon, SBC Communications, Southern Bell, and Qwest, which was founded as an Internet access provider and nearly went bankrupt after investing heavily in optical networks. Qwest became a regional phone company by buying US West, one of the worst-managed Bells, which was notable for poor service and the many lawsuits filed against it in seven different states. Also in the West, SBC took over Pacific Bell and Verizon bought Hawaiian Telephone from Sprint, the long-distance operator. Managers were thus kept constantly busy on the various consolidations, and there was little time for upgrading DSL even as the cable industry was spending $80 billion on improvements in order to offer digital and high-definition television, broadband access to the Internet, and telephone calling. As a result, cable's share of the broadband market increased while high-speed access gained at the expense of the slower, dial-up system. From 2001 to 2003, broadband use doubled from 11 percent to 22 percent and cable's share grew to an estimated 68 percent in 2003 compared to 31 percent for DSL. As these shifts occurred, the Bells lost ground in three ways:

1. When Internet access migrated to broadband, it reduced the renting of second phone lines needed for the dial-up service. The number of residential lines thus dropped, marking the first such decrease since the Great Depression.
2. Users who gave up on their unreliable DSL service switched to cable.
3. Cable began marketing its new phone service to the 90 million cable TV customers, luring 1.7 million of them to switch, with savings of 30 percent on their phone bills.

As the regional Bells stumbled, entrepreneurs took heart, turning to alternate means such as wireless and satellite to deliver Internet service. Technical advances, the growing need for high-speed access for emergency, educational, and entertainment purposes, and the absence of cable and DSL in many geographical areas presented opportunities for small, nimble high-tech outfits, and with financing available as the economy recovered, numerous start-ups jumped into action. Wireless operators offered personalized services to individual homeowners such as the installation of a house antenna aimed at a base station tower to receive the Internet microwave signal. The work could cost up to $400, but consumers willingly paid since served important purposes such as communications and information during an emergency, or was useful in completing job or school-related tasks. Wireless operators usually charged a competitive $40-a-month fee for the broadband service and did not have to pay access fees to the local Bell telephone company. They were therefore profitable with a revenue base consisting of 300 to 500 households and could be run out of a garage in the manner of earlier high-tech firms. In such a favorable environment, eighteen hundred wireless Internet providers have begun operations, with the larger ones offering service to businesses for up to $500 a month.[5]

Competitive Cable

In its house-to-house approach, wireless is following cable's success at first, when it connected its pipeline to individual residences in densely populated areas and clicked on TV service as demand rose. When optical fibers became a superior transmission mode, cable companies upgraded their networks, enabling them to offer interactive game-playing as well as video on demand. Why such innovative and quick action from an industry, especially after its members had become giants contemplating mergers with the likes of AT&T? Organizational theory would have predicted a growing bureaucratic mind-set that stifled creativity. Instead, when market research showed an expanding demand for broadband, cable companies produced a standardized modem that was competitive with the $50 phone modem sold to DSL users. Moreover, part of the upgrading to make cable networks suitable for high-speed transmission had been made, giving cable a $60–$80 billion head start against the Bells. This meant that a local telecom like Verizon would need a huge revenue base of 3.5 to 4.0 million DSL subscribers just to break even. Connection costs were also $150 to $200 greater than for cable service. Such handicaps grew out of a long, government-regulated operating environment in which the phone companies offered universal, secure, and affordable service in exchange for its monopolistic position. Cable companies in contrast had their origins in the rough-and-tumble entertainment business, which forced them to target profitable growth areas and offer more variety and attractive content than rival broadcasting networks. After all, they were competing against free TV programming from CBS, NBC, and ABC. In such a milieu, the cables came to see themselves as underdogs and thus willing to standardize parts in order to keep costs competitive and enter into alliances with rivals to better position themselves in newer markets and services.[6]

As they entered the high-risk TV arena, free market–oriented cable executives like most corporate hypocrites, were not above getting government assistance. Their lobbying resulted in the Cable Act of 1984, which granted a local monopoly to individual franchises. The protection facilitated the building of costly cable connections to homes, apartments, motels, and anywhere else where users had time for more mindless video viewing. The setup was so lucrative that by 1992, sixteen thousand franchisees were jacking up cable rates in areas under their control, setting off cries of price gouging on Capitol Hill. In its inimical way, Congress responded with a follow-up cable law that instead of curbing the abuse, actually raised rates for a third of the complaining customers. It was politically too much and guaranteed a regulatory backlash. In 1994 the rate increase was rescinded by an FCC ruling that simultaneously upended the proposed merger between Bell Atlantic and TCI. In reality, the planned union was aborted because phone-cable technologies were incompatible. Copper phone wiring was too thin to carry broadband, and birth of the dot-com boom gave cable operators a new means for financing their network revamping. They subsequently built their second pipeline to customers, which proved superior to the telephone connection, prompting AT&T and TV broadcasters to acquire major holdings in cable.

Piggybacking on @Home

As the New Economy charged onto the government-built information super highway, cable operators became mesmerized by the business opportunities available in Silicon Valley and even more by the money gushing from venture capitalist firms. Faster than a speeding electron, cables' potentates led by TCI dumped the Neanderthal Bells and negotiated a broadband deal to create the @Home networking firm with top dog John Doerr of the VC outfit Kleiner Perkins Caulfield & Byers. The move secured for cable an ingenious way to build an optical fiber system without adding to its debt load. They would thus escape the resounding collapse suffered by the telecoms as they descended into the snake pit of derivatives and special purpose entities to conceal mounting liabilities. @Home also got into the IPO game at an early stage when the money spigot was turned on and there were less fly-by-night start-ups to sop up the funds. With Doerr on its board and TCI a major investor and customer, the firm received the necessary financing and attracted leading experts, who designed a viable high-speed service by leasing AT&T's fiber-optic lines. Cable companies meanwhile upgraded their lines to provide broadband access to their residential TV subscribers and assembled regional data centers for storing and dispatching information and entertainment content sought by customers. @Home's system clicked on in 1997, and the enthusiastic public reception sent its stock price hurtling skyward from $10.50 at its initial public offering to $60 a share in January 1999. The performance convinced Cox and Comcast, two other major cable firms, to join TCI on @Home's board and use its network. The blue-chip customer base together with its climbing stock price helped @Home secure $9.1 billion to streamline its network and operations, most of which, unfortunately, was never recovered by company earnings. Like the other neophytes, @Home believed that soaring demand for its high-speed system would continue well into the next millennium, and the equally robust stock market would keep funding the start-up's expensive expansion plans.

Not all of its backers shared the rosy outlook. TCI, sensing that the good times were peaking and receiving an offer from AT&T it could not refuse, sold itself and its 40 percent stake in the start-up for $52 billion. Cox, Comcast, Doerr, and his VC firm also sold near the market's top. AT&T, which purchased most of the shares, was consequently left holding the bag in September 2001 when @Home, now merged into Excite@Home, went bankrupt. Burdened by a surfeit of liabilities, the phone giant was forced to sell its broadband unit and end its misadventures in the cable wilderness. Comcast bought the AT&T network, which had cost the phone giant $110 billion to assemble, for $51 billion. Even though times were difficult, the cable operator knew how useful the acquisition would be, especially in its competition with DSL. Comcast's CEO, Brian Roberts, who negotiated the huge deal, justified the $51 billion acquisition by saying, "It was just high-speed Internet—the greatest thing since sliced bread; our network can handle it; let's go."[7] Another big telecom winner was TCI's John Malone, who sold $340 million of AT&T stock that he had obtained when his company was bought by the long-distance carrier.

Telecom Disasters

As a wallflower compared to even other Baby Bells, US West became a takeover target only when Qwest, an optical network start-up and its CEO Joseph P. Nacchio proposed marriage in 1996. The dot-com euphoria was stirring everyone's entrepreneurial juices and the executive was in acquisition overdrive, especially since his company was still small enough to be lassoed by any number of corporate raiders. Bulking up to escape fellow marauders, Nacchio took over LCI International, a long-distance telecom, and followed that by buying US West for $50 billion. In the latter acquisition, Qwest was brushed with a competing bid from Global Crossing, also a fiber-optic networking company that felt that it could transform the sleepy US West and drag it into the Internet Age. Time, however, had run out, with equity markets poised to plunge, when

Qwest completed the takeover. As the combined company's stock price nose-dived, Nacchio began milking the resources of the Bell company to pay off the huge debt incurred during the building and servicing of the optical network, which never attracted much business. Until its alliance with the Baby Bell, Qwest had never made money, and to camouflage this torpid performance it used the hoopla surrounding its high-tech network to bamboozle "the stodgy Bell" into joining it. Nacchio also called his new partner "US Worst," even though the phone company had revenues of $13 billion—dwarfing the $3.9 billion at his start-up. More important, the profits at US West were $3.9 billion.[8] Ignoring such mismatched fundamentals, a glib stock analyst blessed Nacchio's move by declaring, "Qwest is a hybrid—the best of the new and the old. They've got the customers, revenues, and the traffic of a Baby Bell, but they also have state-of-the-art local and national data networks. This is all going to have a happy ending. We're just in the middle of the biggest buying opportunity of our lifetime." [9]

Equally hyperbolic was *Red Herring*'s October 2001 cover story on "Global Qwest," about what its CEO should do to "seize control of the communication world." In order for Qwest—which was having indigestion problems following its US West acquisition—to become an international supercarrier, the magazine recommended that it buy another Baby Bell, Bell South, and either AT&T or Deutsche Telekom. The suggestions were proffered despite the fact that Qwest's debt had mushroomed to $22.9 billion; it had recently written down $3.1 billion of a nonperforming joint venture in the Netherlands, and its stock had fallen by 60 percent.[10] The plethora of ill-informed comments led the Federal Communications Commission to approve the takeover even though it knew little if anything about Qwest, which before combining with US West had operated outside its jurisdiction. Commissioners instead listened to the above hype surrounding Internet operators and convinced themselves that a more entrepreneurial guiding spirit would transform the moribund regional phone company. These hopes were quickly dashed. By April 2002, Qwest, together with Global Crossing and WorldCom, was about to drive the entire telecom sector over the edge with the following dumbfounding numbers describing the carnage:

1. The value of telecom securities sank by $1.4 trillion.
2. Fifteen companies went bankrupt with the largest one, involving WorldCom, yet to occur.

3. Four hundred thousand jobs were lost.
4. Retirement plans of Qwest employees were savaged because 40 percent of the value of their 401(k) accounts were in the company's stock, which fell in value by 80 percent.[11]

As was becoming customary, top corporate insiders at Qwest had dumped their shares before the smashup, with co-chairman Philip Anschutz selling an eye-popping $1.9 billion worth of his holdings and Nacchio raising a more modest $300 million. Since the men chaired the company's board, it was not surprising to see it approve an extension of Nacchio's contract, raising his base salary to $1.5 million even as the company was planning to write down assets by $20 to $30 billion. The huge downsizing did not stop there as, bit by excruciating bit, the whole shebang of management, financial, and accounting irregularities surfaced, necessitating more write-offs, which finally sent Nacchio flying out of the executive suite, headfirst.

Desperation Swaps

The meltdown of dot-com start-ups was understandable given that their financial statements were bereft of earnings and hard assets having resale value. What was surprising was how the spreading debacle consumed corporate giants like Enron, Qwest, Global Crossing, and WorldCom. The collapsing Internet mania may have adversely impacted their broadband units, but other viable operations in long-distance and local calling or energy production and distribution were still generating revenues. These firms also owned considerable assets that could be sold to keep them afloat even during the long dry spell following the crash. Unfortunately, top management with backing from bankers and auditors compromised their viable operations by entering bogus swap and other deals. It would be a netherworld of unregulated financial transactions that the heretofore industry champs embraced to save their crumbling empires, personal fortunes, and vaunted reputations. In fact, they could have cushioned much of the fall by recognizing that the go-go era had ended, and a new paradigm had started, requiring systematic cost-cutting measures such as dismissing overpaid, inept managers, eliminating bonuses and stock options, and cutting extravagant spending like use of corporate jets. Selling nonperforming broadband and other assets and shoring up credit lines would also have helped meet the oncoming austere times. Like protagonists in a Greek tragedy, however, the mere mortals had become addicted to their own visions of grandeur and resisted plotting such a humiliating course of action. Instead, they turned to the obscure swap to lead them back to glory. The swap furthermore proved to be an opportune vehicle because it was:

1. Unregulated, probably due to the varied, complex ways that the exchange could be structured, using at times special purpose and offshore entities.
2. Entered into by private parties which during the telecom bust were desperately grasping at ways to boost the bottom line.
3. Difficult to understand and therefore rarely examined by government regulators, the media, and even investors until their portfolios lost considerable value.
4. Conceived and detailed by Arthur Andersen in a white paper and inappropriately used by Global Crossing and Qwest to create revenue from the transaction. Andersen auditors signed off on the financial statements of both companies.
5. Endorsed by financial experts. One Goldman Sachs telecom analyst reported that Global Crossing's swaps "make sense, they are a normal part of operations . . . the accounting is correct."[12]
6. Used in 1998 by telecom and energy companies in a $1 billion deal to trade long-distance and local calling capacity. Parties to the swap included Williams Communications, a subsidiary of the pipeline and energy Williams Companies, and Winstar, which later went bankrupt.

The Williams-Winstar deal together with the Andersen white paper brought the swap front and center to energy-telecom officials who corrupted the method by using meaningless asset exchanges to increase earnings. This gave the arcane transaction its notoriety just as the manipulation of IPOs compromised the underwriting of dot-com issues. In untainted form, both were and still remain bona fide instruments, with swaps originating in precurrency days as simple barter deals to exchange commodities like food and clothing. With the more recent arrival of the multinational corporation (MNC) operating in a floating exchange rate regime, the swap became a hedging mechanism and was also useful in reducing interest rate costs.

Hedging via a swap is illustrated by the parallel loan in which a U.S.

MNC wishes to lend €1 million to its subsidiary in France but hesitates to exchange its dollars into €1 million at the prevailing $1 = €1 exchange rate. If the euro falls against the dollar when the loan is repaid, the company would incur an exchange rate loss. It thus engages in a swap with a French MNC that wants to lend $1 million to its subsidiary in the United States. The parallel loan swap is made, with the French MNC lending €1 million to the U.S. subsidiary and the U.S. MNC lending $1 million to the French subsidiary. The hedging works because both currencies are not converted and thus the parent companies never incur any foreign exchange risk. The situation becomes more complicated if the MNCs wish to borrow the amounts from a foreign bank while also keeping interest costs low. Then a currency swap can be drawn. These and other swap variations were widely used by major energy and telecom firms in their global operations. They were thus in a position to pervert the legitimate instrument when events turned against them in the late 1990s.

Rise and Fall of Qwest

Before petering out in December 2001, Enron madly arranged swaps with Qwest—both had Arthur Andersen as its auditor—to keep from sinking. Qwest signed on to a quick $500 million transaction to enhance quarterly earnings since it too was hurting for cash because of the massive costs related to its US West takeover. Billions of dollars were also down the drain, spent on building an optical fiber network which, like Enron's broadband unit, was facing a capacity glut. The two companies consequently structured an economically meaningless sale of equal amounts of unused capacity to each other in order to book the $500 million as revenues. The sham transaction was brought to light following Enron's filing for bankruptcy and was part of the $1.01 billion in capacity sold by Qwest in 2001 while it bought $1.08 billion from other carriers. In the same year the company recorded $34 million in sales of equipment to the Arizona School Facilities Board even though the machinery had yet to be delivered. The revelations spurred the SEC to open an investigation into the company's accounting practices, a move that further weighed on the price of its stock, which fell 92 percent from July 2000 to June 2001. The plunge in equity value forced Nacchio to take a $20 to $30 billion write-off for high-priced assets bought during the boom that had swelled its debt to a backbreaking $26.6 billion. The overhang was more than board members could bear, and in June 2002 they ousted Nacchio as Qwest's chief executive.

The new CEO, pressured by prosecutors and regulators, moved to properly record the nefarious dealings of the prior management. More than $1.1 billion of equipment and optical capacity sales and swaps were found to be incorrectly accounted for, leading to a $950 million restatement downward of company revenues. Most of the swaps were arranged with other telecoms such as Global Crossing, FLAG Telecom, and Cable & Wireless, which were facing similar profit shortfalls. In defending their actions, industry managers argued that swap and barter deals were common among telecom carriers and not prohibited by the Securities and Exchange Commission. Stung into action by the glaring oversight, the SEC ruled somewhat belatedly that companies could use swaps to exchange assets, provided the transaction is not booked as a sale. It cited a 2001 swap between Qwest and Global Crossing amounting to $100 million that incorrectly generated revenues at both companies. By the time of the new ruling, however, Global Crossing had already filed for bankruptcy protection, and with Qwest stock trading at $1.50 per share, critics saw the agency move as a way to escape blame for its not-too-diligent oversight of corporate accounting practices. The Justice Department also weighed into the telecom train wreck by charging four Qwest managers with fraudulently inflating revenues to mislead investors. The primary purpose of the indictments was to get the cooperation of these lower-level managers who actually arranged the swaps in implicating top executives who sought the bogus transactions in order to preserve lavish bonuses and obtain contract extensions. They would also be able to make earnings projections that would keep the stock price at lofty levels, enabling insiders to sell their shares for considerable gains and profitably exercise stock options. These financial incentives impelled the bullying of underlings into doing whatever was necessary—legitimate or otherwise—to meet revenue and profit targets.

If these heinous moves were not enough, there were other means by which head honchos could enrich themselves. These cloaked activities depended on the close relationship between the Internet and telephone network, with communications and information traffic sent over both. Dot-com start-ups consequently provided services and products to small Internet-based companies as well as to large telecoms. A company with Qwest's clout could therefore guarantee a start-up's success by placing large orders with the young firm and then publicizing the moves, making them valuable endorsements. To get the Qwest business, dot-com founders discovered that its CEO and other officers were willing to throw them a lifeline, provided they got a part of the IPO action. One such arrangement involved Qwest's executive vice president (EVP) for corporate development, who received options to buy 45,375 shares at $14 per share in an optical switch maker. These were awarded for being a member of the start-up's technical advisory board and became valuable when the small company received a multimillion dollar deal from Qwest that sent its stock to $27 from the offering price of $15 a share. Seeing that there was more growth potential with the young firm, the EVP took a seat on the start-up's board and resigned his Qwest position. Nacchio benefited in another arrangement when the stock he held in a networking start-up was exchanged for 65,112 shares in Lucent Technologies worth $2.1 million. Lucent took over the company before it went public and gave Nacchio its shares in exchange for his holdings in the start-up. These interlocking relationships were only the tip of the iceberg, but they help explain why a seemingly solid telecom sector collapsed so quickly. Top executives were personally invested in the dot-com gold rush and enmeshed their companies in multimillion-dollar deals with the upstarts that produced a backlash when they began to fail. Lucent, for example, bought the small switch maker for $4.5 billion, only to write off the entire acquisition as worthless.[13] Similarly, Qwest overpaid for US West and the building of its optical fiber network, necessitating billion-dollar write-downs in goodwill. Equally important, the shady dealing undermined investor confidence in telecoms, sending their stocks plummeting and Global Crossing and WorldCom into bankruptcy. In the end, Qwest escaped from such a fate when it was rescued by the reliable earnings power of its once maligned partner, US West.

Global Crossing

Without a Baby Bell to keep it afloat, Global Crossing hurtled into bankruptcy in January 2002, wiping out the $20 billion of investor funds raised to underwrite its ocean-spanning optical networks. The company, founded in 1997 by Gary Winnick, was ultimately sold for $750 million. Its rapid rise and fall paralleled the dot-com boom-and-bust cycle with a final, desperate use of bogus swaps hastening its precipitate ending. Winnick also erred mightily in losing to Qwest in the bidding for US West and thus had no means for paying the interest on the company's huge debt when capital markets tumbled. This would be ironic because Winnick had made his mark in the securities business before starting Global Crossing. He furthermore sold debt securities at the hotbed of high finance, Drexel Burnham Lambert, during the heyday of its "junk-bond king" Michael Milken. Winnick thus experienced the subsequent implosion that sent his sidekick to prison for security violations but apparently learned little from the run-in, perhaps because he was not criminally charged. In 1997, it was on to Global Crossing and the laying of eight thousand miles of fiber-optic lines across the Atlantic Ocean for hundreds of millions of dollars. Winnick also used wave division multiplex technology for his Atlantic Crossing 1 cable line, which increased its carrying capacity ten thousand times compared with older cable systems. The same scale-up factor was employed to estimate monthly revenues for a fully functional AC-1 and with an older line charging $10,000 a month; his perfunctory math arrived at monthly revenues of $100 million. Flaunting such a red-hot number in the raging bull market and using contacts made as a junk bond peddler, Winnick got a tremendous reception on Wall Street for his company's IPO, and it brought in $318 million to the start-up even though its founder had never worked in telecommunications. The market capitalization of Global Crossing would go on to reach $38 billion—more than Ford Motor Company—within one year of going public. Incoming cash from the sale of securities swelled to $20 billion and accelerated Winnick's expansion of his network into a global system with a trans-Pacific line following AC-1. Commitments from AT&T and Deutsche Telekom for use of AC-1 circuits also were seen as endorsements of Winnick's business plan, except that these were seasoned long-distance carriers, and they became disillusioned with Global Crossing's stiff fees and inept handling of technical glitches in its network. They furthermore did not have to tolerate the poor service, with AT&T and MCI forming a joint venture to lay their own transoceanic line. Other upstart telecoms, generously financed by Wall Street, also entered the optical network market and the resulting glut and falling price for their long-distance, high-speed service whiplashed Global Crossing and Qwest into acquiring hard assets like US West, which had more durable earnings.

For buying other companies, both telecoms had high-flying stock that was as good as cash in the late 1990s. Global Crossing consequently acquired Global Marine in a stock deal worth $855 million. Frontier Communications, a long-distance carrier, was bought for $11.2 billion in a deal that sent US West to Qwest. Without the Baby Bell's earnings, the situation at Global Crossing turned desperate after the stock market crash dried up funds and pummeled its stock, making it useless for more acquisitions. Deals with dot-coms also went down the drain when they went belly-up. As an example, the September 2001 bankruptcy of Web host Exodus Communications severely impacted cash-starved Global Crossing by ending the $500 million worth of business Exodus had contracted to send to it. Global Crossing had also sold a $1.9 billion subsidiary to the dot-com firm for which it received Exodus stock, which was now worthless. In an effort to keep their own stock price aloft, executives at Global Crossing, like their counterparts at Qwest, fell back to writing bogus swaps to generate artificial revenues that would lull investors into holding their shares even as Winnick and other top managers were dumping their stock.

To assist in the financial engineering, Global Crossing hired Joseph Perrone, the Andersen accountant who had co-authored the white paper on capacity swaps, as its executive vice president for finance. Perrone recommended that contracts governing the sale and purchase of equal amounts of excess capacity be made at least sixty days apart to avoid the impression that these were part of the same round-trip transaction. Global Crossing would thus sell $100 million worth of capacity to another party, wait sixty days, and then buy back the capacity rights. Cash was received and paid to create a payment trail that backed the sale and purchase. The company was further aided in the subterfuge by the common occurrence of these deals in the industry, where they were known as indefeasible right to use (IRU) sales. Such a sale could be legitimately employed by a carrier to serve customers over lines it did not own. Rather than build a new line, it would contract with the line's owner for any unused capacity.[14] Global Crossing's IRU deals, however, served no useful purpose—except for falsely generating revenue—since demand for use of optical networks had evaporated. Qwest was the first to use the illicit procedure in 1999 and was followed the ensuing year by Global Crossing, which booked its sales up front instead of over the life of the contract. Purchases on the other hand were capitalized, thus creating earnings in the year the sale and purchase occurred. This accounting irregularity can be described using a $100 million IRU sale that allowed the buyer to use capacity for a ten-year period. The full amount of the sale was booked in the first year. If Global Crossing then bought back the $100 million of capacity, the purchase was expensed using straight-line depreciation over ten years, resulting in a $10 million expense in the first year. Subtracting the $10 million from the $100 million in revenues yielded "earnings" of $90 million. As fictitious numbers, the dollar amounts could not be used to pay bills and interest costs, and inevitably unpaid creditors and mounting liabilities would shove the swappers into bankruptcy. This is indeed what happened to Global Crossing and other high rollers.

In 2000, Global Crossing signed a $180 million swap deal with 360networks and attempted to do another one in March 2001. Time was needed for Winnick and other insiders to sell their securities before outside investors realized how financially untenable the company's situation had become. Winnick outdid everyone by receiving $735 million for his shares while six members of the board collectively sold only $582 million worth of their shares. Under such leadership, the company—not too surprisingly—never recorded any bona fide earnings, and the desperate circumstances now necessitated a second swap with 360networks. The two insolvent partners, however, without any hard cash to offer, could not reach agreement. Regulators too were becoming aware of the extensive use of the nefarious swap as a cascade of telecom swappers began falling into a financial black hole. Winstar Communications filed for bankruptcy in April 2001, PSInet in May, and 360networks followed in June. The big energy enchilada—Enron—with its broadband unit, went bust in December, with Global Crossing filing for court protection in January 2002. By then Winnick had made off with so much loot that *Fortune* dubbed him "the emperor of greed" for treating Global Crossing as "his personal cash cow—until the company went bankrupt."[15] The name-calling made little difference to the company's winners and losers, with Winnick riding off into the sunset to settle into his $92 million Bel-Air estate in Southern California, leaving a maddening crowd of losers to their own yelling and screaming. They should have learned something from their losing ways like: "Where were the danger signs? They were staring investors right in the face. Global Crossing's SEC filings showed that the company had lost money eight straight quarters going back to 1999. Total debt as a percentage of its capital grew from 24 percent in September 2000 to 41 percent the next year; experts consider anything higher than 15 percent to be a warning sign."[16] Had the media published the doleful performance before the dominoes fell, allied customers, suppliers, employees, and investors may have escaped with more of their hides in tact. Unfortunately, most of these innocent bystanders were too busily engaged as customers, suppliers, employees, and investors to detect what the bogus swapping was wreaking, and it would take the truly calamitous fall of WorldCom to see how tragically broken the system actually was.

Trail-Blazing WorldCom

When WorldCom sprang its surprise bid for MCI on October 1, 1997, the superlatives belched from the lips of Wall Street analysts hailing Bernard J. Ebbers, its chief executive and chairman, as an Internet kingpin, semilegend in high finance, and visionary of the telecom and digital revolutions. It would be a spectacle of no mean disproportions, featuring WorldCom with annual revenues of $7 billion and $30 billion in stock market value offering to pay $30 billion in an all-stock deal for MCI Communications, which was three times its size. To consummate the deal, WorldCom fearlessly upped the bid to $37 billion as an irrationally exuberant Wall Street cheered. With a fellow Southerner from Hope, Arkansas, in the White House, Ebbers—who taught Sunday school in Mississippi—confidently expected that his time for stardom had arrived, and the MCI maneuver was simply another, albeit giant, step toward reaching parity with AT&T. The CEO had furthermore carefully timed his deals to take advantage of the deregulation winds that were blowing Ma Bell's monopoly apart. Big windbags had also been courted in the media and on Wall Street who, when signaled from his headquarters in Jackson, Mississippi, brayed their overwhelming approval. The noisy endorsements gave Ebbers the credibility he needed to assemble a corporate empire in the manner of Bill Gates at Microsoft, Steve Case at America Online, and Jeff Bezos at Amazon.com.

Bernie Ebbers also owed much to MCI because it had successfully brought the landmark antitrust lawsuit against AT&T that prompted him to focus on telecommunications. The resulting court-ordered consent decree broke up Ma Bell and deregulated the long-distance end of the business, which Ebbers entered with the acquisition of LDDS in 1983 despite having no industrial experience. At any rate, no entity—least of all his giant long-distance competitor AT&T—knew how deregulation would play in a regime formerly controlled by the Bell system. Ebbers actually made his move on MCI after AT&T's CEO Bob Allen ignored his calls to discuss an alliance. The harried executive could be excused for the slight since he was then preoccupied with the Telecommunications Act of 1996, which was poised to unleash the Baby Bells in his territory. While the new development would particularly vex Allen, Ebbers was reveling in the gamesmanship of the Internet era, where growing fast trumped all other business plans. He would furthermore get Wall Street's generous financing for the fifty deals that were stitched together, making WorldCom big enough to take over MCI. Such ambitious deals were pursued even when his company was still an unknown entity named LDDS. In 1993 a $2.2 billion deal brought in Metromedia's long-distance service. The following year the satellite company IBD was acquired for $700 million, and the Wiltel fiber network was bought for $2.5 billion in cash. By 1995, LDDS was the country's fourth-largest long-distance carrier and, signaling its worldly ambitions, renamed itself WorldCom. Number one in the sector was a floundering AT&T followed by MCI, which was carpet-bombing Baby Bell and AT&T subscribers with $25 checks to get them to switch their local and long-distance service. MCI nearly went broke in the process, paving the way for its takeover by the Ebbers empire. He would accomplish the spectacular feat by shrewdly taking advantage of momentous industrial and technological shifts that were in play in the late 1990s. These seismic movements included:

1. Deregulation of telecom, with the new environment presenting opportunities, which were seized.
2. Commercialization of the Internet, making business data transmission over WorldCom's growing network quite profitable.
3. Repeal of the Glass-Steagal Act, which had separated investment from commercial banking. Underwriting initial and secondary public offerings became Wall Street's breadwinner, endearing wheeler-dealers like Ebbers to the captains of high finance.
4. The explosion of media coverage of these events, elevating entrepreneurs to the level of rock stars and giving them a platform from which they could launch the takeover of giant companies like US West and MCI.
5. The Netscape IPO, which established that a company's stock market value was more important than earnings or assets, thus beginning the IPO and dot-com booms.
6. Financial engineering involving derivatives, special purpose entities, and IPOs that flabbergasted regulators, resulting in lax, counterproductive, or nonexistent oversight and easy manipulation of the books by empire-builders.

In this highly charged atmosphere, Bernie Ebbers moved with lightning speed, striking a $14 billion merger in 1996 with MFS Communications, which provided local phone service in major cities. Together with the 1997 acquisition of Brooks Fiber Properties, a smaller local telephone operator, WorldCom became the first major carrier in both local and long-distance markets. MFS also brought UUNet Technologies into the fold, having acquired the large Internet backbone firm prior to its merger with WorldCom. UUNet's activities complemented acquisition of networks from Compuserve and America Online, making WorldCom the largest carrier of business data traffic. In the pell-mell merge-and-acquire (M&A) race, top management was guided by the spectacle of either becoming a dominant player or being subjected to the humiliation of being taken over by a faster-moving entity. There was also the problem of keeping abreast of technical advances, which M&A solved by bringing in better transmission facilities and new Internet, Web hosting, and wireless services without the need for huge research and development expenditures.

On the other hand, the downside to the strategy lay in the failure to properly integrate disparate business units as well as implement suitable controls on the behemoth that was being created. The chaotic situation ultimately led the company to file for bankruptcy protection, with a court examiner finding that "with respect to WorldCom, absent diligent attention by the Internal Audit Department to financial control systems, the risk of financial statement fraud was high due to the complexity and dispersed nature of the Company's organization and financial operations."[17] The report also noted that WorldCom's independent auditor, Arthur Andersen, had found "significant risk" in management's "overly aggressive revenue or earnings targets" and its "accounting and financial reporting" and concluded that the company was a "maximum risk client."[18] In spite of the deterioration, Ebbers was already addicted by his M&A success and was not prone to slow the torrid growth pace.

MCI Takeover

It was consequently a transformed Bernie Ebbers who launched what would become the largest merger of its time. What also got his juices flowing included the snub from AT&T's CEO and the hotly contested bidding for MCI, first against a bigger and bumbling British Telecom (BT) of the United Kingdom and later against a late entrant, GTE. BT had begun the campaign to take over MCI a year earlier by agreeing to purchase for $37 a share the 80 percent of the company it did not already own. It intended to use MCI as a means for entering the huge U.S. market as well as augment its plans to become a global player. Unfamiliar with the brawling M&A situation in the United States, BT's shareholders expressed strong reservations about the purchase price and pressured top management to lower its offer to $32 a share. This blunder immediately brought forth the surprise bid from the ever-opportunistic Ebbers, who calculated correctly that with a $9 billion premium, his offer to MCI shareholders would not be refused. He also gambled on winning the support of MCI's top executives and board. This would be easier given the BT affront and his riding in as a white knight who would restore MCI's honor. Ebbers was also on terra firma against the foreigners and explained their clumsy move with a terse "They just don't live here."[19] To calm MCI shareholders concerned about how the much smaller WorldCom would finance the takeover of their company, Ebbers pointed to his numerous acquisitions over the past twelve years that had pushed WorldCom's stock price up by twenty-six times while BT's stock barely budged. The increase was ascribed to the successful integration of the acquired companies, resulting in considerable cost savings. The explanation may have been far from what transpired, but it was received enthusiastically by MCI shareholders who were desperately hoping to cash in on the dot-com mania. Ebbers embellished his pitch by citing how the merger would reduce network operating costs by $1.8 billion since each company could use the other's network without paying or building new lines. By using WorldCom's local lines, for example, MCI could forgo spending $800 million. More savings of $1.2 billion were possible by eliminating duplicate staff services in advertising, human resources, corporate finance, accounting, and other overhead areas.

After winning over MCI, Ebbers personally approached top BT executives, who were now smarting from the rude toppling of their best-laid plans. BT still owned 20 percent of MCI and had no desire to exchange its shares for stock in that wretched WorldCom. To salve wounded egos, Ebbers offered $7 billion in cash—giving BT a handsome $3 billion profit—for the 20 percent stake, which the Britishers accepted before returning home. Before these negotiations were finalized, however, GTE joined the battle with a $40 all-cash bid for MCI. The cash payout made the offer particularly attractive compared to WorldCom's deal, which entailed an exchange of MCI stock for volatile shares in the smaller company. To clinch the deal, Ebbers upped his offer to $51 a share and offered the chairmanship of the merged companies to MCI's chairman. Other executives were also promised key positions in the combined enterprise. Upon announcement of these terms, Wall Street was taken aback by the extravagant terms and sent WorldCom stock down by $2 a share. Ebbers reacted at warp speed, promising that $20 billion in savings would be achieved over the next five years, earnings would grow by 20 percent in the first year of the merger, and combined revenues would increase by 25 percent annually. These glib promises were enough to eliminate GTE as a rival and forge a corporate empire with $32 billion in revenues, 20 million long-distance customers, and 70,000 employees in 200 countries. The grand conquest, however, was not enough for Bernie Ebbers. On October 4, 1999, he made a $129 billion stab for Sprint Corporation, and in this attempt would come up empty-handed.

End of WorldCom

Before the monumental move, WorldCom's stock was trading at its all-time high of $62 a share before falling sharply to less than $50 at the time of the Sprint announcement. Other disturbing noises were coming from the financial front. Budgeted revenue numbers were missed starting in the first quarter of 1999, and management reacted to the shortfall by drawing down reserve accounts in order to pad revenue figures. A major acquisition furthermore was needed to replenish the reserves, and together with losses arising from the dot-com bust prompted WorldCom to bid for the large local carrier Sprint with its captive customer base. The target company, however, was also a major long-distance operator that competed with WorldCom, and its possible disappearance moved the U.S. Justice Department to block the merger on antitrust grounds. It was a major setback.

> When the government ultimately refused to approve the Sprint merger in July 2000, and signaled that it would not be sanctioning other large mergers, WorldCom did not have adequate excess reserves to draw down as a vehicle to increase earnings going forward. Shortly after this time, the Company took the brazen and radical step of converting substantial portions of line cost expenses into capital items. These conversions ultimately added approximately $3.8 billion improperly to income. The disclosure of these improprieties was the subject of the June 25, 2002 restatement announcement.[20]

Manipulating Reserves

Setting up and drawing down reserves were subjective procedures that required an estimate of how much should be set aside to cover possible contingencies like uncollected payments from deadbeat customers, lay-off costs following an acquisition, or an adverse legal or tax judgment arising out of a lawsuit or merger. How much to put in each reserve and when to terminate it were furthermore discretionary decisions by management, and the situation was made murkier at WorldCom because of its grab bag of mergers and acquisitions. The closing of duplicate facilities and the culling of redundant workers in the wake of the 50 to 60 alliances invariably produced innumerable reserve accounts to cover contingencies. From 1999 to 2001, over $2 billion was placed in reserves reflecting the high takeover rate, and their use to manipulate earnings became quite tempting. Management could easily inflate an account by placing "excess" profits into a reserve by using an accounting entry and then releasing them when the earnings were needed. Smoothing the numbers in this way enabled management to continuously meet ambitious earnings targets, which in turn drove up its stock price. The higher price could then be used to make acquisitions in an empire-building scheme that no one excelled in more than Bernie Ebbers. His gung-ho takeovers thus financed themselves while providing a legitimate reason for their occurrence, which was never questioned by authorities even as the accounts soared to well over $2 billion. Investors were also lulled by the increasing earnings and stock price, with the charade further abetted by the creation of reserves as special, onetime charges. Although these depressed earnings, the one-time hit was generally ignored by analysts and investors as long as earnings from continuing operations remained strong.

In 2000 the clandestine raison d'être for WorldCom's mountainous reserves was actuated as the economic slowdown crippled sales and management searched for ways to boost earnings. The Wall Street collapse further hacked away at its stock price, and the crumbling financial picture could hardly have come at a worse time. The company was in the midst of its largest takeover—that of $129 billion Sprint—which would unravel if earnings fell. Consequently, management called on the reserves to juice earnings in every quarter of 2000 by over $2 billion. The sudden reserves drawdown can be contrasted to the years before and after 2000 when only $172 million and $78 million were taken out of the accounts.[21] The abusive tactics, however, were not enough to close the Sprint deal, which was barred by the Justice Department. Ironically, WorldCom had grown too big for the government to sanction its takeover of another telecom titan. And with no major acquisition allowed, the use of reserves to pad earnings ended. The billion-dollar accounting irregularity furthermore came to light only after WorldCom's bankruptcy filing, when new management examined the books. Prosecutors were flummoxed with the convoluted practice because, in a criminal trial of the company's former chief financial officer, they now had the nearly impossible task of explaining to a jury why and how securities laws were violated. This was also the case in another irregular accounting maneuver of capitalizing operating expenses, as it too was never challenged by the Securities and Exchange Commission until after Enron and Global Crossing imploded.

Capitalizing Expenses

The new ploy centered on WorldCom's $35 billion fiber-optic network that had been built to cash in on the global data communications business. The vast system was underwritten mainly by the sale of bonds during the boom years, increasing the company's notes payable and long-term debt from $3.4 billion in December 1995 to $21.1 billion in December 1998 and $30.2 billion in December 2001. Because other giants like Qwest and Global Crossing were borrowing heavily to build capacity, interest rates on long-term bonds were pushed higher and credit rating companies began downgrading such securities, especially after a severe glut loomed over the data transmission market. WorldCom stood in the midst of the maelstrom, with 60 percent of its networks bringing in no revenues, and networks furthermore burdened by multibillion-dollar contracts that the company had signed with other carriers. These line costs, primarily covering the use of local lines owned by the Baby Bells, came to $8.1 billion in 2001 and, added to the interest charges, compelled WorldCom's financial officer, Scott Sullivan, to capitalize them, in clear violation of accounting rules. It was an absurd thing to do, but these were no longer normal times at the company. In July 2000 the Sprint acquisition was quashed, and from that time to the beginning of 2001, WorldCom's stock price plunged from $44 to less than $20 a share. In November the company cut its financial estimates for the following year, which accelerated the falling price. To stem the deterioration, Sullivan recharacterized $3.8 billion of line costs as "prepaid capacity," in the process removing them as expenses for the year and shifting them to capital accounts, where they would be depreciated over a period of

Table 9.1

Effect of Line Cost Recharacterization on Reported Income (in $millions)

Quarter	Income (Loss) before reserves added ($)	Reserves addition ($)	Income after addition ($)
1st quarter 2001	217	771	988
2nd quarter 2001	(401)	560	159
3rd quarter 2001	102.3	743	845
4th quarter 2001	(540)	941	401
1st quarter 2002	(578)	818	240
Total	(1,200)	3,833	2,633

Source: First Interim Report of Dick Thornburgh, U.S. Bankruptcy Court Examiner for the Southern District of New York. In re: WorldCom, Inc. et al. Debtors, Chapter 11, Case No. 02-15533 (AJG). Washington, DC: Kirkpatrick & Lockhart LLP, November 4, 2002, p. 109.

years.[22] The effect of these accounting moves is shown on Table 9.1 for the four quarters of 2001 and the first quarter of 2002.

In three of the five quarters, the recharacterizations turned losses into income gains. The second quarter, for example, had a loss of $401 million until $560 million in line costs were removed from the income statement and placed on the balance sheet. This resulted in a gain for the quarter of $159 million. For all of 2001, $1.684 billion was recharacterized, turning the year's loss of $621.7 million into a profitable one of $2.393 billion. It would, however, be a bad time for manipulating the books. Throughout 2001, the Raptors were sending Enron Corporation into free fall, with accounting scandals dragging down the heads of Global Crossing and Qwest. The optical-fiber capacity glut further forced WorldCom to cut earnings estimates for 2002, just as it had done for the prior year, and write down $15 billion of acquired assets. The blows kept raining down on the company and its chief, Bernie Ebbers:

1. On March 12, the SEC at long last began an inquiry into its accounting practices.
2. On April 3, the company laid off 10 percent of its workforce.
3. On April 24, the credit rating on its debt was cut.
4. On April 29, Ebbers was ousted as CEO.

Securing His Future

Building an empire by buying other companies with daring abandon, Bernie Ebbers also insatiably borrowed to add to his personal property holdings, especially in Deep South timberland. It was furthermore these personal dealings that led to his ouster when his indebtedness soared to over $1 billion, with $400 million borrowed or guaranteed by the company. Authorization for the loans and guarantee payments came from the compensation committee of WorldCom's board, and when he failed to repay the money, he was abruptly dismissed. Generous amounts were also extended by Citigroup—$552 million—and the Bank of America—$253 million—with the latter repaid in full. Six other banks funded $124.2 million of Ebbers's binge buying. These proceeds went into the purchase of a Louisiana rice and soybean farm for $14 million, a 500,000-acre Canadian ranch with 20,000 head of cattle for $65 million, a Georgia shipyard for $14 million, and a Mississippi trucking company for $28.5 million. The bulk of the loans—$658 million—was used to buy 548,000 acres of timberland in Mississippi, Alabama, Tennessee, and Louisiana. The banks moreover eagerly loaned him the money because the WorldCom CEO could steer significant investment banking their way that generated huge fees for underwriting the debt issues which the company floated to build its transoceanic and transcontinental optical network. Advisement fees on all its mergers and acquisitions were also up for grabs and, not too coincidentally, Citigroup, which loaned more than half of the total in bank loans, in return received the lion's share of WorldCom's investment banking largesse. Ebbers further facilitated his billion-dollar borrowing by collateralizing the loans with his 20 million shares of company stock. The lenders were consequently covered as long as the stock price climbed, but the situation turned dicey after the market crashed. With the stock dropping in 2000, Ebbers received margin calls from his broker, seeking additional security or he would suffer the sale of his shares. As the squeeze tightened, the CEO turned to his company and its directors for assistance with the implied threat that his large stock holdings would be sold if he did not meet margins calls. It was an effective ploy because one of the directors, Stiles A. Kellet, Jr., approached by Ebbers, held stock worth $100 million, which would plummet in value if Ebbers dumped his shares.[23] Other directors held smaller amounts, but all were anxious to prevent any panic selling that would depress the price before they cashed out. Thus, in clear violation of their fiduciary duties, members of the board's compensation committee, chaired by Kellet, authorized the loans and guarantees to serve their own interests. In 2000, $76.8 million was loaned, and the following year $59.9 million in loans and guarantees were disbursed. By 2002, WorldCom's end was looming and company coffers were raided, with Ebbers receiving $263.8 million in loans and guarantees. The looting's details were revealed following his resignation:

> A review of WorldCom documents and Mr. Ebbers' own records suggests that, during the period when WorldCom was extending Mr. Ebbers hundreds of millions of dollars in credit, he used more than $27 million for purposes unrelated to his margin calls, including payments of $1.8 million for the construction of his new home, $2 million to a family member for personal expenses, approximately $1 million in loans to his family, his friends, and a WorldCom officer, and payments of $22.8 million to his own business interests.[24]

As rudderless WorldCom went to hell in a handbasket, credit rating agencies suddenly realized that things were amiss and downgraded its bonds five days before the company dismissed its CEO. Ten days later, Moody's and Fitch took harsher action and cut the bond ratings to junk status even as Ebbers had already left the firm with $400 million in loans. His colleague Kellet, who helped Ebbers get the money, also departed with plenty to spare by selling his holdings in WorldCom stock for $53 million. Other investors were in a less enviable position. From a high of $120 billion in July 1999 to its bankruptcy filing in July 2002, the market value of WorldCom's shares plunged to $335 million—a loss of $119.6 billion—while bondholders witnessed their $1,000 corporate bonds fall to $150, with losses totaling $25.5 billion.

In their covert action to artificially boost earnings while unloading their portfolios, company officials were aided by the zealous stock recommendations of its principal investment banker, Salomon Smith Barney (SSB), which had received $107.1 million in fees from WorldCom between October 1997 and February 2002. The remuneration was in turn the source of Jack B. Grubman's $20 million annual compensation as Salomon's telecommunications analyst who, not surprisingly, unceasingly promoted the company's stock even as it entered its death throes. His "buy" recommendation, Salomon's highest rating, was given to WorldCom and downgraded to "neutral" after the SEC began its inquiry and the stock had fallen to $6 a share. SSB found another ingratiating way to ensure that it would keep receiving the lucrative investment banking fees from WorldCom. In addition to the effusive ratings from Grubman and the $552 million in loans to Ebbers from its parent bank Citigroup, Salomon allocated close to 1 million IPO shares in hot Internet start-ups to the CEO. Tens of thousands of shares also went into the personal accounts of CFO Scott Sullivan and Stiles Kellet, head of the board's compensation committee. These were cashed for gains of $11 million by Ebbers and $7 million by the others. The activity, known as "spinning," moreover defrauded investors and unjustly enriched the insiders. To thwart the practice, New York attorney general Eliot Spitzer brought suit in September 2002 against five top telecom executives including Ebbers and Joseph Nacchio of Qwest seeking the return of $1.5 billion in IPO profits. The following year Salomon and its analyst Jack Grubman were made to pay for the blatant conflict of interest involving quid pro quo IPO allocations, fraudulent research reports, and investment banking fees. SSB agreed to settle civil charges by paying $150 million in penalties, $150 million representing the disgorgement of profits arising from its conflicted activity, and $100 million to advance independent research and investor education. Salomon and First Boston also agreed to end the spinning of IPO shares. Grubman was barred for life from the securities industry and fined $15 million for his fraudulent recommendations. The biggest Wall Street firms also agreed to separate their investment banking from in-house stock research to ensure that recommendations are honestly arrived at and not used for attracting clients and customers.

There would be additional retribution and reforms before and after the bankruptcy filing of WorldCom in July 2002. In the same month the passage of the Sarbanes-Oxley Act prohibited corporations from making personal loans to their executives. The new law also changed the way accountants performed their audits, with this reform highlighted by the conviction of Arthur Andersen for obstructing justice and the resignation of Harvey L. Pitt as chairman of the SEC for his "inept" handling of the corporate accounting and Wall Street scandals.[25] The widespread irregularities would also lead to the indictment of Scott Sullivan on charges of securities fraud and making false reports to the SEC in an action by federal prosecutors to get WorldCom's former CFO to implicate his mentor and boss, Bernie Ebbers. The drawn-out criminal procedures would keep the sordid practices in the spotlight as a beacon that warned the investing public that their interests are rarely protected on Wall Street. It is therefore incumbent that due diligence be performed before funds are committed and resulting portfolios be sufficiently diversified with a variety of instruments to safeguard against any train wreck of dot-com or WorldCom proportions.

—— Chapter 10 ——

The Revolution Lives

Jeffrey Skilling, having just resigned from the chief executive position at still-mighty Enron, avowed the continuation of the Internet Revolution in the August-September 2001 issue of *Business 2.0*. He passed along a prescient observation that, in spite of the dot-com implosion, the revolution lived on:

> There have only been a couple of times in history when those costs of interaction have radically changed. One was the railroads, and then the telephone and the telegraph. And I think we're going through another one right now. The costs of interaction are collapsing because of the Internet, and as those costs collapse, I think the economics of temporarily assembled organizations will beat the economics of the old vertically integrated organization.[1]

Unfortunately, Skilling would never reap the fruits of such productivity-enhancing changes because his career and company were collapsing faster than those integration costs. More than three years after the company crumbled, Skilling was indicted for allegedly manipulating Enron's financial statements, pleaded not guilty to all forty-two counts, and was released after posting a $5 million bond. The event was overshadowed by two ongoing corporate malfeasance trials involving more flamboyant executives: Martha Stewart of Martha Stewart Living Omnimedia and Dennis Kozlowski of Tyco International. Stewart was accused of lying to federal agents in the sale of four thousand shares of a company in which, as a passive investor, she had no management role. The $240,000 value of her holdings represented a drop in the bucket compared to Kozlowski's spending of Tyco's money, which included $29 million for property in Florida, $14 million to refurnish his New York apartment on Fifth Avenue, and a $1 million birthday party for his wife on the Mediterranean island of Sardinia. The courtroom battles were further joined on July 7, 2004, when Kenneth Lay was indicted for falsifying Enron's financial statements. He immediately blamed others particularly his CFO Andrew Fastow for the alleged criminal activity even though he had been Enron's CEO for fifteen years.

Conspicuous Consumption and Pay

Unnerving as the monetary details were—Stewart spent $17,000 annually for a weekend chauffeur and for having her well-coiffed hair done, and Kozlowski purchased a $6,000 shower curtain and $15,000 umbrella stand—investors at the time of the trials were not moved to dump their shares in corporate America. The stock market had turned upward and they were making money again. Besides, greedy executives were right behind Hollywood stars and aging politicians in ostentatious spending, and they could furthermore dip into the company till as they repeatedly did during the long economic expansion and bubble years of the late 1990s. The scandalous behavior was uncovered after Wall Street plunged, and continuing investigations and more trials knocked the socks off dot-com founders and telecom bigwigs and embroiled capitalism's bastion, the New York Stock Exchange, and its chairman, Richard A. Grasso. Rising through the ranks, Grasso took over leadership of the NYSE in 1995 just as equity trading was poised to climb and shower money by the bucketful on specialists and members of the Big Board. The exchange, which already dominated smaller venues like Nasdaq, increased its share of U.S. stock trading from 70 percent, when Grasso's tenure began, to 90 percent in 2003, when he was forced to resign. Why did the NYSE dismiss him after he had compiled such an outstanding record? Like the imperial corporate chiefs whose heads had rolled before his, Grasso had become addicted to the perquisites and excessive pay of the bubble years and could not wean himself fast enough from his overly fat paycheck when the Big Board tanked and investors lost $7 trillion. Someone had to pay for the flood of red ink coursing through the canyons of Wall Street, and Grasso became a target when, in August 2003, it was revealed that he had received a $139.5 million employment contract. Managers at powerful investment banks, brokerage firms, and pension funds were particularly outraged because they were being continuously hounded by clientele and the media about mounting account losses. They now had a fall guy, and because such institutions controlled the exchange's board, Grasso was asked to submit his resignation on September 17, 2003.

Freewheeling Funds

Throughout the Big Board's hubbub, the giant $7 trillion mutual fund industry stood mute, fervently praying that some of their own irregular trading procedures would not be brought to light. Unfortunately, Eliot Spitzer, attorney general of New York, had noticed, and sixteen days prior to Grasso's ouster filed suit against the hedge fund Canary Investment Management for illegal trading in the stock mutual funds of Janus Capital Group, Strong Financial, Bank One, and Bank of America. As a private entity, Canary managed the investments of its limited partners and catered to wealthy individuals capable of investing hefty amounts approaching or exceeding $1 million. With a small staff of five employees and largely unregulated by agencies like the Securities and Exchange Commission, the hedge fund could quickly move large financial amounts to take advantage of price movements in fast-paced currency, security, and commodity markets. Returns during the late 1990s were spectacular for hedge and mutual funds, but after the bust, losses mounted and customers began to withdraw their money and close accounts. Both fund types desperately sought to keep their remaining business, with the mutual funds allowing big investors like Canary to illegally trade after hours to ensure that their buying and selling of mutual funds were made at prices that turned a profit and made them happy. With large trading gains, the hedge funds could in turn attract more investors. Canary was also permitted to trade in and out of mutual funds, a practice known as market timing that was not permitted by smaller investors. These investors were thus deceived by the mutual funds into thinking that they were doing business on a level playing field, when in reality special treatment had been accorded larger investors. A few days after being charged by Spitzer, Canary agreed to a $40 million settlement of fines and restitution and agreed to end the irregular trading. The matter, however, did not end there as more companies came under investigation for allowing improper trading in their mutual funds, and these resulted in the following action:

1. Executives and brokers at Alliance Capital Management and Prudential Securities were disciplined. Alliance later agreed to refund $250 million to investors and cut its fees by about $350 million.
2. The chief executive of Putnam Investments resigned under pressure.

3. The two founders of PBHG Funds were fined and accused of fraud.
4. Security Trust Company of Phoenix, a mutual fund intermediary, was shut down and executives charged with securities fraud.
5. The founder of the Strong Mutual Funds was accused of making $600,000 by trading in his own funds and relinquished control of the company.

Congressional lawmakers predictably jumped before the news cameras and parceled out blame for the scandal to lax oversight, greedy executives and employees, and devilishly complicated trading instruments and practices for which they were partly responsible. The irate posturing by politicians was, as usual, too late to prevent the fleecing of 95 million mutual fund investors by fund managers who were offering market timing and trading after hours to large institutions to gain their business. As the scandals spread, a deepening gloom gripped the small investors who never seemed to catch a break in this funny-money game. Would they always get the short end of the stick? IPOs, dot-com issues, the telecom crash, derivatives, special purpose entities, and now mutual funds all robbed the little guy of his hard-earned money. Why had it become such a routine? Like the technology undergirding the information superhighway, the financial underwriting of the Internet Revolution reached an incredibly sophisticated level that individual investors had to do their homework in order to play with the pros. Otherwise they were vulnerable to talking heads on money shows recommending some sure way for beating the odds. Usually there is a self-serving angle like buying the expert's book of tips promising remarkable returns with minimum risk, or simply handing the portfolio to an experienced money manager at a mutual fund, which then charges for overseeing the account. In the latter case a diversified investment plan is supposed to be created in consultation with the investor, which is then added to from paycheck to paycheck to produce a secure retirement nest egg. Unfortunately, what resulted in the last bull market was quite different as account managers bought high-risk dot-com or telecom issues for accounts that were wiped out when the markets plunged. The Wall Street scandals thus exposed the myth that even small portfolios would be conscientiously managed by brokerage houses and mutual funds, when in reality they were ignored or used to generate fees by excessive buying and selling of nondescript securities. And why would a fund manager look after puny accounts when commissions and bonuses were earned by advising and trading for major investors? The lesson therefore for new, disillusioned, or fleeced investors is not to rely on the securities industry, and to learn the rules and fees that will enable them to manage and trade for their own accounts. Then they can keep control of their investments and also learn how to research a broad range of securities that yields a diversified portfolio, with only small amounts invested in risky issues. If there is no time for such rudimentary preparation, then securities trading should not be attempted and the investor should keep his money in a government insured, commercial bank savings account. The temptation to make a killing when markets rally should also be firmly resisted, particularly when pundits again start pushing their tips on getting rich fast.

Markets Recover

Following a mild recession, monumental bankruptcies, and devastating losses in dot-com and telecom issues, capital markets unexpectedly began recovering a short three months after WorldCom's implosions even as prosecutors were having a field day exposing Wall Street tricksters and corporate gluttons. Lows for the savagely brutal bear market were reached on October 9, 2002, when the Dow Jones industrial average closed for the day at 7,286, well below the record high of 11,722 at the end of the great bull market on January 14, 2000. Nearly three years of doom and gloom had engulfed the securities business, and the October 9 low would be tested but not breached in March 2003 when the Iraq war began. From there, the Dow surged to close the year at 10,453 for an annual gain of 25.3 percent. Most of the buying that propelled the rally occurred in tech issues, with the Nasdaq index, heavily weighted with such companies, climbing 50 percent for the year. The turnaround in technology was totally unexpected with Wall Street still smarting from the mauling it had received in the dot-com and telecom meltdowns. Books and magazine columns by burnt investors eulogized the Internet's death and warned that securities' trading was for fools and suckers.[2] These doleful accounts proved highly misleading, appearing as they often do near the depths of a bear market when investors should be preparing to enter and not flee the trading arena. At any rate, most investors had been knocked out of the game when their portfolios were routed in the market's collapse, which, as depicted on Figure 10.1, encompassed three sharp downturns. The graph excludes the sell-off caused by the September 11, 2001, terrorist

Figure 10.1   **The 2003 Rally Following the October 2002 Low**

Source: Adapted from "Dow Closes Above 10,000 for First Time in 18 Months," *New York Times*, December 12, 2003, p. C1.

Notes: (1) October 9, 2002. DJIA closed at low of 7,286; (2) March 11, 2003. DJIA closed at 7,524 prior to start of Iraq war on March 21.

attack on the World Trade Center and Pentagon that closed exchanges for six days. A rally followed their reopening, leading Wall Street to believe that recovery was taking place, only to see those hopes dashed when markets lurched downward. The five-year bottom of October 2002 would also be difficult to pinpoint because of the steep slide in March 2003. Even stalwart investors had sworn off stock trading well before these nerve-racking dips. Those that survived and even prospered during this wrenching period had sold all or a major part of their holdings during the boom and invested gains in bonds or real estate, which both soared as the Federal Reserve forced short-term interest rates to sixty-year lows. At the same time, equity prices were driven to bargain-basement levels by panic selling, making them attractive again as investments even though buying sentiment had largely disappeared. Making investment moves contrary to what most people recommended thus would have been highly profitable in the last boom-and-bust cycle. In more volatile periods, moreover, being a contrary investor has been quite rewarding, turning it into a mantra to buy low near the market's depths and sell high despite what others are saying or doing.

Other aphorisms can also be applied to manage the vicious vicissitudes in stock prices. For one, big booms are generally followed by major busts, making it incumbent that gains are taken during the good times and portfolios diversified in preparation for the ensuing meltdown. A second lesson is the paucity of worthwhile information in the media and on Wall Street. Spadework needed to uncover profitable trades must therefore be done by individual investors. This is supported by the sustained rally that began at the end of 2002, when the bear market and prosecutors had silenced most pundits and stock analysts. Those who issued recommendations were furthermore predicting that the devastation would continue because of the coming Iraq war, the high unemployment rate, and terrorism activity. This leads to a third aphorism, which predicts that bull markets climb a wall of worry. Indeed, during the gloomy depths of 2002, a rally began sending the Dow upward for 2003.

The pithy statements may be good as general guidelines, but how does an investor decide which stocks will lead a recovery? The crash made this task easier because most issues had fallen to penny-stock price levels—less than $10 a share. Shares in well-known companies could consequently be purchased at dirt-cheap prices that would turn into handsome gains as markets recovered. Furthermore, it was not difficult to determine which ones to buy among the plethora of downtrodden securities. The dubious ones had no earnings while potential investment candidates were profitable even during the exceptionally difficult years of 2000 to 2002. Internet-related issues had also become attractive investments as the worldwide number of Net users continued to climb exponentially. As indicated in Figure 10.2, their numbers rose by over 100 million between 2001 and 2002, even after the crash had no longer made investing in dot-com shares a popular activity. Champions of the Internet like Henry Blodget ironically had been vindicated just when their advocacy of such stocks as Amazon.com and Yahoo! was needed. Coinciding with increasing Internet use has been the availability of digitally driven devices, many of which, like handheld computers and communicators, could access the Net. Digital cameras, DVD machines, MP3 players, and cellular phones also participated in the worldwide growth as sales of desktop computers, telephones, and TV sets remained flat or declined. Use of all these

Figure 10.2   **Growing Internet Use**

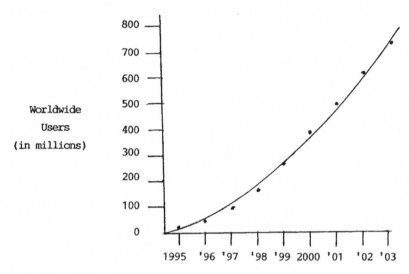

Source: "The Growing Web," *Wall Street Journal*, February 9, 2004, p. R3.

devices was projected to climb to 3.1 billion units in 2004 from an estimated 2 billion in 2002 and 1.25 billion in 2000.[3]

Gains in Information Technology

The new wireless products that were successfully launched have especially benefited their companies' stocks in the 2003 rally as sales and profits were earned, many for the first time. This success in turn resulted in a 46.6 percent return in 2003 for shares in the information technology (IT) sector, which was the best performer of ten sectors in the Standard & Poor's index. Intel, a major IT company, contributed to the sector's strong showing when its shares soared by 105.8 percent. In contrast, the telecommunications sector had the lowest return, of 3.3 percent, in spite of the growth in cellular phone use. Local and long-distance calling, still the mainstay of most telecoms, was flat or falling with WorldCom, renamed MCI, still in bankruptcy.

Winners abounded on the Nasdaq, where Intel trades, with smaller issues having their best annual gains ever, even though many of these had no earnings. In these cases the high-risk, high-reward correlation was in play in which booming markets lift smaller, riskier issues much

Table 10.1

Large Internet Stock Gains in 2003

Stock	% Gain	Earnings per share (¢)	Industry
Mobility Electronics	1,076	Loss	Mobile computing components
Netopia	948	Loss	Wireless broadband
Epicor Software	920	Loss	E-business & enterprise software
Ditech	776	Loss	Optical networking
Ask Jeeves	607	46.2	Search engine
Corillian	596	Loss	Online financial services
Akamai	522	Loss	E-business computer services
Ceragon Network	485	Loss	High-capacity wireless network equipment
ECollege	435	5.4	Online collegiate services
Avaya	428	12.7	Communications using Internet protocols
Research in Motion	409	Loss	Wireless Internet services
Netflix	396	Loss	Online entertainment
Microstrategy	247	Loss	Web services
Red Hat	217	4.7	Linux operating system
Amazon.com	178	Loss	E-retailing
Yahoo!	175	36.9	Portal, directory, search engine
E*Trade	160	51.5	Online securities trading
Intel	105	85.0	Microprocessor chips
eBay	90	68.0	Web auctioneer
Cisco	85	61.1	Networking hardware

Source: "Outlook: The Markets," *New York Times,* January 2, 2004, pp. C1–C13.

faster and higher than bigger, better-known stocks. The high fliers also have a comparatively small number of outstanding shares, often less than 30 million, and a rumor or press release can propel them to stratospheric prices. This can be compared to Intel, which has 6.67 billion shares outstanding and requires heavy buying from large institutional pension and mutual funds to increase its price. The rapid risers, it should be mentioned, also tend to be the fastest decliners when markets crumble, and insiders exit before the bad news is released. Hence, the illiquid trading situation in tandem with the stock's low price frequently whiplash these speculative securities up as well as down. The biggest gainer on Table 10.1, Mobility Electronics, is a case in point. The provider of components for mobile computing started 2003 at 76 cents and finished the year at $8.94 for a gain of 1,076.4 percent, even though it had no earnings. Speculators who purchased $10,000 of Mobility shares saw their investment rise by a multiple of 11.7 to $117,631. Such a killing is an example of a high-risk, high-return investment that pays off, usually when robust times follow a severe market collapse. In most instances the investor would have lost a big part if not all of the $10,000. The odds thus favor investments in companies that have good management, exceptional product lines, and clear growth potential. All three attributes are important, particularly in the tech sector where product life cycles are shortened by rapidly occurring advances. An innovation may give a start-up a rousing sendoff in wireless devices, Web services, or optical networks, but competitors soon begin marketing an improved version of the product, which cripples sales and sends the company into a free fall.

There are a number of ways to quantitatively analyze such a dynamic situation and they begin by assigning a high probability like 95 percent to the event that the investment becomes worthless. Such odds dictate that under most conditions, the stock should best be left alone. On the other hand, when the issue has been battered and the price remains near its bottom for a prolonged period of time, a turnaround situation is possible where handsome gains, as in the case of Mobility, can be realized. Under more ordinary conditions, the expected payoff of an investment in Mobility can be calculated by multiplying the two extreme outcomes, a $107,631 gain or a $10,000 loss, by their respective probabilities as indicated below:

$$\text{Expected payoff} = (\$107,631 \times 0.05) + (-\$10,000 \times 0.95) = -\$4,118$$

The negative payoff or expected loss indicates that the investment generally loses money and therefore should be undertaken with funds that are expendable. It should also be made in conjunction with funds placed in more conservative instruments like AAA investment-grade bonds yielding 6 percent. Larger amounts like $100,000 can be put in such bonds because of the very low probability of losses. The bonds will add $6,000 in interest to the portfolio that changes the negative return of −$4,118 to a positive payoff of $1,882. The portfolio can be further enhanced by adding a second stock such as Intel. The extreme payoffs for a $20,000 investment in the semiconductor company can be a doubling of its stock price, which happened in 2003, or a loss of the entire investment of $20,000. When multiplied by probabilities of 75 percent and 25 percent, the expected payoff of such an investment is $10,000. Thus if the $20,000 investment in Intel is added to the portfolio, it increases its expected payoff to $11,882. The numerical exercise, although based on arbitrarily assigned probabilities, validates the need for diversification, especially when speculative, high-tech issues are involved. In this way, the portfolio's risk of a loss is diminished, and it also gives the investor an opportunity for huge gains in the event that the three securities perform as they did in 2003. The return then totals $133,631, with $107,631 derived from the high-flying issue, $20,000 from a more conservative stock, and $6,000 from the bonds. In an average performance, the Mobility stock incurs a loss of $4,118, Intel gains $15,000, and the bonds pay interest of $6,000. In the worst scenario the bonds still pay $6,000 while the stock investments lose 100 percent and 50 percent of their values. The portfolio suffers a paper loss of $20,000 but is still held together by the bonds and Intel stock, with the latter having lost 50 percent of its value. Investors, such as retirees, who are unable to bear such losses, should not be investing in stocks. Those able to incur more risk for higher returns can more aggressively invest in speculative issues like those listed at the top of Table 10.1. It should be noted that they will probably fail to duplicate their gains and may even be delisted from the Nasdaq if their prices tumble because of a lack of earnings. Even if they prosper, their returns may still be far lower than in 2003. At the close of trading on March 2, 2004, three of the ten largest gainers on Table 10.1 are lower in price from their close at the end of 2003. All have no earnings, as does a fourth issue that had little movement in its price. In contrast, the three stocks with earnings were trading higher. The price movements further indicate that 2004 will not be as good for small issues as the prior year, and about half of the largest gainers will drop in price in 2004. The market recovery also ensures that innumerable start-ups will appear to challenge these companies with new wares and services, and those that succeed will replace the top gainers in 2004. The volatile situation makes it necessary that investors do the homework to uncover the new winners or, failing that, bet on established companies like Cisco, Amazon.com, Yahoo! and eBay, with considerable backup from bonds in case the stocks nose-dive.

Search Wars

Companies with strong high-tech franchises are apt to benefit greatly in the current expansion because customers have come to depend on them for advanced components and unique services. Research and development programs moreover continued during the slowdown, keeping them on top of technical advances while management restructured operations and formed new alliances. The belt-tightening improved balance sheets, and at Yahoo! a new CEO, Terry S. Semel, was appointed to steer the company through the dot-com flameout. While weaker competitors went belly-up as online ads fell, a formidable challenger—Google—emerged in early 2003 and overtook Yahoo! to become the leading U.S. search engine company. Its service captured 35 percent of the market, compared to Yahoo's 27 percent at the end of the year, and the two leaders were followed by AOL and Microsoft MSN with close to 15 percent each. Ask Jeeves rounded out the top five search firms, and in March 2004 it agreed to acquire Interactive Search Holdings for $193 million in cash. As Table 10.1 indicates, 2003 was an exceptional year financially for the once hard-pressed Ask Jeeves, with its stock climbing by 607 percent and its earnings per share exceeding those of the larger Yahoo! Its lowly market share of 3.5 percent, however, needed a significant boost—supplied by the Interactive acquisition, which doubled its share of the market—if it wanted to remain a competitor in the search field. It was eager to consummate the deal before Interactive's stock took off and before another company entered the bidding. Another small search company, Mamma.com, for example, rocketed from $4.05 to $10.10 in one day, March 2, 2004, after reporting earnings for the latest quarter following a year of losses. Ask Jeeves in turn soared by 40 percent two days later, following its takeover of Interactive, which now also owned Excite.com. Inktomi furthermore had been acquired earlier by Yahoo! in order to reduce its reliance on Google.

With online advertising rebounding by 20 percent in 2002, climbing from $6 billion to $7.2 billion, such Internet-related companies have once again become hot takeover candidates because they offer sophisticated marketing tools to advertisers that are capable of turning Web clicks into sales. When an ad is clicked showing interest in a product, a free gift or chance at winning the item induces the viewer to send in personal information, which the advertiser then uses to call on the customer to make a timely sales pitch. The immediate attention given potential buyers easily accomplishes more for the seller than expensive TV ads that generally fall on deaf ears. Furthermore, for TV viewers interested in the merchandise, there is no follow-up and the ad is then forgotten. Television advertisers also have difficulty determining the effectiveness of their ads and are unable to collect information on the customer since purchase is done, anonymously, at a retail outlet. Internet use has also closed much of the gap with

ade by the 18 million Linux users and furthermore remain untied
roprietary systems like Microsoft's Windows and Sun's Solaris.[5]

The operating principles adhered to by the Linux community in shar-
g information include the free use of the OS even in the development
f commercial products and services. Modifications to the code, how-
ver, must be posted and made available to others. Whether these changes
re incorporated into updated versions of the operating system is de-
ided by Linus Torvalds, based on the merits of each contribution.
orvalds is in a position to do this because he developed and posted the
inux program on the Web, which users could download and use. The
ystem's decidedly unorthodox origins—Torvalds gets no royalties from
he OS, which was released in 1991—grew out of its developer's fear of
ecoming "too shortsighted. You have a 'this is what we need' mentality
in commercial applications], and you blow everything else off. But you
want the commercial side, because commercial forces end up listening
o different customers and meeting different needs compared to those
doing it just for fun."[6] With such eclectic thinking behind the software's
development, it is understandable how the OS found its way into a variety of devices thrown up by the digital revolution. Besides its use in
large and desktop computers, Linux guides character creation at Pixar
Animation Studios and runs Motorola cell phones, Sony game consoles,
and TiVo recorders. Furthermore, the applications were developed without a concerted research and marketing effort because, in the absence of
royalty payments, funding was unavailable. Torvalds also eschewed the
anti-Gates role that Silicon Valley was hoping he would assume to lead
the open-source forces against Microsoft. As he explained in an inter-
view in the *New York Times,* "Microsoft just isn't relevant to what I do.
That might sound strange, since they are clearly the dominant player in
the market that Linux is in, but the thing is: I'm not in the 'market.' I'm
interested in Linux because of the technology, and Linux wasn't started
as any kind of rebellion against the 'evil Microsoft empire.' Microsoft
really has been one of the least interesting companies. So I've never
seen it as a 'Linus versus Bill' thing."[7]

The Perfect Nonstrategy

The for-and-against commercialism, while resisting counterproductive
skirmishing with Bill has proven to be a perfect nonstrategy that has
allowed Linux to thrive in Microsoft's backyard and keep the movement

TV viewing, with 26 percent of Americans using their free time to go
online compared to 28.5 percent who watch TV. These shifts together
with the use of potent marketing techniques resulted in an 84 percent
increase in ad revenues for Yahoo! and a 175 percent rise in its stock price
even as it was losing its lead in Web searches to Google.

Google Arrives

> Every few years, a rising superstar goes public in a blaze of headlines,
> speculation, and energy. . . . A hot IPO can even burn a hole in the zeit-
> geist, creating an entrance for a fresh batch of products, companies, and
> visionaries to spill out on society, changing it forever. Already, the Google
> IPO seems to be heralding a great new round of public offerings—by late
> January [2004] 24 tech companies were registered with the Securities
> and Exchange Commission.[4]

Wired magazine, from which the preceding excerpt was taken, can be
excused for waxing hot about Google's IPO going supernova sometime
in 2004. The publication had survived an advertising drought that nearly
silenced its printing presses and was searching for a messianic coming
that would rejuvenate its anemic pages and lengthen its subscription
lists. Its hyperbolic cover story on Google mania would consequently
have been dismissed as being too self-serving, were it not for the $10
billion Bill Gates supposedly offered to buy the search firm. If true, it
would have been a double-edged development for the company, whose
revenues from Web site ads were estimated to be less than $1 billion.
With the high valuation placed by Gates on Google, there was also the
recurring specter of Netscape being mauled by the software giant. Moreover, after having its offer to buy Google rejected, Microsoft announced
plans to build a competing search engine. Google aficionados, however,
were unimpressed. The richest man in the world had already underestimated the commercial importance of search technology, and Gates had
been chastened by the antitrust suit that nearly broke Microsoft in two.
The courts may not be so lenient a second time around.

Another potent authority has also weighed in on prospects for the
big software company. In 2003, while the tech-heavy Nasdaq soared
by 50 percent, its star listing—Microsoft—went up by a mere 5.9 percent. And why was the stock so lackluster when its ally Intel in the
Wintel duopoly was climbing by 105 percent? None other than
Microsoft's CEO and chairman were dumping hundreds of millions of

dollars of their holdings, depressing the stock's price and indicating that there was not much optimism about Microsoft's future. At the same time Ask Jeeves and Yahoo! were bounding ahead by 607 and 175 percent, respectively, even in the face of an onslaught from Google. This suggests that any titanic battle of search engines may very well be between Yahoo! and Google, with Microsoft more of a spectator. Moreover, the expected battlers—unlike Netscape, which had no earnings—are in strong financial shape, with revenues from online ads and funds from the investment community giving them the means to keep their front-running positions. From 2002 to 2003, Google was buoyed by a 620 percent rise in revenues, allowing the company to nearly triple its workforce by hiring 850 employees. While the number is impressive, many in the huge freshman class were attracted by the mother lode of the IPO gold mine and may depart the firm after cashing in their shares. These deserters, however, will not be abandoning a sinking ship. Google's co-founders Sergey Brin and Larry Page knew what they were doing when they built their search engine to rank Web sites in various categories according to their popularity. This made searches highly efficient because results listed those sites where the desired information was most likely to be found. Other search services in contrast, which failed to rank information found in the vastness of cyberspace, usually produced a lengthy list of irrelevant or outdated material. To assist online shoppers, moreover, related ads were placed close to the citations the search produced, and these could be clicked on and lead to a possible purchase. Thus, Google's searches often resulted in sales, endearing the service to advertisers as well as buyers, who got what they were looking for. In addition, Google allows marketers to open ad accounts online using a credit card. Key AdWords would be specified that described the merchandise or service being marketed. When a shopper enters a search word, Google presents the results from its ranked index of 3.3 billion Web pages, and next to the listing places a two-sentence boxed ad linked to an appropriate advertiser. The advertiser pays $1 to $2 each time the ad is clicked, and the clicks are correlated with sales to produce a quantitative measure of the ad's effectiveness. The ads have been so successful at generating sales that marketers are increasing their search-related advertising by 34 percent for 2004 while planning to spend half as much on other online promotions like banner ads which are widely used by MSN, Yahoo!, and AOL. Google's unique search and advertising method also ensures a successful public offering of its stock, with capital raised from the IPO enabling the start-up to develop more cutting-edge

technology, acquire other companies, expand its servic markets. Even in its primary search business, Google ha 90 percent of the existing Web sites, and the job become since cyberspace continues to expand. Competitors more behind the 3.3 billion pages already indexed by Google. gine AlltheWeb has done 3.2 billion pages; Inktomi, the engine, did 3.0 billion; Ask Jeeves did 1.5 billion; and Al billion. With competition already intense, Microsoft set to ness, and smaller firms like Mamma.com planning on get of the market, the ensuing search wars may lead to new roa information superhighway. Nevertheless, with funding arriv Wall Street and Madison Avenue for targeted search ads, tl to create more order out of the Internet's chaos will undoubt

Open-Source Advances

Planning for battle against flyspeck search companies, gia has already received a thousand small and not-so-small cuts ing forces backing the freely distributed Linux operating sy Linux users total 18 million worldwide, and it will soon ov as the leading OS for servers that run large corporate data well as the Internet itself. Google's one hundred thousand operate its twelve computer centers, for example, use Linux stalwarts like IBM, Oracle, HP, and Dell have also climbed open-source movement, partly to escape a Netscape-type bl that could result from an overdependence on Microsoft's systems software. Intel abetted the movement by producing chips compatible with Linux, and with the economic downtu sales of more expensive PCs, discounters like Wal-Mart have fering Linux-based computers for $200. Being able to offer lc bigger machines is also prompting manufacturers like IBM an use Linux, with Dell selling its servers, like its PCs, over the Cost comparisons also moved E*Trade to replace sixty of its ers, costing $250,000 each, with eighty Linux machines cost $4,000 apiece. Morgan Stanley, the investment banker, is follow and is expecting to save $100 million in operating costs over fi\ by replacing four thousand servers with Linux-run computers. N these buyers are supporting the open-source movement in order t on the free software upgrading posted on the Web by users of tl proprietary Linux program. They thus can take advantage of ad

away from the IPO money madness of Wall Street. Meanwhile, IBM, Netscape, and AOL have suffered ugly and sometimes deadly scrapes with the software kingpin—which might also include Google in the future. The absence of royalty payments as well as corporate structure, moreover, makes Linux an amorphous target that is difficult to attack, sue, or vote against as in a proxy battle. The situation further permits Linux to upgrade its software and expand into high-growth businesses. Such success perplexes management gurus, other talking heads on cable TV, and assorted journalists, making for a dearth of books, newspaper headlines, and thirty-second sound bites about the nonstrategy. The nondescript Torvalds is equally unfabulous, with reporters from *Wired* and *Business Week* relying on his increasing "paunch" to liven up their stories. And why shouldn't Torvalds grow fat and lazy? There are no IPO shares to hand out or global markets to fight over. There is only the software to improve, and in that job Torvalds's forte is manifestly evident. He leads by being a nonleader of twelve worldwide lieutenants who voluntarily "maintain" the code. Decisions are arrived at by consensus, and although he has the final say on any modification, Torvalds would "much rather have 15 people arguing about something than 15 people splitting into two camps, each side convinced it's right and not talking to the other."[8] Debate thus continues, and until an amiable conclusion is reached there will be no ill will because promotions, bonuses, and executive perquisites are not at stake. Different motivations also prompt the worldwide cadre of diligent programmers to submit contributions, with the majority seeking only professional recognition for their efforts. It is a situation similar to Tim Berners-Lee's online release of his World Wide Web. The Internet Revolution is thus proceeding with big and small steps being taken for both altruistic and commercial reasons. Anti-Microsoft zealots disagree about Linux's significance and argue that the system may be "a technical success, but as a business, it's a flop. . . . Who is Linux's Bill Gates or Steve Jobs? Not Linus Torvalds. He supports desktop Linux but does little proselytizing." Even Eric Schmidt, CEO of Google, argues that "Open source is a technology innovation strategy looking for a business model."[9] The criticism is misplaced because, even though Linux is currently a flop in desktop computers,

> Advances to Linux come out all the time, and are quickly made available free of charge [because] unlike a commercial software company, Mr.

Torvalds doesn't need to hold back improvements to get people to pay for an upgrade. No wonder he and the Open Source software movement continue to represent one of the most important forces in all technology. Mr. Torvalds has long predicted that Linux will eventually win on the desktop, too. That's starting to happen, not in the home, but on "fleets" of desktops, where lots of workers all use the same collection of three or four programs.[10]

Linux's growing importance also made the open source movement an alternate way for incorporating advances into software systems. It accomplishes this without the need to kowtow to financial bigwigs or erect an imperial hierarchy that promotes officious self-dealings, illegal conflict of interest, and wasteful bureaucratic infighting which were all on disgusting display in recent business and Wall Street scandals.

Violent Arrival

On the home entertainment front, Microsoft's multibillion-dollar game plan for growth stalled with its Xbox video player. This was predictable given the peculiar origins of interactive video gaming—far from the logical constructs of software enterprises—which appeared to burst from the head of Nolan Bushnell, founder of the game producer Atari, to capture every kid's imagination. It has bypassed music, TV, and Hollywood movies to become the most popular form of entertainment and has taken over the living room because kids and now adults have fallen under its spell. Microsoft typically failed to anticipate the phenomenon's commercial impact, which earned $28 billion in 2002, with Gates noticing its 20 percent growth rate only when PC software sales slowed. Even in his corporate army of highly paid, so-called best and the brightest programmers and managers, few if any saw Pac-Man, Mario, and Lara Croft charging down everyone's streets and onto the small screen, in the process giving Sony, which entered the business in 1995 with its first game player, an insurmountable lead. Its second-generation game console, PS 2 has already sold 60 million units worldwide, and in fiscal 2002 was responsible for 70 percent of Sony's operating profit. Unfortunately for the company, computer entertainment, which houses video games, accounts for 13.1 percent of sales and is being overwhelmed by the slowdown in the huge consumer electronics division that brings in 63.1 percent of its sales. The rut is further exacerbated by lagging results in music and movies, which deepens Sony's dependence on computer games and its "entertainment czar," Ken Kutaragi. Just as Torvalds single-handedly developed the first Linux operating system, Kutaragi directed Sony's move into games from the time he arrived at the company in 1975. In the process he battled the daimyo of consumer electronics, particularly TV executives, who ruled the Sony kingdom and dared to call them "old guys [who] should step aside to make way for the young."[11] This insolent comment was made in 1995 following the launch of the first PlayStation, which surged past Nintendo's player, the former leader in video gaming with its popular Mario and Donkey Kong games. Sega, another leading Japanese competitor, would also fall to PlayStation as Sony proceeded to sell 100 million units of the console, aided in large measure by the 1,000 games that ran on the new platform. In contrast, Nintendo's N64 machine was played with 276 game titles while Sega's Dreamcast player played 192.[12] Sega, following the introduction of PS 2 in 2000, dropped out of the video game hardware business to concentrate on producing games. Months later, Microsoft launched its Xbox console, with Bill Gates selling the first unit in New York's Times Square at the stroke of midnight. While the Xbox was produced using cutting-edge technology, there were few hit games to propel its sales. As such, its entrance into video games—though widely anticipated—failed to duplicate Sony's success with PlayStation.

The Hollywood Factor

Sony too once lacked experience in the business, but the Tokyo-based company was a giant in consumer electronics and worked continuously with TV executives and programmers. It also owned the Columbia and Tri-Star Hollywood film studios as well as CBS Records and was thus familiar with creating entertainment products. These ventures made its corporate hierarchy receptive to making a substantial investment in digital video games even though it meant overruling TV warlords who wanted to stick with their analog format. There was also Kutaragi, who actively pushed to set up the Sony Computer Entertainment company, even threatening to leave Sony if the games unit was not created. The brash engineer familiarized himself with games by playing his son's Nintendo set, and finding its sound quality poor, invented a chip that improved the player's sound processing, which was then sold to Nintendo. This laid the groundwork for an alliance between the two companies in which Sony's CD-ROM technology would be used by Nintendo in its next generation of machines. Nintendo, however, walked out of the project and partnered with Philips, the European electronics manufacturer and Sony competitor. Kutaragi immediately saw this slap in the face as a way to move Sony into video games and make Nintendo pay dearly for insulting Japan's most innovative company. Adding further insult to injury, Sony also approached and was rebuffed by then number two game-maker, Sega. The Sony proposal was shelved by Sega's board, which dismissed it with the following contemptuous remarks: "What are you crazy? Sony doesn't know anything about building a game system, and they don't know anything about software. Why would you want to partner with them?"[13] The twin affronts were presented to Sony's chairman, Norio Ohga, by Kutaragi, along with his recommendation to develop the PlayStation. According to Kutaragi, "Mr. Ohga responded with energy, saying that if that's the way I was going to say it, then show him the proof that I could do it. Then he boiled over, clenching his fists and bellowing, 'Do it!'"[14] It was a landmark decision that threw Sony's manufacturing and marketing heft into a fray that transformed kiddy game-playing into interactive entertainment for alpha males who were tiring of passively watching movies, TV, NASCAR runs, and sporting events. The 18- to 34-year-olds wanted to take part in more of the action, which Sony, with its experience in Hollywood films and pop music, provided, and it seized the market from Nintendo and Sega. Nintendo would further paint itself into the kiddy corner with its highly successful Pokémon franchise while violent (*Mortal Combat,* 1992) and busty Lara Croft (*Tomb Raider,* 1995) titles began to attract adults. In the ensuing battle, Nintendo also continued the practice of signing exclusive licensing agreements with firms that developed games for its console, the Nintendo Entertainment System (NES). Sony in contrast "welcomed all comers. As a result, it covered all the bases more quickly in terms of consumer preferences. It was easy to find several games in each category, whether baseball, football, fantasy role-playing, fighting, or racing games."[15] Sony also assisted game developers by switching the PlayStation's memory system from cartridges used in NES to its own, cheaper and easier to mass produce compact disk-ROM unit. This enabled "companies to release more titles in smaller production runs. They could then quickly pump out millions of hit games—just as Sony had always done in the hits-driven music business."[16] The technical innovations and firepower from its game developers overwhelmed the competition and transformed the business, giving Sony 47 percent of the worldwide game console market, leaving Nintendo with 28 percent and

Sega with 23 percent. It also crowned Kutaragi as Sony's games czar, paving the way for a top corporate appointment and leading to the development of PS 2, especially after he predicted that Microsoft would enter the market. Convergence of the boxes—TV, PC, game players—had taken hold in electronics, prompting Bill Gates to call on Sony executives to ask about using Microsoft's software in PS 2. To no one's surprise the software titan was gently turned away, who then characteristically flew into a rage and returned to headquarters muttering dark forebodings about PS 2 threatening his PC franchise.[17] With Gates enraged, Microsoft went into overdrive, with Sony now the villain, to ensure that Windows would run the entertainment units in the living room as well as kitchen appliances and mobile gadgets even though the company lacked experience in consumer products. It had furthermore blundered by letting its klutzy chief executive take control of a game plan that required partnering with funky developers who were in no mood to answer to the likes of Bill Gates. Japan Inc., Hollywood, and Silicon Valley were thus arrayed against Microsoft from the start, forcing it to swim off alone in treacherous waters where a thousand Captain Ahabs—not to forget Big Blue (IBM)—were set on beaching the software whale.

PS 2

Sony meanwhile had been working on PS 2 for the five years prior to March 2, 1999, when it publicly released plans calling for its commercial launch the following year. Its premiere wowed players and game developers with its 128-bit microprocessing chip, called the Emotion Engine, endowing characters with human-like reactions and motions. With more than three times the processing power of the Pentium III, the fastest PC microprocessor, sales of games created for the new console began outrunning sales of PC-run games. By the end of 2001, console game sales reached $9.4 billion in the United States with PC games behind at $1.4 billion. Brisk sales of the PS 2 thus grew out of the machine's hold on top-selling games including the popular *Grand Theft Auto 3* and forced Microsoft, which had introduced the Xbox in 2001, to assign game development to nine hundred in-house programmers. The company also attempted to convince the Lara Croft–Tomb Raider producers to make an Xbox version of the all-time, best-selling franchise, but the suggestion was rejected. Eidos, Lara Croft's corporate developer, then announced that a new game of the popular raider's adventures was forthcoming for Sony's PS 2.[18] Another major developer, Electronics Arts, also shifted its hardware base from PC to game console after sales of the first PlayStation began surpassing home computer sales. As a result, the PS not only transformed electronics games from kiddy cartoons to adult entertainment fare, but moved games from the nerdy and dull computer box to a digital screen with high-definition picture clarity, stereophonic audio, and the player's ability to control the screen's environment and events. With the new technology, Electronics Arts successfully developed "God games" into a billion-dollar franchise played mainly by teenage girls simulating people's lives. The electronic dollhouse runs exclusively on PS 2. The affinity between game producers and the first PlayStation ensured the successful launch of PS 2, with shipments to retailers reaching 70 million by the end of 2003 compared to 13.7 million Xboxes. In order to remain competitive, Microsoft has cut prices twice, with the Xbox now selling for $149, but the strategy has been thwarted by the $99 price tag on Nintendo's console, the Game Cube. Its low price has lifted Game Cube's sales, which now outpace those of Xbox. The industry currently awaits the next major development in hardware, which is expected to be the PlayStation 3 that Sony maintains "will have 1,000 times the performance of the PlayStation 2."[19] Because game developers had trouble working with the parallel architecture of PS 2, Sony released details of the next-generation machine to familiarize them with its performance capabilities, which would help them create games for its debut. A prototype of PS 3, called GScube, has also been developed to aid game writing. The concern is warranted because games now require $10 million and about three years to develop, with the strong profit potential—hundreds of millions, even billions of dollars—encouraging the huge outlays. There is also some talk about online gaming, where strangers in distant lands play against each other. Sony and Microsoft are competitively setting up their units to enable such play on the Web, but any payoff appears far in the future. They therefore along with Nintendo are placing more of their efforts on next-generation game players while cultivating developers whose titles will determine who wins the battle of the boxes.[20]

Another Deal of the Century

The entertainment world was jolted on February 11, 2004, when Comcast, the largest cable operator, offered $48.7 billion in stock to take over the

Walt Disney Company. Like the AOL–Time Warner merger, the proposed alliance would unite a producer of well-known entertainment content and properties—movies, TV broadcasting, sports channels, theme parks—with Comcast, which transmitted such programming through its cable systems. Given the failure of the AOL merger, what compelled Comcast with 2003 revenues of $18.3 billion to move on the larger conglomerate Disney with revenues of $27.1 billion? Was it again some fuzzy notion of cashing in on synergies by a would-be media mogul? In giving his reasons for the deal, Comcast CEO Brian Roberts appeared to echo AOL chief Steve Case's remarks by saying, "The bottom line is that we think it will accelerate the digital future."[21] Roberts was referring to Comcast's broadband services which, if the deal went through, would carry Disney's entertainment to new viewers using the Internet. Comcast's cable system had two years earlier been augmented by the hefty $50 billion acquisition of AT&T Broadband, and Roberts was looking for new business to carry on his cable and high-speed networks. With the AT&T addition, moreover, Comcast possessed the technology for distributing video programming, which neither AOL nor Time Warner had when they merged. And before the capability could be developed, the dot-com crash crippled AOL's Internet service, turning Time Warner's shareholders and managers against the merger.

The problematic takeover of Cap Cities ABC by Disney is also making its presence felt in the current Comcast-Disney maneuvering. Michael Eisner, chairman and CEO of Disney, engineered the $19 billion purchase, and with ABC's ratings among major TV broadcasters now fourth behind even Fox, it has undermined Disney's leadership and prompted Comcast to act. The cable company was itself responding to competitive pressures arising from the acquisition of DirecTV's satellite distribution system by Rupert Murdoch's News Corporation, which can now transmit its creative content from Fox studios and other production units over its own satellite system. It no longer has to depend on independent distributors and can even charge producers for distributing their programs and airing them on its TV stations. This development motivated Comcast, lacking programming content to carry over its system, to search for a content supplier to fill its lines. And as its CEO quickly discovered: Who has better content than Disney? Disney was furthermore in the midst of an internecine battle over Eisner's stewardship of the entertainment empire, and major Disney stockholders were calling for his resignation. In addition to tiring of his nineteen-year tenure, critics were outspoken about his dispute with Jeffrey Katzenberg, one of the company's most creative executives, who reinvigorated animated production. His departure was followed by the money-losing ABC acquisition; a $1.6 billion loss on an Internet portal investment, Go.com; and the failure to reach a new deal with Pixar, which supplied Disney with some of its hit films. Disney's CEO also nixed the Comcast proposal even as its stock has outperformed Disney's because Wall Street was impressed by Comcast's management and the way it profitably integrated AT&T Broadband into its operations. With the acquisition, the cable company offers TV, high-speed Internet connections, and even telephone service to subscribers and, by merging with Disney, its vast entertainment productions can be distributed as well. The possibilities were detailed in a letter to Disney by Brian Roberts, Comcast's president and CEO:

> Together, we could unite the country's premier cable provider with Disney's leading filmed entertainments, media networks and theme park properties. In addition to serving over 21 million cable subscribers, Comcast is also the country's largest high-speed Internet service provider with over 5 million subscribers. . . . Disney's content [can be delivered] through existing distribution channels and technologies such as video-on-demand and broadband video streaming and other emerging technologies.[22]

For Disney shareholders, Roberts also noted how Comcast stock outperformed the S&P 500 index by "more than 2 to 1 since Comcast went public in 1972."[23] While Disney's board took the Comcast offer to merge under advisement, it did at a later shareholder's meeting split the company's chairman and CEO positions, which forced Eisner to give up the former. It was a step toward a post-Eisner era, and whether the future called for a Comcast role depended on how persuasive Roberts was in explaining Disney's need for his company's distribution system. The merger, for example, could increase profits by creating more cable channels using repackaged Disney programming. The new channels could then be bundled with popular media properties like the ESPN sports channel or local ABC broadcasts. Boosting ABC's ratings would also allow it to charge higher advertising rates that could turn its $36 million operating loss into annual profits of $800 million to $1.3 billion as earned by other top primetime networks. ABC moreover is only a stone's throw behind Fox, with the latter having 9.98 million viewers in the 2003–4 season and ABC 9.97 million. Overtaking Fox is therefore possible by adding viewers from Comcast's 21 million cable and 5 million broadband subscribers. Comcast's "on-demand" service can also distribute Disney's sports and news programs to help Comcast retain digital subscribers and compete against satellite-TV operators. The service allows users to pay for the convenience of watching programs whenever they want to. This will help the network cope with busy viewer schedules, which caused the downturn in ABC's ratings because much of the audience was not at home when the programs were broadcast. Such use of advanced technology that better serves customers has boosted Comcast's earnings and stock market valuation and given it the opportunity to acquire Disney, even though it is a smaller company. Its stock is valued at $70 billion compared to Disney's valuation of $56.4 billion. The more robust equity markets are also aiding the Comcast bid by motivating large Disney investors to vote for the merger and exchange their stock holdings for shares in the smaller but faster-growing company, which could yield bigger financial returns. Even if the bid fails, it will have awakened Disney to the possibilities of using the Internet to distribute its entertainment fare. In such ways is the information superhighway being extended with the use of digital and financial engineering methods.

Wireless Combination

Transforming events have also engulfed the huge telecom industry, with Global Crossing crawling out of bankruptcy and WorldCom attempting to do the same under its new name MCI. Bernie Ebbers, its infamous co-founder, was finally indicted on March 3, 2004, for his part in the largest corporate fraud case in U.S. history. The indictment was announced by the U.S. attorney general, who charged that Ebbers "directed co-conspirators to make false and fraudulent adjustments to WorldCom's books and records."[24] One of Ebbers's most trusted co-conspirators, former CFO Scott Sullivan, pleaded guilty to the illegal accounting and was cooperating with prosecutors against his erstwhile boss in hopes of receiving a lighter sentence.

While the curtain was coming down on Ebbers, a new chapter was being written, with remnants of the AT&T monopoly forging a union that would produce the largest wireless company in the country with 46 million users. Cingular Wireless, a 60–40 joint venture between Baby Bells SBC and BellSouth, agreed on February 17, 2004, to buy AT&T Wireless for $41 billion in cash. The acquired company had been spun off from AT&T and, because of the intense competition in mobile phones, had put itself up for sale as capital ran out to upgrade its network infrastructure. Because of its deteriorating service, disgruntled customers were leaving the company. At their end, SBC and BellSouth had to act as their local phone markets were being invaded by mobile and long-distance companies. Voice over Internet Protocol technology was further muddying the waters, with cable companies and AT&T using it to break into the local calling business. Wall Street is also warming to the idea and has funded two New Jersey start-ups with $100 million to send telephone calls over the Internet. The heightened competition moved SBC and BellSouth to overpay for AT&T Wireless in order to take it from Britain's Vodafone, which was also actively bidding for the company. Even after the takeover, however, it remains uncertain how the Bells through their Cingular joint venture will be able to develop the wireless and data transmission assets of AT&T Wireless into profitable operations. As huge telecom enterprises, it was expected that SBC and BellSouth could have uncovered and pursued these possibilities as opposed to buying in so late in the game after competitors had set up shop in their own backyards. Considerable investment in time and money is now needed to meld networks, technologies, management structures, and business systems, and these adjustments may push the Bells further behind as technology and the competition rapidly advance.

—— Chapter 11 ——
Epilogue: Downloading Music and Doing No Evil

On March 24, 2004, the five-year investigation by the European Commission into the anticompetitive practices of Microsoft culminated in a ruling against the company's bundling of new programs with its Windows operating system. Specifically the case focused on the Windows Media Player, which when offered with the Windows operating software sent sales plummeting for the front-running media playing software of RealNetworks, Microsoft's much smaller rival. The commission concluded that the effect was too similar to the Netscape browser battle in which Microsoft's bundling of its Internet Explorer software with the operating system doomed the smaller browser company. In attempting to blunt the extension of the Windows monopoly to new areas, the commission, however, was acting after much of the damage had been done, and the ruling, while forcing the software giant to remove WMP from one version of Windows, did not return the market to the time before Microsoft's entry. All that the regulatory agency could do was appoint a monitor to ensure that the two versions of Windows—with and without WMP—were comparable and that Microsoft did "not give PC manufacturers a discount conditional on their buying Windows together with the Windows Media Player."[1]

This was little consolation for RealNetworks, which was still left to compete with Microsoft, with the world's largest software company required only to offer Windows in Europe with and without the media player. Since there would be no price difference between the two packages, little impact on buyers was anticipated, as they would continue to buy the version that gave them the WMP. Sales of the player would thus be boosted by the Windows monopoly, which in the end could hamstring RealNetworks in the same way that bundling overwhelmed Netscape. The problem is compounded by the financial situation facing RealNetworks, which has been in the red for the last four years as a result not only of its battle with Microsoft, but due to the highly successful entry of Apple Computer into digital music. Under the direction of its celebrated CEO Steven P. Jobs, the PC company launched a two-pronged strategy consisting of its iPod digital MP3 music player and its iTunes online music store from which individual songs on major record labels can be downloaded for 99 cents. While the small charge keeps iTunes in the red, sales of iPod at over $300 each nearly tripled to $391 million, sending Apple's share of the music player market to 25 percent in the two years since its introduction. The surge in revenues of the pricey device more than doubled net income at Apple, with iPod's popularity increasing sales at the iTunes Music Store by tenfold. Apple's success undoubtedly cut into RealNetworks' subscription music business, where songs could be listened to but not stored on a PC and therefore only rented by the subscriber. Lacking the expertise to design and produce a device like iPod, RealNetworks remains undaunted by Apple's surge since it has been able to get its software on 7 million cell phones in deals with leading manufacturers like Nokia and Motorola and mobile operators like Vodafone and Sprint. In effect, hardware development, an extremely competitive business with small profit margins, is being left to established makers while it enhances its service of unlimited music listening for a nominal annual fee. Rob Glaser, founder and CEO of RealNetworks, feels that Apple and his company's Rhapsody music service can both grow in the burgeoning business and furthermore, "It's not bad to have a leading competitor that takes a different strategy from yours" to keep you competitive and at the forefront of technology.[2] Thus, while songs downloaded (purchased) from iTunes jumped from 30 million to 50 million between January and March 2004, titles listened to on Rhapsody rose from 42 million to 48 million in the same three months. The number of subscribers also climbed from 250,000 to 350,000 in the third quarter of 2003. In response to the Apple challenge, RealNetworks established a RealPlayer Music Store where subscribers can download and own song titles for 79 cents each. Nonsubscribers can also make purchases, but are charged 99 cents. In addition, program offerings were expanded to include computer games, NASCAR races, professional basketball games, and news. These can be downloaded for a $5- to $10-a-month subscription fee and were well-received, with revenue from such programs doubling to comprise 75 percent of all company revenue. At the same time, revenue from software fell to 25 percent as part of a concerted move to reduce dependence on markets in which the company competes against Microsoft. The diversification away from music is also wise because of the way Steve Jobs streamlined music retailing by placing his iTunes music store at its nexus. He accomplished this even as record companies were suing teenagers for pirating songs using Napster software. Convincing corporate executives that their litigation was counterproductive, Jobs persuaded them instead to sell their titles on iTunes for a nominal amount and concentrate their efforts in what they do best: creating hit tunes and developing new artists to generate sales. These are necessary because the popularity of songs and musicians is short-lived. The ubiquitous and continuously open online store was offered as an ideal distribution channel, and Jobs used these obvious attributes to convince record companies to make their titles available on iTunes. The mobile iPod player with its ability to hold ten thousand songs on its hard drive was another ingenious development that complemented the iTunes store, and Jobs expanded its marketing appeal by making the store's software compatible with Windows PCs. IPod, however, is operated with Apple's software, and it plays only songs downloaded from iTunes. Apple has also forged an alliance with Hewlett-Packard, allowing the latter to sell iPods under its brand name and giving HP computers the ability to download music from iTunes. In addition, a smaller and cheaper $249 iPod has been developed to keep Apple ahead of competitors like Sony, Dell, and discount retailer Wal-Mart.

On May 4, 2004, Sony joined the music-downloading fray with its Connect Web site offering five hundred thousand titles that can be listened to on one of the 2.5 million music players it has already sold in the United States. In following Apple's game plan, the electronics giant had decided that purchasing songs as opposed to listening to them while subscribing to a service was a better approach to the digital music market. With the Connect service, moreover, it has introduced a fourth format for downloading music that competes against those of Microsoft, RealNetworks, and Apple. Its entrance is thus a blessing because of the choices available, and a curse for consumers and the industry because the market will sustain only one standard. The move to a more lucrative film downloading service is also clouding any resolution in music technology. Both Sony and Microsoft are planning to launch portable video players in 2004, with Microsoft's entry, the Portable Media Center, expected to cost between $400 and $700 and be capable of storing 175 hours of video. Microsoft, unlike Sony, however, has no movie-producing studio and therefore is dependent on Hollywood for films to play on the PMC. It subsequently signed a deal with Disney in February 2004 to do just that, with the movie producer formatting its films to enable their PC downloading using the Windows Media Player for viewing on the Portable Media Center. Comcast, which lacked Microsoft's Internet technology, then dropped its plans to merge with Disney. The latter's deal with the software powerhouse was prompted by the piracy of feature films, which had doubled in one year to over sixteen million more files that were freely available on the Internet in March 2004. Spreading broadband connections and advanced compression technology—available with Microsoft software—paradoxically spurred the piracy by reducing download times from a lengthy seven hours per film in 1999 to only one hour now. Microsoft has also developed digital-rights management programs that protect movie studios from the pirating of their films and gives them control over what devices they can be shown on. Microsoft is using the antipiracy software and new Portable Media Center to lure other film producers to sign onto its video transmission service and overcome the reluctance in Hollywood of doing business with Gates and Company. The piracy problem, however, hangs over the industry like a sword of Damocles, and its resolution will probably depend on the success of Microsoft's player and software. These products could then become the centerpiece of digital video the way Apple's iPod and iTunes has revolutionized music distribution.[3]

The restructuring of Apple away from PCs to consumer entertainment and the European Commission's ruling against Microsoft are examples of how the Internet has become ensconced in nearly all aspects of business and society. It allowed Steve Jobs to rejuvenate his company and the music industry, and as he entered the winner's circle with his iPod and iTunes successes, Gates was receiving a black eye in Europe and being forced to unbundle his media player from Windows. Microsoft was also sued by RealNetworks for $1 billion in damages on antitrust grounds, which further tarred the giant company's reputation. Also like Apple, the diminutive RealNetworks successfully reoriented its business to include news and sports programming, which takes it beyond software and Microsoft. While it remains in competition with Apple, there are still major differences between their music service. Apple's iTunes is an online store where songs are purchased, and Rhapsody is a service that rents its music. Both companies furthermore remain wary of competition from Sony and Microsoft, which are entering the digital media business albeit as latecomers. They are also suffering from lagging growth in their traditional profit centers, and this opens opportunities for nimble, innovative companies which, as shown by Apple's move into music, can result in breakthroughs even for an aging entrepreneur like Steve Jobs.

No-Evil Underwriting

The widely anticipated Google IPO and the robust performance of equity markets in 2003 signaled the return of investor confidence to high-tech issues, and the renewed financing will accelerate the continued expansion of the Internet. A net $152.8 billion flowed into stock market funds in 2003, contrasting sharply with the $27.8 billion outflow in 2002 when capital markets were still reeling from the dot-com bust. Because of eroded investor sentiment, Google held off from going public even though its popular search engine had already made it profitable. The company broke into the black in 2001 and had a net income of about $100 million for each of the succeeding two years. Google's cash vaults—already holding $455 million—will soon be bursting at the seams as it files to raise $2.7 billion, when its shares are first offered to the public. It will be the largest Internet-related IPO in history, and investor demand for the shares is expected to give the firm a market valuation of $25 billion as well as make multibillionaires of its young founders Larry Page and Sergey Brin, vaunting each of them past Donald "You're fired" Trump, whose net worth stands at $2.5 billion. There is as usual a more formidable billionaire who is planning to use his Windows monopoly to smash another Internet start-up, but the firepower behind Bill Gates's ambitions will be dampened by Google's rallying cry to do no evil, which has propelled the company to the front ranks of other portals, past Yahoo! and Microsoft's MSN. Its search engine directs 75 percent of Net users seeking Web site information, making it the Internet's gatekeeper. How did it reach these heights in such a Microsoft-infested environment? For one thing, its founders were determined not to bring forth another Gates or Trump enterprise that operated by instilling shock, awe, and fear in competitors and employees. In other words, Google did not want to morph into a company that "will just suck dollars" from its customers.[4] Page and Brin's original ambition was to establish the search business and then sell it to Yahoo! But the stock market gods intervened, forcing the two founders to develop and launch the company guided by their instincts and learning from the $7 trillion debacle of jerry-built corporate empires and Internet start-ups. They realized that "searching and organizing all the world's information [is] an unusually important task that should be carried out by a company that is trustworthy and interested in the public good."⁵ These goals would furthermore be carried out by:

1. Emphasizing an "atmosphere of creativity and challenge [that encourages employees] to spend 20 percent of their time working on what they think will most benefit Google."
2. Maintaining a "long-term focus" without regard to swings in its stock price and quarterly profits.
3. Making "our search results the best we know how to produce."
4. Establishing the Google Foundation to which "employee time and 1 percent of Google's equity and profits in some form [will be contributed]. We hope someday this institution may eclipse Google itself in terms of overall world impact by ambitiously applying innovation and significant resources to the largest of the world's problems."⁶

Google's efforts at circumventing Wall Street's tainted IPO process furthermore prompted its founders to propose an auction-based system that the company will use to control the pricing and allocation of its shares. In booming dot-com days, investment bankers led by notorious wheeler-dealers like Frank P. Quattrone determined the price of coveted IPO issues and gave them to favored clients like Bernie Ebbers of WorldCom, who in turn steered considerable underwriting business to Quattrone's bank. Skewed research reports hyped the securities to ensure that they soared in price after being offered to the public, at which time, inside investors dumped their shares for fast and fat gains at the expense of later, smaller investors. The system worked because the investment bank purposely left enormous amounts of money on the table to enable the initial "pop" or run-up in price that rewarded favored clients with quick and easy gains. This was accomplished by lowballing the IPO's offering price, which shortchanged the company issuing the stock. For abetting such activity, Quattrone was found guilty of obstructing the government's investigation into his IPO dealings a week after Google publicly announced how its shares would be floated using a "Dutch auction." The search firm had already shied away from the traditional underwriting process when it decided to not go public in 2000 even after being badgered to do so by venture capitalists and Wall Street bankers. It further banned the bankers from its offices while it developed its IPO plan, and because its founders did not want to be encumbered by speculation over quarterly profit estimates, the company will refrain from giving "guidance" on how earnings are shaping up. As Page and Brin put it: "A management team distracted by a series of short-term targets is as pointless as a dieter stepping on a scale every half hour."[7] This leaves media pundits and stock analysts with little to go on in creating their hype, but at any rate, Internet chat rooms and individual investor Web sites have supplanted many if not all of these talking heads on television. Obviously, Google does not want to endear itself to such dethroned "experts," who darkly hint that the auction may be a bust as overly eager investors bid up the stock price to ridiculous levels only to see it fall after trading begins. Better to leave the initial pricing, they say, to investment bankers who will estimate demand for the issue by huddling with large institutional investors. A price is then set that matches supply with anticipated demand. In such a process, large investors from the start are in close contact with the underwriters, giving them an advantage in getting large allocations of hot new issues. The "little guy" on the other hand is left out of the loop. In implementing the nontraditional Dutch auction, Google's founders say that: "It is important to us to have a fair process for our IPO that is inclusive of both small and large investors [and leads to] a share price that reflects a fair market valuation."[8] And while the dark mutterings from Wall Street continue, its bankers dare not antagonize Page and Brin for fear of being left out of the lucrative investment loop that they once controlled. As such, they will adhere to the new underwriting rules that now opens bidding to the masses. Individual investors will still have to have a brokerage account at one of the underwriters as well as submit a price that is high enough to buy the shares. After all bids are in, Google will award the shares to the highest bidders and thus receive most of the proceeds from the stock sale. Then the market takes over: Investors can sell their shares if the stock surges above the price they paid. The stock can also tank and give the company and its auction process a black eye. It can dodge such a result by setting a low offering price for successful bidders. It will also suggest a price range to eliminate bids that are either too high or too low. The corporate guidance will probably lead to a price close to what most investors expect and in addition keep the stock from gyrating wildly following the IPO. If this occurs, Google will help bury the sordid financial manipulations that brought Wall Street to its knees and the information superhighway to a near dead end. It will also go a long way toward reforming the IPO and investment banking process that underwrites much of the innovative development of the Internet.

Notes

Notes to Preface

1. See the author's Letter to the Editor, "Lessons to Be Learned from 401 (k) Disasters." Money & Business section, *New York Times,* October 19, 2003, p. 2.
2. Floyd Norris, "The Bounceback Year: Energized by the Economy, Stocks Advance Forcefully with Small Issues in the Lead." *New York Times,* January 2, 2004, pp. C1-C6.
3. See the author's Letter to the Editor, "Municipal Bonds, for the Long Run." Money & Business section, *New York Times,* September 22, 2002, p. 10.

Notes to Chapter 1

1. OECD, *A New Economy?* (Paris: Organization for Economic Cooperation and Development, 2000).
2. James Grant, "A Foreseeable End to the Fed's Magic." *New York Times,* April 20, 2001, p. A19.
3. "Excerpts from Report by Greenspan at Senate." *New York Times,* July 17, 2002, p. C8.
4. Jacob M. Schlesinger, "Did Washington Help Set Stage for Current Business Turmoil?" *Wall Street Journal,* October 17, 2002, p. A12.
5. "Excerpts from Report by Greenspan."
6. Alex Berenson and Chris Gaither, "Cisco, Internet Power, Adds Evidence of Frail Economy." *New York Times,* April 17, 2001, p. C4.
7. "And Then There Were . . ." *New York Times,* February 11, 2001, sec. 3, p. 4.
8. Jonathan Weber, "Story of a Startup." *Industry Standard* (May 14, 2001): 5.
9. Michael Dell, *Direct from Dell* (New York: HarperBusiness, 1999), p. 127.
10. Jeffrey D. Sachs and Andrew Warner, "Globalization and International Competitiveness: Some Broad Lessons of the Past Decade." In *The Global Competitiveness Report, 2000* (New York: Oxford University Press, 2000), pp. 19–20.
11. Stephen D. Oliner and Daniel E. Sichel, "The Resurgence of Growth in the Late 1990s: Is Information Technology the Story?" Finance and Economics Discussions Series, Washington, DC: Federal Reserve Board, May 2000. Downloaded from www.federalreserve.gov/pubs/feds/2000/index.html.
12. Ibid., p. 2.
13. Jeremy Greenwood, "The Third Industrial Revolution: Technology, Productivity, and Income Inequality." *Economic Review,* Federal Reserve Bank of Cleveland (quarter 2, 1999): 10.
14. Jonathan Dee, "Playing Mogul." *New York Times Magazine,* December 21, 2003, pp. 36–41.

15. David Bank, "Sponsors Target Technology in Developing Nations." *Wall Street Journal*, July 16, 2001, p. A6.

16. Scott Thurm, "Cisco Posts Period Loss of $2.69 Billion." *Wall Street Journal*, May 9, 2001, p. A3.

17. Saul Hansell, "An Ambitious Internet Grocer Is Out of Both Cash and Ideas." *New York Times*, July 10, 2001, pp. A1 and C10.

18. Russ Mitchell, "Don't Lose Your Nerve." *Business 2.0* (May 15, 2001): 5.

19. "Thinner, Much Thinner." *New York Times*, July 27, 2001, p. C6.

20. Charles Gasparino, "Merrill Must Pay in Wake of Analyst's Call on Tech Stock." *Wall Street Journal*, July 20, 2001, pp. C1 and C13.

21. John Heilemann, "Andy Grove's Rational Exuberance." *Wired* (June 2001): 140–41.

Notes to Chapter 2

1. OECD, *A New Economy?* (Paris: Organization for Economic Cooperation and Development, 2000), 62.

2. Janet Abate, *Inventing the Internet* (Cambridge, MA: MIT Press, 1999), ch. 2.

3. Leslie S. Hiraoka, "U.S.-Japanese Competition in High-Technology Fields." *Technological Forecasting and Social Change* 26 (1984): 1–10.

4. Edward A. Feigenbaum and Pamela McCorduck, *The Fifth Generation* (Reading, MA: Addison Wesley, 1983), p. 12.

5. Anthony B. Perkins and Michael C. Perkins, *The Internet Bubble* (New York: HarperBusiness, 1999), pp. 40–44.

6. Feigenbaum and McCorduck, *The Fifth Generation*, p. 121.

7. Office of Technology Assessment, *Information Technology and R&D: Critical Trends and Issues* OTA-CIT-268 (Washington, DC: U.S. Congress, February 1985), pp. 75–76.

8. Ibid., p. 81.

9. Andrew Pollack, "Slugging It Out on the Software Front." *New York Times*, October 16, 1983, pp. F1 and F8.

10. John Markoff, "Ending PC Chaos in the Workplace." *New York Times*, September 9, 1988, pp. D1 and D3.

11. Dylan Loeb McClain, "The Kitchen Sink Operating System." *New York Times*, May 21, 1998, p. D5.

12. Stratford P. Sherman, "Microsoft's Drive to Dominate Software." *Fortune* (January 23, 1984): 82–90.

13. Michael A. Cusumano and Richard W. Selby, *Microsoft Secrets* (New York: Free Press, 1995), chs. 1–2.

14. Karen Southwick. *High Noon* (New York: John Wiley & Sons, 1999), p. 14.

15. Ibid., p. 29.

16. Randall E. Stross, *eBoys* (New York: Crown Business, 2000), p. xv.

Notes to Chapter 3

1. Jeffrey S. Young, *Cisco Unauthorized* (Roseville, CA: Forum, 2001), p. 26.

2. John Markoff, "Ending PC Chaos in the Workplace." *New York Times*, September 9, 1988, pp. D1 and D3.

3. Tim Berners-Lee, *Weaving the Web* (San Francisco: HarperSanFrancisco, 1999), p. 18.

4. Ibid., p. 107.

5. Robert Harris, *A Guidebook to the Web* (Guilford, CT: Dushkin/McGraw-Hill, 2000), pp. 11–12.

6. Kara Swisher, *aol.com* (New York: Times Business, 1999), p. 61.

7. Michael A. Cusumano and Daniel B. Yoffie, *Competing on Internet Time* (New York: Free Press, 1998), p. 9.

8. Anthony B. Perkins and Michael C. Perkins, *The Internet Bubble* (New York: HarperBusiness, 1999), p. 70.

9. Ibid., p. 99.

10. Michael Dell, *Direct from Dell* (New York: HarperBusiness, 1999), pp. xii and 30.

11. William A. Niskanen, *Reaganomics* (New York: Oxford University Press, 1988), pp. 36–40.

12. Edward M. Gramlich, "Social Security Reform in the Twenty-First Century." *The Frank M. Engle Lecture* (Bryn Mawr, PA: American College, 2001), p. 5.

13. Perkins and Perkins, *Internet Bubble*, p. 6.

14. Swisher, *aol.com*, p. 55.

15. Ibid., p. 67.

16. Ibid., p. 99.

17. Ibid., ch. 11.

18. Cusumano and Yoffie, *Competing on Internet Time*, p. 116.

19. Ibid., p. 112.

20. Jim Clark, *Netscape Time* (New York: St. Martin's Press, 1999), p. 253.

21. Cusumano and Yoffie, *Competing on Internet Time*, pp. 115–17.

22. Steve Lohr and John Markoff, "Deal Is Concluded on Netscape Sale to America Online." *New York Times*, January 25, 1998, p. A1.

Notes to Chapter 4

1. "How Corrupt Is Wall Street?" *Business Week* (May 13, 2002): 39–40.

2. Floyd Norris, "Amazing Amazon: Losses Grow as They Seem to Shrink." *New York Times,* February 2, 2001, p. C1.

3. "Can Amazon Make It?" *Business Week* (July 10, 2000): 38–43.

4. Jennifer Waters, "Amazon Shares Drop After Downgrades." CBS. MarketWatch.com, January 31, 2001.

5. Gretchen Morgensen, "Requiem for an Honorable Profession." *New York Times,* May 5, 2002, sec. 3, p. 3.

6. Saul Hansell, "Amazon Loss Soared 543% in 4th Quarter." *New York Times,* February 3, 2000, pp. C1 and C10.

7. Quotes from "Amazon's Amazing Ambition," in Survey of E-commerce, *Economist* (February 26, 2002): 24.

8. Gary Hamel, *Leading the Revolution* (Boston: Harvard Business School Press, 2000), p. 222.

9. Jonathan Weil, Alexei Barrionuevo, and Cassell Bryan-Low, "Andersen Win Lifts U.S. Enron Case." *Wall Street Journal,* June 17, 2002, p. A1.

10. Robert Spector, *amazon.com.* (New York: HarperBusiness, 2000), pp. 9–43.

11. G. Bruce Knecht, "How Wall Street Whiz Found a Niche Selling Books on the Internet." *Wall Street Journal,* May 16, 1996, p. A1.

12. Kevin Werbach, "Amazon's Secret Sauce." *Business 2.0* (June 2002): 124.

13. "Reaching for More." *New York Times,* September 30, 1999, p. C25.

14. "Going Down with the Dot-Coms." *New York Times,* March 11, 2001, sec. 3, p. 14.

15. Mylene Mangalindan, "Online-Jobs Niche Sparks Yahoo's Bold Move." *Wall Street Journal,* December 24, 2001, p. B4.

16. Mylene Mangalindan, "Yahoo Says Its Online Sales Volume Jumped 86%." *Wall Street Journal,* December 27, 2001, p. B2.

17. John Gaffney, "The Online Advertising Comeback." *Business 2.0* (June 2002): 118–120.

18. Miki Tanikawa, "A Cautious Sibling Waits to See What Works." *New York Times,* March 11, 2001, sec. 3, p. 14.

19. Fred Vogelstein, "Looking for a Dot-com Winner? Search No Further." *Fortune* (May 27, 2002): 65–68.

20. Mylene Mangalindan, "Yahoo Tops Profit Forecast on 47% Revenue Jump." *Wall Street Journal,* April 10, 2003, p. A3.

21. *Industry Standard* (August 6, 2001): cover page.

22. Randall E. Stross, *eBoys* (New York: Crown Business, 2000), pp. 48–49.

23. Ibid., p. 57.

24. Saul Hansell, "Meg Whitman and eBay, Internet Bubble Survivors." *New York Times,* May 5, 2002, sec. 3, p. 17.

25. Benjamin Mark Cole, *The Pied Pipers of Wall Street* (Princeton, NJ: Bloomberg Press, 2001), pp. 76–77.

Notes to Chapter 5

1. Lisa Bannon, "The EToys Saga: Costs Kept Rising But Sales Slowed." *Wall Street Journal,* January 22, 2001, p. B1.

2. Saul Hansell, "Amazon's Risky Christmas." *New York Times,* November 28, 1999, sec. 3, pp. 1 and 15.

3. Ibid.

4. Bannon, "EToys Saga," pp. B1 and B10.

5. Matt Richtel, "EToys to Lay Off Its Remaining Workers." *New York Times,* February 6, 2001, p. C8.

6. Michael Sokolove, "How to Lose $850 Million—And Really Not Care." *New York Times Magazine,* June 6, 2002, p. 66.

7. Stephen Paternot and Andrew Essex, *A Very Public Offering* (New York: John Wiley & Sons, 2002), p. 101.

8. Joseph Nocera, "Why Is Bill Gross Still Smiling?" *Fortune* (March 5, 2001): 73.

9. Ralph King, "Falling Idol." *Business 2.0* (August/September 2001): 122.

10. Ibid., pp. 120–24.

11. Norm Alster, "What's That Rumble in Venture Capital Funds?" *New York Times,* March 3, 2002, sec. 3, p. 4.

12. Gretchen Morgenson, "Buy, They Say. But What Do They Do?" *New York Times,* May 27, 2001, sec. 3, p. 1.

13. Susan Pulliam and Randall Smith, "At CSFB, Lush Profit Earned on IPOs Found Its Way Back to Firm." *Wall Street Journal,* November 30, 2001, p. A11.

14. Michael Siconolfi, "Underwriters Set Aside IPO Stock for Officials of Potential Customers." *Wall Street Journal,* November 12, 1997, pp. A1 and A14.

15. Pulliam and Smith, "At CSFB."

16. Randall Smith and Susan Pulliam, "CSFB Settles 'Pervasive' IPO-Profit Scheme." *Wall Street Journal,* January 23, 2002, p. C16.

17. Julia Boorstein and Matthew Boyle, "The Billion-Dollar Losers Club." *Fortune* (June 11, 2001): 127–28.

18. Mark Leibovich, "MicroStrategy's CEO Sped to the Brink." *Washington Post,* June 6, 2002, pp. A1 and A16.

19. Ibid., p. A16.

20. Mark Leibovich, "Once Defiant, Microstrategy Chief Contritely Faces SEC." *Washington Post,* January 8, 2002, p. A12.

21. Mark Leibovich, "At the Height of a Joy Ride, Microstrategy Dives." *Washington Post,* January 7, 2002, p. A10.

22. Jared Sandberg and Deborah Solomon, "WorldCom Board to Begin Search for New CEO." *Wall Street Journal,* September 11, 2002, p. A3.

23. Stephen Labaton, "Praise to Scorn: Mercurial Ride of S.E.C. Chief." *New York Times,* November 10, 2002, p. 24.

24. Frank Rose, "The $7 Billion Delusion." *Wired* (January 2002): 69.

Notes to Chapter 6

1. Floyd Norris, "Microsoft in the Court of the Investor." *New York Times,* June 8, 2000, p. C1.

2. Joel Brinkley, "Microsoft Breakup Is Ordered for Antitrust Law Violations." *New York Times,* June 8, 2000, p. A1.

3. Thomas Penfield Jackson, "Text of the Order to Split Up Microsoft." *New York Times,* June 8, 2000, p. C12.

4. Joel Brinkley and Steve Lohr, "Retracing the Missteps in the Microsoft Defense." *New York Times,* June 9, 2000, p. C9.

5. "Key Sections of the Decision by the United States Court of Appeals." *New York Times,* June 29, 2001, p. C8.

6. Stephen Labaton, "Appeals Court Voids Order for Breaking Up Microsoft But Finds It Abused Power." *New York Times,* June 29, 2001, p. C7.

7. Key Sections of the Decision by the U.S. Court of Appeals. *United States v. Microsoft Corporation.*

8. Ibid.

9. Labaton, "Appeals Court Voids Order."

10. Nicholas G. Carr, "IT Doesn't Matter." *Harvard Business Review* (May 2003): 41–49.

11. Ian Mount, "Attention Underlings: That's Mister Conway to You. And I Am Not a People Person!" *Business 2.0* (February 2002): 54.

12. John R. Wilke and Don Clark, "Despite Settlement, Microsoft Faces More Legal Challenges." *Wall Street Journal,* November 4, 2002, p. A1.

13. David Bank, Mylene Mangalindan, and Rohn R. Wilke, "Oracle Sweetens Its PeopleSoft Bid." *Wall Street Journal,* June 19, 2003, p. A3.

14. Leon Erlanger, ".Net May Be the Biggest Change to Microsoft's Strategy Since It Introduced Windows 3.0." *Internet World,* www.internetworld.com (April 15, 2001): p. 7.

15. William M. Bulkey and Robert A. Guth. "IBM, Microsoft Hunt Same Prey: Small Customers." *Wall Street Journal,* June 25, 2003, p. B1.

16. Stewart Alsop, "Eating My Own Words." *Fortune* (February 18, 2002): 64.

17. Lee Gomes and Don Clark, "Java Is Finding Niches But Isn't Yet Living Up to Its Early Promises." *Wall Street Journal,* August 27, 1997, p. A1.

18. David Kirkpatrick, "The Future of IBM." *Fortune* (February 18, 2002): 62.

19. Steve Bodow, "Microsofter." *New York Times Magazine,* November 24, 2002, p. 74.

20. Erick Schoenfeld, "This Is Your Father's IBM, Only Smarter." *Business 2.0* (May 2002): 54.

Notes to Chapter 7

1. "Welcome to the 21st Century." *Business Week* (January 24, 2000): 37–8.

2. Anthony Bianco and Tom Lowry, "Can Dick Parsons Rescue AOL Time Warner?" *Business Week* (May 19, 2003): 87.

3. Patricia Sellers, "Ted Turner: Gone with the Wind." *Fortune* (May 26, 2003): 126.

4. Saul Hansell, "America Online Agrees to Buy Time Warner for $165 Billion; Media Deal Is Richest Merger." *New York Times,* January 11, 2000, p. C11.

5. Steve Lohr, "Medium for Main Street." *New York Times,* January 11, 2000, p. C10.

6. Amy Harmon, "How Blind Alleys Led Old Media to New." *New York Times,* January 16, 2000, sec. 3, pp. 1 and 14.

7. Ibid., p. 1.

8. Alex Berenson and Bill Carter, "When Everything New Becomes Dizzingly Newer." *New York Times,* January 11, 2000, p. C10.

9. Lohr, "Medium for Main Street."

10. Peter Coy and Catherine Yang, "Running the Numbers on the Deal." *Business Week* (January 24, 2000): 39.

11. "Open Letter." *Red Herring* (February 2002): 21.

12. "Can These Two Make the Marriage Work." *Business Week* (January 15, 2001): 58–59.

13. Lohr, "Medium for Main Street."

14. Franklin Paul and Tom Johnson, "AOL looks ahead, but stock drops." CNNfn, January 12, 2001, http://money.cnn.com/2001/01/12/deals/new_aol.

15. Mark Gimein, "You Bought. They Sold." *Fortune* (September 2, 2002): 64–74.

16. David D. Kirkpatrick and David Carr, "A Media Giant Needs a Script." *New York Times,* July 7, 2002, sec. 3, p. 10.

17. Saul Hansell, "Can AOL Keep Its Subscribers in a New World of Broadband?" *New York Times,* July 29, 2002, p. C1.

18. Julia Angwin. "Cable Deal Brings Expansion to America Online—at a Price." *Wall Street Journal,* July 21, 2002, p. B1.

19. Amy Harmon, "Culture Clash Seen in Merger of Companies." *New York Times,* November 24, 1998, p. C4.

20. David D. Kirkpatrick,"Ouster at AOL, But Where Does Trail End?" *New York Times,* September 1, 2002, sec. 3, p. 1.

21. Matt Murray, "Options Frenzy: What Went Wrong?" *Wall Street Journal,* December 17, 2002, pp. B1 and B2.

22. Kara Swisher, *aol.com* (New York: Times Business, 1999), p. 303.

23. Steve Lohr and John Markoff, "Deal Is Concluded on Netscape Sale to America Online." *New York Times,* January 25, 1998, p. C5.

24. Alec Klein, "Unconventional Transactions Boosted Sales; Amid Big Merger, Company Resisted Dot-Com Collapse." *Washington Post,* July 18, 2002, p. A1.

25. Julia Angwin and Martin Peres, "Officials Probe AOL's Actions with Partners." *Wall Street Journal,* August 26, 2002, pp. C1 and C7.

26. Klein, "Unconventional Transactions Boosted Sales."

27. Julia Angwin, "SEC Requests Documents from AOL." *Wall Street Journal,* July 30, 2003, p. A3.

28. Martin Peres, "AOL Swings to Profit, Boosted by Film, Cable." *Wall Street Journal,* April 24, 2003, p. B3.

29. David Carr, "A Star Is Born (If AOL Rebounds)." *New York Times,* January 19, 2003, sec. 2, p. 11.

Notes to Chapter 8

1. Robert Bryce, *Pipe Dreams* (New York: Public Affairs, 2002), chs. 12 and 37.

2. "The Role of the Board of Directors in Enron's Collapse." Report 107–70 prepared by the Permanent Subcommittee on Investigations of the Committee on Governmental Affairs, Washington, DC: U.S. Senate, July 8, 2002, p. 11.

3. Bryce, *Pipe Dreams,* p. 135.

4. U.S. Senate Report 107–70, p. 6.

5. Arthur Levitt and Paula Dwyer, *Take on the Street* (New York: Pantheon Books, 2002), p. 143.

6. Kurt Eichenwald, "Company Man to the End, After All." *New York Times,* February 9, 2003, sec. 3, pp. 1 and 12.

7. Kurt Eichenwald and Diana B. Henriques, "Enron Buffed Image to a Shine Even as It Rotted from Within." *New York Times,* February 10, 2002, sec. 3, pp. 1, 28, and 29.

8. Jerry Useem, "And Then, Just When You Thought the 'New Economy' Was Dead." *Business 2.0* (August–September 2001): 74 and 76.

9. Eichenwald and Henriques, "Enron Buffed Image," p. 28.

10. U.S. Senate Report 107–70, p. 7.

11. Bryce, *Pipe Dreams,* p. 84.

12. Ibid., pp. 217–21.

13. David Barboza, "Enron Trader Had a Year to Boast of, Even If. . . ." *New York Times,* July 9, 2002, pp. C1 and C6.

14. David Barboza, "Former Officials Say Enron Hid Gains During Crisis in California." *New York Times,* June 23, 2003, 1 and 24.

15. Federal Energy Regulatory Commission. "Final Report on Price Manipulation in Western Markets: Fact-Finding Investigation of Potential Manipulation of Electric and Natural Gas Prices." *Docket No. PA 02-2-000,* Washington, DC (March 2003): ES-2.

16. Rebecca Smith and John R. Wilke, "Enron Ex-Trader Admits to Fraud in California Crisis." *Wall Street Journal,* October 18, 2002, p. A3.

17. Bryce, *Pipe Dreams,* p. 191.

18. Yochi J. Dreazen, "Behind the Telecom Glut." *Wall Street Journal,* September 26, 2002, pp. B1 and B8.

19. Dennis K. Berman, "Innovation Outpaced the Marketplace." *Wall Street Journal,* September 26, 2002, pp. B1 and B8.

20. William C. Powers, Jr., Raymond S. Troubh, and Herbert S. Winokur, Jr., "Report of Investigation by the Special Investigative Committee of the Board of Directors of Enron Corp" (February 1, 2002): 5. Online at www.chron.com/Enron under Powers Report.

21. Rebecca Smith, "A Blockbuster Deal Shows How Enron Overplayed Its Hand." *Wall Street Journal,* January 17, 2002, A1 and A6.

22. U.S. Senate Report 107–70, p. 7.

23. Alexie Barrionuevo, Jonathan Weil, and John R. Wilke, "U.S. Charges Fastow with Fraud in Enron Case." *Wall Street Journal,* October 2, 2002, p. A4.

24. Powers, Jr. et al., "Report of Investigation," p. 8.

25. Bethany McLean and Peter Elkind, "Partners in Crime." *Fortune* (October 27, 2003): 90.

26. Robert Bryce, *Pipe Dreams,* ch. 22.

27. U.S. Senate Report 107–70, pp. 21 and 24.

28. Kurt Eichenwald, "Merrill Reaches Deal with U.S. in Enron Affair." *New York Times,* September 18, 2003, pp. A1 and C5.

29. Kurt Eichenwald and Riva D. Atlas, "2 Banks Settle Accusations They Aided in Enron Fraud." *New York Times,* July 29, 2003, pp. A1 and C7.

30. Jonathan Weil and John Wilke, "Senate Panel Chides SEC for Falling Short in Enron Regulation." *Wall Street Journal,* October 7, 2002, pp. C1 and C11.

31. Floyd Norris, "A Warning Shot to Banks on Role in Others' Fraud." *New York Times,* July 23, 2003, p. C7.

32. Eichenwald and Atlas, "2 Banks Settle," p. A1.

33. U.S. Senate Report 107–70, pp. 43 and 45.

34. Ibid., p. 45.

35. Eichenwald, "Andersen Guilty in Effort to Block Inquiry on Enron." *New York Times,* June 16, 2002, pp. 1 and 20.

Notes to Chapter 9

1. Reed E. Hundt, *You Say You Want a Revolution* (New Haven, CT: Yale University Press, 2000), pp. 54–55.

2. Ibid., p. 55.

3. Ibid., pp. 26 and 134.

4. Katie Hafner, "Digitally Disenfranchised." *New York Times,* August 6, 2001, pp. C1 and C3.

5. Matt Richtel, "Fast and Furious: The Race to Wire America." *New York Times,* November 16, 2003, sec. 3, pp. 1 and 10.

6. Shawn Young and Peter Grant, "How Phone Firms Lost to Cable in Customer Broadband Battle." *Wall Street Journal,* March 13, 2003, pp. A1 and A6.

7. Ibid., p. A6.

8. Deborah Solomon, "How Qwest's Merger with a Baby Bell Left Both in Trouble." *Wall Street Journal,* April 2, 2002, pp. A1 and A10.

9. Diana Asher, "The New Wave in Communications." *On Investing* (spring 2001): 34.

10. Om Malik, "Qwest's Napoleonic Ambitions." *Red Herring* (October 15, 2001): 47–52. In the same issue, see an Open Letter to Joseph Nacchio from the editors, p. 104.

11. Gretchen Morgenson, "Telecom, Tangled in Its Own Web." *New York Times,* March 24, 2002, sec. 3, p. 7.

12. Dennis K. Berman, Julian Angwin, and Chip Cummins, "As Market Bubble Neared End, Bogus Swaps Provided a Lift." *Wall Street Journal,* December 23, 2002, pp. A1 and A10.

13. Gretchen Morgenson, "Deals Within Telecom Deals." *New York Times,* August 25, 2002, sec. 3, pp. 1 and 10.

14. Simon Romero and Seth Schiesel, "The Fiber Optic Fantasy Slips Away." *New York Times,* February 17, 2002, sec. 3, pp. 1 and 7.

15. Julie Creswell and Nomi Prins, "The Emperor of Greed." *Fortune* (June 24, 2002): 107.

16. Arthur Levitt and Paula Dwyer, *Take On the Street* (New York: Pantheon Books, 2002), p. 144.

17. First Interim Report of Dick Thornburgh, United States Bankruptcy Court Examiner for the Southern District of New York. In re: WorldCom, Inc., et al. Debtors, Chapter 11, Case No. 02-15533 (AJG). Washington, DC: Kirkpatrick & Lockhart LLP, November 4, 2002, p. 55. Available at http://news.findlaw.com/hdocs/docs/worldcom/thornburgh1strpt.pdf.

18. Ibid., pp. 50–51.

19. Steven Lipin and John J. Keller, "WorldCom's MCI Bid Alters Playing Field for Telecom Industry." *Wall Street Journal,* October 2, 1997, p. A1.

20. First Interim Report of Dick Thornburgh, p. 8.

21. Ibid., p. 108.

22. Jared Sandberg, Deborah Solomon, and Rebecca Blumenstein, "Inside WorldCom's Unearthing of a Vast Accounting Scandal." *Wall Street Journal,* June 27, 2002, p. A20.

23. Susan Pullian, Deborah Solomon, and Carrick Mollenkamp, "Former WorldCom CEO Built an Empire on Mountain of Debt." *Wall Street Journal,* December 31, 2002, pp. A1 and A6.

24. First Interim Report of Dick Thornburgh, pp. 73 and 80–81.

25. "Cleaning Up Dodge." *Wall Street Journal,* October 10, 2002, p. A14.

Notes to Chapter 10

1. Jerry Useem, "And Then, Just When You Thought the 'New Economy' Was Dead." *Business 2.0* (August–September 2001): 74.

2. See, for example, David Denby, *American Sucker* (New York: Little, Brown, 2004).

3. "Digitally Driven." *New York Times,* August 29, 2002, p. C1.

4. Michael S. Malone, "Surviving the IPO Fever." *Wired* (March 2004): 114.

5. Jim Kerstetter, Steve Hamm, Spencer E. Ante, and Jay Greene, "The Linux Uprising." *Business Week* (March 3, 2003): 78–84.

6. Gary Rivlin, "Leader of the Free World." *Wired* (November 2003): 206.

7. David Diamond, "Questions for Linus Torvalds: The Sharer." *New York Times Magazine,* September 28, 2003, p. 23.

8. Rivlin, "Leader of the Free World."

9. Russ Mitchell, "Open War." *Wired* (October 2001): 136–37.

10. Lee Gomes, "For Linux's Torvalds, Software Is Improved with Little Fanfare." *Wall Street Journal,* June 9, 2003, p. B1.

11. Robert A. Guth, "Sony Is Grooming Game Maverick for the Next Level." *Wall Street Journal,* November 18, 2002, pp. A1 and A19.

12. Mark Frauenfelder, "Death Match." *Wired* (May 2001): 150–53.

13. Mike Dolan, "Behind the Screens." *Wired* (May 2001): 149.

14. Ibid.

15. Dean Takahashi, *Opening the Xbox* (Roseville, CA: Prima Publishing, 2002), p. 16.

16. Dolan, "Behind the Screens," p. 148.

17. Takahashi, *Opening the Xbox,* pp. 13–14.

18. Joseph Pereira, "Showdown in Mario Land." *Wall Street Journal,* April 19, 2002, p. A13.

19. Paul Boutin, "Next Box." *Wired* (May 2001): 141.

20. Jonathan Dee, "Playing Mogul." *New York Times Magazine,* December 21, 2003, pp. 36–41.

21. Bruce Orwall and Peter Grant, "Rebuffed by Eisner, Comcast Makes $48.7 Billion Offer to Acquire Disney." *Wall Street Journal,* February 12, 2004, p. A1.

22. "Excerpts from Comcast Letter Informing Disney of Bid." *New York Times,* February 12, 2004, p. C6.

23. Ibid.

24. Susan Pulliam, Almar Latour, and Ken Brown, "U.S. Indicts WorldCom Chief Ebbers." *Wall Street Journal,* March 3, 2004, p. A12.

Notes to Chapter 11

1. "Excerpts from Ruling in Europe and Microsoft's Response." *New York Times,* March 25, 2004, p. C11.

2. Steve Lohr, "Musical Chairs with the Big Boys." *New York Times,* March 21, 2004, sec. 3, p. 9.

3. Paul Sloan and Geoff Keighley, "The Offer Hollywood Can't Refuse." *Business 2.0* (May 2004): 88–96.

4. Melanie Warner, "What Your Company Can Learn from Google." *Business 2.0* (June 2004): 104.

5. Amy Harmon, "Is a Do-Gooder Company a Good Thing?" *New York Times,* May 2, 2004, sec. 4, p. 12.

6. Larry Page and Sergey Brin, "Letter Is Manifesto of Founders." *Wall Street Journal,* April 30, 2004, p. A10.

7. Kevin J. Delaney and Robin Sidel, "Google IPO Aims to Change the Rules." *Wall Street Journal,* April 30, 2004, pp. A1 and A10.

8. Randall Smith and Susanne Craig, "Auction Promises to Bid Adieu to Tradition." *Wall Street Journal,* April 30, 2004, p. C1.

Bibliography

Abate, Janet. *Inventing the Internet.* Cambridge, MA: MIT Press, 1999.

Berners-Lee, Tim. *Weaving the Web.* San Francisco: HarperSanFrancisco, 1999.

Bryce, Robert. *Pipe Dreams: Greed, Ego, and the Death of Enron.* New York: Public Affairs, 2002.

Clark, Jim. *Netscape Time.* New York: St. Martin's Press, 1999.

Cole, Benjamin Mark. *The Pied Pipers of Wall Street.* Princeton, NJ: Bloomberg Press, 2001.

Cusumano, Michael A., and Daniel B. Yoffie. *Competing on Internet Time.* New York: Free Press, 1998.

Cusumano, Michael A., and Richard W. Shelby. *Microsoft Secrets.* New York: Free Press, 1995.

Dell, Michael. *Direct from Dell.* New York: HarperBusiness, 1999.

Feigenbaum, Edward A., and Pamela McCorduck. *The Fifth Generation.* Reading, MA: Addison-Wesley, 1983.

First Interim Report of Dick Thornburgh. U.S. Bankruptcy Court Examiner for the Southern District of New York. In re: WorldCom, Inc. et al. Debtors, Chapter 11, Case No. 02–15533 (AJG), Washington DC: Kirkpatrick & Lockhart LLP, November 4, 2002. http://news.findlaw.com/hdocs/docs/worldcom/thornburgh1strpt.pdf.

Hiraoka, Leslie S. "U.S.-Japanese Competition in High-Technology Fields." *Technological Forecasting and Social Change* 26 (1984): 1–10.

Hundt, Reed. *You Say You Want a Revolution: A Story of Information Age Politics.* New Haven, CT: Yale University Press, 2000.

Levitt, Arthur, and Paula Dwyer. *Take On the Street.* New York: Pantheon Books, 2002.

OECD. *A New Economy? The Changing Role of Innovation and Information Technology in Growth.* Paris: Organization for Economic Cooperation and Development, 2000.

Office of Technology Assessment. *Information Technology and R&D: Critical Trends and Issues,* OTA-CIT-268. Washington, DC: U.S. Congress, February 1985.

Paulson, Ed. *Inside Cisco.* New York: John Wiley & Sons, 2001.

Perkins, Anthony B., and Michael C. Perkins. *The Internet Bubble.* New York: HarperBusiness, 1999.

Powers, William C., Jr., Raymond S. Troubh, and Herbert S. Winokur, Jr. "Report of Investigation by the Special Committee of the Board of Directors of Enron Corp." February 1, 2002. www.chron.com/Enron.

Rust, Roland T., and P.K. Kannon, ed. *e-Service: New Directions in Theory and Practice.* Armonk, NY: M.E. Sharpe, 2002.

Southwick, Karen. *High Noon*. New York: John Wiley & Sons, 1999.
Spector, Robert. *amazon.com*. New York: HarperBusiness, 2000.
Stross, Randall E. *eBoys*. New York: Crown Business, 2000.
Swisher, Kara. *aol.com*. New York: Times Business, 1998.
Takahashi, Dean. *Opening the Xbox*. Roseville, CA: Prima Publishing, 2002.
U.S. Senate Report 107–70. *The Role of the Board of Directors in Enron's Collapse*.
    Permanent Subcommittee on Investigations of the Committee on Governmental
    Affairs, Washington, DC: U.S. Senate, July 8, 2002.
Young, Jeffrey S. *Cisco Unauthorized*. Roseville, CA: Forum, 2001.

Index

Leslie S. Hiraoka is Professor of Management Science at Kean University of New Jersey, where he developed and was the first chairman of the Department of Management Science. He is the author of *Global Alliances in the Motor Vehicle Industry* (2001) and, based on the book's research, was awarded the first Shigeo Shingo Prize in Excellence in Manufacturing, named for the noted Toyota production expert. Dr. Hiraoka was guest editor and contributor to a special issue on Industrial Policy and Technological Competitiveness for the *International Journal of Technology Management* (1989) and a contributor to the *Wiley Encyclopedia of Electrical and Electronics Engineering* (1999) on Human Resource Management. He was an AACSB–Sears Roebuck Federal Faculty Fellow at the U.S. Department of Commerce in Washington, D.C., and has testified before congressional House and Senate subcommittees.